STILL MORE
VOICES FROM
PRISON WALLS

by
WILLIAM CAWMAN

Author of
Voices from Prison Walls
More Voices from Prison Walls
Yet More Voices from Prison Walls

SCHMUL PUBLISHING COMPANY
NICHOLASVILLE, KENTUCKY

Cover image copyright: <a href="https://www.123rf.com/profile_kleberpicui">kleberpicui / 123RF Stock Photo</a>. Used by permission.

Published by Schmul Publishing Co.
PO Box 776
Nicholasville, KY USA

Printed in the United States of America

ISBN 10: 0-88019-620-3
ISBN 13: 978-0-88019-620-8

Visit us on the Internet at www.wesleyanbooks.com, or order direct from the publisher by calling 800-772-6657, or by writing to the above address.

CONTENTS

FOREWORD

As this is the fourth volume of these letters written month by month from behind prison walls, little introduction need be given again except to say that God's work among the prison population of our country still lies very close to His heart. It does to my heart as well, and I am thoroughly convinced by frequent heartfelt reports from the many readers that it lies close to your hearts as well.

There will be no class distinctions in heaven; no résumés will be presented there; no titles of distinction will be even thought of. There will be but one class of people in heaven—those "who have washed their robes, and made them white in the blood of the Lamb." And, all hail! Blood of Jesus! For it reaches the most defiled!

Someone, learning of this the fourth volume of letters being published, asked, "Twenty years from now will you publish another four volumes?" That may depend upon the continuation of the fervent prayers whose answers have given birth to the first four. Whether twenty years or not, the song says and we repeat, "We'll work till Jesus comes!"

May God use the following pages to His glory alone!

Your Brother in Christ,
WILLIAM CAWMAN

...h one and I thank you for your love to me. You ...terested to know that I tell these precious young ...t I have parameters for the Grandpa relationship. ...three rules connected with it. (1) As of this past year ...to be twenty-nine years of age or younger. (2) They ...want to go to heaven and be striving to get there; how- ...s for life— once they are adopted if they begin to wan- ...ay I am coming after them. (3) Grandpa is only Grandpa ...days of the year; he takes December 25 off.

...right, now let me move to the real purpose of this ...r. Do you remember the little man from Mexico that I ...te about several months ago who is very small of stat- ...e and he was provided what looked like the largest size ...nter coat available? Well, he has continued to shine and ...alk in the light, and one night this month he gave a testi- ...mony in the Sunday night service. He said that his sister came to visit him and she told him, "If it is Jesus who has changed you like you are now, I want Him." It's hard to imagine such a little fellow, so shining with happiness and grace, ever being anything different, but he does show the marks of a past life that was not a bit good. He is marked with many tattoos from the street gangs, even though he was not very old when he came to prison. He also has many years yet to go, but it does not seem that fact is dimming his joy at all. Isn't it so good that we can say, "But God!"

Over the years I have noticed something very repetitive that finally came through very clearly to me. So many times I have had this same experience: the first visit with a man brings tears and sobs to his eyes. He is broken and feels so keenly his need and wants to visit again soon. We visit again, and again, and then he begins to slump away and finally evades the vis- its. It has happened so many times that it is heart-breaking, but then one day recently I thought of Felix as he heard Paul for the first time. The Scripture tells us that he trembled dur- ing that first visit, but he told Paul to go his way for the time, and that when he had a more convenient season he would call

love you ea
might be i
people tha
There are
they had
have to
ever, it
der aw
for 36
Al
lette
wr
ur
w

1
THEY'RE NOT ALL IN YET

January 1, 2013

CAN IT BE THAT another year is gone? One year that great eternal reward with Jesus! What else is living for? I first want to say that I so much appr all that you, my Christian family, have done during this year to help fill the void that I have been so conscious of in t translation of my dear wife to her eternal home. I apologize that I have just not felt my heart able to send out Christmas cards since I am but half here, but I do so much appreciate all the ones I have received. Many of them contained notes of love that I feel so unworthy of, but it has drawn me so much closer to my family in Jesus. I thank every one of you who have called, written, sent notes of encouragement, and prayed for me. I have treasured it all, even though so unworthy of it. I love you, each member of my family.

God has been so good this past year in countless ways. Many young people and children have come and asked if I would be their Grandpa, and it has melted my heart that the love of Jesus shines so lovely through young hearts. It has certainly gone a long way to filling the vacancy that I feel so much. I for him. The next verses tell us that he did have a more convenient time and sent for him often, but there is no record that he ever trembled again. Could it be that this is repeated over and over in one life after another?

How many that we meet on the street or in the stores have already had an encounter with truth that made them tremble, but they relegated their response to it to a more convenient season and have never trembled again. David said, "Surely goodness and mercy shall follow me all the days of my life...," but that is contingent upon us doing something more than nothing about it. As I walk around through the prison I can see ever so many faces that once were tear-stained, so many eyes that once had a longing expression in them; but now they are apparently settled into the life-style of a convict, with their focus taken up by the activities around them.

Thank God, this is not the case with all. God has been really moving in on our classes in Christian Living. We are studying the Second Work of Grace and oh, how alive the subject becomes again and again. God's clear anointing has been upon this that Jesse Peck calls *The Central Idea of Christianity*. At the same time, other teachers are coming in and teaching them that they cannot lose their salvation and that they cannot live in this life free from sin. What a failure Calvary was, according to that doctrine of devils. Recently the men have come to class desiring to hear the real truth regarding these things, as they know full well that what they listened to was not.

One teacher emphasized the impossibility of losing one's salvation from the theory that once a person is a son, he is always a son. I told them that spiritual things must be compared with spiritual things, not with natural things. The Bible says that "flesh and blood shall not inherit the kingdom of God," and that what is true in the flesh is not true in the spiritual. For if it was, not one of them could be saved, including myself, for we were at one time sons of Satan. Immediately a round of happy applause went through the room as they declared, "I'm not a son of Satan anymore!"

I then asked the class why anyone would desire to labor so ardently to prove that one could not lose his salvation instead of laboring that hard to not do it. Then I asked them if they thought that I could ever lose my deusselflexer. They looked at me with knit brows and said, "Your what?" "My deusselflexer." "We don't know what that is." "Yes, but do you think I could lose it?" "We can't know whether you can lose it because we don't know what it is." "Yes, and that's exactly the problem we are up against here. How can we know whether we can lose our salvation if we don't understand what salvation is?" "Oh, yes, we see." "Well, then, what is salvation?"

After a few stabs that very well evidenced the point at hand, someone replied, "It is being saved." "Exactly right!" "Being saved from what? Falling out of a cherry tree?" "No, saved from sin." "Yes, that's right, as well as from the consequences of sin." "So if a man has been saved from his sin and walks with God for a while and then goes back into sin again, what on earth is he saved from? What is it that he can't lose?" By this time the class was in shouting happy agreement and we proceeded on to look at how we can get cleansed from the carnal mind that wallows in these errors. Have you thanked God recently that you ever heard of a cure that goes deeper than the problem? If not, do so now, please!

The men have begun their own study times on the cell blocks and are just really enjoying this wonderful teaching of the finished work of Jesus. They love to come up in a group before class and tell me what they have been feasting on. Please pray for them specifically for this: full salvation, properly understood, is beautiful beyond all description. But if it stops with a mental understanding and worship, it becomes the most subtle form of idolatry there is. Jesus clearly castigated those who loved to call Him Lord and Master, but did not do the things which He said. Will you please help us pray that out of these classes will come a harvest of fully sanctified men, dead to self and sin and alive altogether unto God?

There is one officer who never fails to stop me and share a word of spiritual enrichment with me, and he loves to have me do the same. One day he opened the door where I was waiting for an interview and said, "Chaplain, I want to tell you that nothing in the world matters to me anymore except to be right with God." Yesterday he stopped me on the compound and said, "Do you know that God is our Father, and that He has given us of His Holy Spirit to dwell within us, and that He has said, 'Be ye holy, for I am holy?' That means that with His Spirit within us every step we take becomes holy ground." I said, "That's good, Brother, thank you for that." What kind of a prison would we have if every officer was like him?

My supervisor said that he would like to have a Christmas Eve service for all of the men who wanted to attend, but of course since we do not mix the various sections of the prison that would require five separate services that evening. I told him our church would do their best to provide the services and he was very happy with that. At 5:30 we were to have a service in the minimum unit outside the main perimeter and a service in the prison hospital. I requested that we also be able to do room to room visitation that evening for the bedfast men who could not get out to the service. Then at 7:30 we would divide the group into three groups and have a service in each of the facilities.

Knowing that we would be rather short staffed to provide an effective choir for three spots at once, I asked the very conservative Mennonite Church in town if they would care to join us. A group came with us and when we got to the prison in plenty of time to have everyone cleared for security, the officer in the front lobby told me that out of the usual 400± officers on duty for that shift, fifty-seven had called off. This left them a bit paranoid because it is not infrequent at all for there to be outbreaks and fights over Christmas because of the intensity of emotions. He said that the lieutenant had said we could only have a half hour for each service.

My supervisor was there to make sure all went well and I told him so he called the lieutenant in charge and explained to him what dedication it was for all these people to leave their homes and their own churches and come in for the men in prison. The lieutenant backed down and all went well. We had a good service in the minimum unit while a smaller group went to the hospital. While several were giving the program, which was Christmas songs and Scriptures and a reading, two of the brethren went upstairs and asked about visitation from room to room. Thank God (a definite answer to prayer for that evening) both a nurse and young officer were very commodious and almost became a part of the team as the officer would ask the men in bed one by one if they wanted a visit from the minister, and even promoted it. They were able to minister even longer than the specified time there.

Then we met in the main hallway and divided into three groups and went to the three chapels inside the prison. I believe over eighty men were in attendance at one and over 100 at the other two. Knowing the men as I have for so many years now, I could easily see deep emotions welling up within them. Men in prison learn not to show their outward emotions, as it is perceived as a sign of weakness, but they were really feeling the presence of God deep within and expressing it as well. We urged them to open their hearts and let Jesus come in if He was not there so that they could really know the glory of the real meaning of Christmas. God alone knows all the impact that night had on these precious lives.

Christmas is a very difficult time for men in prison. If one would walk into a tier of cells on Christmas day he might well hear grown men sobbing their hearts out. Why need there be all this heartache? Sin. Aren't you glad that one day soon God will by the Word of His mouth expunge the entire universe of every trace of Satan's ugly work— even the memory of it! Lord, hasten the day!

But for now— there is work yet to do. God has really been moving consistently in two of the groups in particular and my heart cry is that out of the group we will see, not one or two, but a harvest of washed and sanctified vessels to the honor of the Gift of Christmas. I told one of the groups on Christmas Eve that I did not know what would happen if every one of them would open their hearts fully to Jesus and let Him enter, but I would be most willing to find out!

And so we enter another year of unfathomable mercy — leaning hard on Jesus alone.

William Cawman

╫

February 1, 2013

As my schedule is now arranged I have only one regular Bible study on Friday evenings (two on Tuesday evenings) and so this past Friday was one-on-one interviews, both morning and afternoon. Is there a typical interview? I have not found it in fourteen years, but maybe you would be interested in peeking in on this particular day. We will take them one by one as it actually was.

(1) He is a black man, forty-one years of age, but looks vibrant and younger than that with a pleasant facial expression. He just recently joined my class and this is our first private visit. He begins to unfold his history. He has been to college and is an ex-navy man with several bars of honor on his jacket, which of course is now traded for the same khaki as all the others about him. He has earned several medals in the military and upon release started his own business of detailing private jets and yachts. He began to list the well-known people he has detailed jets or yachts for and has shaken many a big-time hand.

When he returned from the military he found that his wife had wasted every dollar he made on party clothing, to the point where she had even sold everything he owned in the house to buy more clothes. Partying was her specialty and love and she could not be persuaded to release the addiction, so he divorced her. Then he married again and this wife he really loved but he began, out of greed, to sell drugs from his detailing shop, and he was caught. Immediately his wife left him and for about ten years he went straight downhill in addictions and wasted living. All of his bright beginning was squandered, just like the Prodigal Son, and he found himself on the bottom and facing prison. After a bit of sobering reflection he began coming to Christian Living class and is recognizing that he is hearing there what his life has been missing all these years. He promised to seriously seek the Lord, and so please pray for him that he will turn his whole life completely over to God.

(2) In the corner of the room nearest the door in one of my classes sits an "old man." So he looks and acts. He comes in either with walker or wheelchair and fumbles his way to his seat and listens very attentively. I decided it was time to get acquainted with him before he would slip downhill any further and be gone. I called him down for a visit and discovered that he is three years younger than myself! That's enough to squelch any desire one might have to look in the mirror! He has had brain surgery, a heart attack, and now has Bell's Palsy, which certainly accounts for his much antiquated appearance.

A very quiet-tempered man, he nonetheless proved to be a perfectly untutored heathen as pertains to any knowledge of divine things. He expressed a desire to get out of his condition, but asked this pathetic question: "Chaplain, I say prayers every morning and I'm trying to read the Bible, but am I supposed to be getting something out of it?" Oh, how my heart longed to lead him to Jesus Who prayed, "Father, the hour is come; glorify Thy Son, that Thy Son may glorify Thee: As Thou hast given Him power over all flesh, that He should give eternal life to as many as Thou hast given Him. And this is life eternal, that they might know Thee the only true God, and Jesus Christ, whom Thou hast sent."

He lives in a four-man cell with Muslim cellmates. Oh, how much I wish he could know Jesus! What else does he have?

Will he even live till his release date? I think of how happy my life is with Jesus and a wonderful Christian family and then I look into his twisted face and so wish I could share my Jesus with him. "But the way of transgressors is hard. The wages of sin is death." Please pray that he will really find not "something," but "Someone!"

(3) Next at the door appears a man I have not met, but who has turned in a request to see the chaplain. He has both sides of his head shaved off and a Mohawk extending down over his forehead like a forelock. He has a hole in each ear lobe about 3/8" in diameter where whatever had been inserted before DOC [Department of Corrections] made him remove them. He has two conspicuous holes in his lower lip. He is tattooed with very obnoxious embryo angels in half-developed fetal positions and many other things, most of which he has done himself, as he is a tattoo artist.

But he is now sitting in front of the chaplain asking if there is something better.

What if there was not?

And there is not— that is, except for Jesus. Sin is absolutely helpless to correct itself. There is not one ray of hope offered in Scripture that supports the modern religious programs of self-help and self-reform, no matter how many "steps" they prescribe. The Tower of Babel never reached heaven and never will. There is, however, a remedy and a thoroughly satisfactory one, too— the cleansing Blood of Jesus Christ! I am very eager to see just what the Blood can do for this artifact of Satan's obnoxious artwork. He desires to visit more and we will. Will you pray?

(4) A few weeks ago a man appeared in my Bible studies who caught my eye and my mind with the immediate thought, "Is that a woman?" Small of stature with perfectly white but short hair, the face could have been either one or the other. I had not yet put a name to the face when I received a request for a visit, so in the door he came. I greeted him and asked how things were going and he began his tale.

He claims he has been a homosexual all his life, even though he was married to a woman for thirteen years and had a child. He is suffering with advanced AIDS as well as other physical problems, as his countenance well reveals. He tells me the officers hate him and openly show it, and even as he was coming down to see me one of the officers said to another, "I can't stand that man!"

I suppose there's little danger of an ego trip when living under those kinds of evaluations. He is but fifty-two years old, but I would have thought fifteen years older than that. His question: "Is there any real hope that I could be different? I'm not at all happy with myself." I began to try to show him just how God felt about him; that if he would seek for God's power to stop all sinning in his life, he could then ask God to correct what was wrong and give him victory over it.

He said he would really like that, but admitted that he did have a lover that he really did not want to lose. If God had a bargain basement or an auction block He would be bombarded with applicants, but that "strait gate" beyond which lies the "narrow way" leaves many still unwilling to part with the pleasures of sin. If they only knew!

(5) Then some of you who have gotten these letters for a long time would remember perhaps a man several years ago who was doing so well, but was accosted by a female officer and when he fled from her, like Joseph, and told the sergeant, was moved to another facility and immediately faced persecution. He became discouraged and faded back into the shadows and has remained there for a long time. At times I would put him on the appointment sheet for a visit and a few times he came, but he has spent way too long in a howling wilderness.

Recently I put him down for another visit and he really broke down in front of me and admitted that he was not happy with the state he was in. I begged him to earnestly seek God again and come back into the good way and he promised he would. He, too, needs prayer.

There were one or two more that day that did not leave much to write about, but this sample of needs will help you perhaps to know better how to pray for these lives who did not have the opportunities many of us did.

There has been a continuing move and deepening conviction and understanding of heart holiness among two of the classes in particular. We are praying and believing for God to give us some more genuinely sanctified men.

Today I had a very special interview. A man who has been in a few Bible studies now, I called down for a get-acquainted visit and found him to be my brother! He has been born of the same Father that I have and he is as happy about it as I am. The further the visit proceeded the happier we both got until we ended up in each other's arms. He hardly gave a thought to God or spiritual things until after he landed in prison in 1998 for a double murder, drug related.

On the night that he was arrested he sat up in his jail cell thinking up just how he was going to fabricate a string of lies to get himself out of his trouble. All of the sudden a Voice spoke to him as clearly as an audible voice, saying, "Tell the whole truth and the truth will set you free." He went before the judge and confessed it all, just as it happened. Coming away with a thirty-year sentence he again heard that Voice, saying, "Give Me your all." He there and then opened his heart and cried out to God and Jesus came in. He has walked in that Light ever since and has found it to shine ever brighter.

As I asked him further of his present relationship, he freely confessed that he at times finds things within him that are not like Jesus and he instantly cries out to God for victory over them and is thereby kept from sinning. I began to point him to the all-cleansing Blood that can deliver us from those ugly things within, and his face began to shine even brighter. "I want that!"

Let me tell you, in case you didn't know it before, there's power in a born-again soul! There's power to live above sin. There's power to shine with joy for Jesus. And there's power to instantly brighten up to the light of holiness without a kickback. This man is on his way into the fullness of God's predestinated plan for him— *to be conformed to the image of His Son!* Can you feel my excitement?

And then I have had a couple of visits with another younger man who realizes his life has been what he does not want it to be and has from all appearances really been born again. When I question him about a real and living relationship with Jesus, he excitedly and brightly affirms that he is living right there and wants more. It is one more reminder that the Holy Spirit is still faithfully brooding over this sin-devastated world and is calling souls to Jesus.

And listen to what happens when a soul, no matter where they have been or what they have done, responds to that call: "Verily, verily, I say unto you, He that heareth my word, and believeth on him that sent me, hath everlasting life, and shall not come into condemnation; but is passed from death unto life. Verily, verily, I say unto you, The hour is coming, and now is, when the dead shall hear the voice of the Son of God: and they that hear shall live. For as the Father hath life in himself, so hath he given to the Son to have life in himself."

By the way, don't miss the context here: this is not referring only to the final resurrection of the righteous, but also to the glorious moment when a soul who has been "dead in trespasses and sins" hears the heavenly call and opens the door. "Behold, I stand at the door, and knock: if any man hear my voice, and open the door, I will come in to him, and will sup with him, and he with me." And this precious promise was spoken to the very church age we are living in.

Many there are whose one-time Christian radiance has succumbed to an upside-down smile, as they deem this present day as having slipped over the edge of the divinely possible— or at least probable. Not so! There is still drawing love in the call of Jesus and power in His precious Blood. If you cannot find it, some others are, and oh, how glorious it is to listen to a man, once a child of wrath, now tell with rapture what Jesus is doing in his heart! I love it! Pray for more and more. What else in this world has any meaning left in it?

I want to thank God for some of our officers who are ever so friendly and supportive of our efforts. The class in Facility 1 has grown too large for the fire regulations for the classroom, so the officer is having the dividing partition rolled back every week to accommodate the larger number. He is such a warm, friendly and helpful man that we cannot but thank God for having him there.

I want to close with this statement: "I am encouraged!"

William Cawman

March 1, 2013

WELL, GOD HAS DEFINITELY been answering your prayers and there is a real "sound of a going in the tops of the mulberry trees" in more than one area. Just in this past month several men have been getting awakened to a real sense of need, and God has met some of those needs.

Just yesterday I visited with a young man who had asked for help and he really seems to give good testimony that God has forgiven his sins and given him new life within. When I asked him if he was finding a clear witness that his sins were forgiven and that he was a child of God, he responded most heartily that he certainly did, and it was growing brighter all the time. He had several questions to ask and as I tried to give him the answer from God's word, he beamed and said, "That's exactly what I thought! Wow!" He has now joined the class and is definitely not just there for something to do. It is very obvious that there is a lot of damage from the rocky road that Satan drew him down all his life so far, but he is surely finding something better now.

It is so rewarding, even though many are still struggling to be a Christian without Christ within, that some others are finding the reality of what God can really do for them. Please keep praying that the awakening will increase in scope and depth. Two of the classes in particular are so open and vibrant with the truth of holiness that it is thrilling to teach and preach to them. Our textbook is such a skeletal outline of the way of holiness that we often do not even get a point it lists all covered in one class period, but that is all right. We just want them to not only learn it mentally, but experience it all the way through.

It is such a glorious privilege to be able to take other ministers in from time to time, as well as having others from our church volunteer to cover classes also. God has chosen that in the mouth of many witnesses His word would accomplish its purpose. Often when we have a church revival, we clear the evangelist to go in to minister to the men in prison also. Last month I told you about a man who was saved in 1998 in his county cell after a Voice told him to tell the truth and the truth would set him free. He found such a precious relationship with Jesus that he has not lost it since. When I asked him if he ever encounters elements within that are not like Jesus and would like to rise up in his heart, he readily responded "Oh yes, but I don't give in to them. God gives me victory over them." Isn't that good as far as it goes?

Many people do not keep that well saved, and of course one cannot, once he knows there is a deliverance and fails or is slow to go on to receive it. When I told him there was a deliverance from those things within until they would not ever rise up and bother him again, he beamed with joy and declared at once he wanted it. Then later he told me that the last evangelist we had brought in (which was the only one he had ever heard) was speaking to them when all of the sudden a light went on inside of him and he at once said to himself, "That is what Chaplain Cawman has been talking about— now I see it all so clearly." And he agrees with it and wants it too.

Isn't it wonderful how God can take our clumsy efforts and stack them up in the corner until another brother comes along and lights the fuse that sets the whole stack on fire? I just love

God, don't you? After I visit with this man for a few minutes I feel like I've had a wonderful church service. I believe him to be a good candidate for "Now therefore give me this mountain, whereof the Lord spake in that day; for thou heardest in that day how the Anakims were there, and that the cities were great and fenced: if so be the Lord will be with me, then I shall be able to drive them out, as the Lord said."

On a Tuesday evening I was standing in the doorway greeting the men coming into Bible study. A man who has been there for several months stopped and began to tell me something about a man who had just been moved to that facility from another one (in the same prison). The second man is the one I wrote about who had been accosted by a female officer and had suffered persecution because he would not yield to her. Do you remember that for some time he had gone into discouragement and despondency, but that recently he really took hold again as I begged him to not stay in that trap of Satan but to pray through again? Well, I let what the first man said just go without comment, but it did bother me.

The following class time on Thursday, we had not begun before the first man wanted to say something. He openly confessed that he had misunderstood the second brother and had allowed a wedge to come between them. He begged the class and myself to forgive him as well as the other man and then went on to say, "The real problem is W—— is the one who needs to die! Every bit of trouble I've ever had has been what is still in me!" What a clearing of the atmosphere it brought to the whole classroom. Apparently God still honors the route of "Confess your faults one to another, and pray one for another..." It was not hard to start discussing our topic for the day ("present your bodies a living sacrifice...") in that cleared atmosphere.

Can God save a pedophile? It's too late to ponder that question— He already did. A forty-six-year-old white man came to us a few weeks ago under a heavy load of guilt and sin. He had been molested as a boy, and then had turned around and repeatedly molested the children of the woman he married. Once in prison, he began to reflect on his behavior and became completely snowed under with a sense of guilt and worthlessness. He actually hated himself for who he was and what he had done. We began to point him to the cleansing Blood and to the cross of Jesus, where all that guilt and sin could be nailed and he could be set free, a new, different man from the one he hated. He grasped hold of that hope and began to really seek God for forgiveness.

What a change! He is now beaming with joy and happiness, and when I ask him how he is doing he replies, "Wonderful, absolutely wonderful! I know He forgives me and I am finding communion with Him every day." His life of sin has left his body wrecked, and unless God chooses to heal him, he may not have much longer to live. He is very diabetic and because he ignored that his kidneys are now shutting down. They wanted to start him on dialysis, but he did not give his consent yet because he wants to hear from God as to what he wants him to do. He said, "I'm willing for whatever He wants of me, but I'd have to say that my heart longs to just go home to be with Him. He is the only One who has ever satisfied me like this!"

Another recent contact is a young man who seems very intelligent, had his own auto repair business, but fell into sin and now regrets it immensely. He came in two days ago and seemed so depressed and discouraged. When I began to inquire about it, he said he just can't stand living among and seeing all the evil that surrounds him in the prison. The atmosphere is not what he wants or is used to. He said the other day the officers were cursing at the men coming away from Bible study and then when he started up the stairway to his cell, blood was all over the steps where an officer had beat on an inmate.

Then he told me that he had married only a year before coming into the prison and his wife promised him she would stand by him for the four years of his sentence, but that after only a year, she left him. My heart went out to him and I began to try to point him to the One who is the answer to it all. After a bit he looked at me with longing eyes and said, "Chaplain, everything you are saying to me makes sense and I see it all very clearly, and I want it." Oh, how my heart longs in times like these to just be able to impart even a minute of the precious presence of Jesus, but that I cannot do. In Him alone is life; He is the source, we but the empty channels through which He flows. Oh God, keep me clean and pure so that only Jesus is seen!

Have you ever pondered the ramifications and potentialities of that frightening Scripture, "But evil men and seducers shall wax worse and worse, deceiving and being deceived"? That need no longer be considered a prophecy of things to come— it is here in all its fury. As if there are not sufficient false religions and cults in the world, new ones seem to be cropping up all over. My supervisor is almost completely occupied with finding out just which ones are recognizable legally and what their recognized practices are in order to allow or disallow them access.

Last week a new (unheard of before, and yet claiming to be older than all the rest) cult of some kind sent an official looking letter asking admittance to teach the men and claiming to be the reincarnation or something like that of all the old heathen beliefs. Maybe they found them in the recycle can, I don't know. They want to come in and teach heathenism— admittedly! And by that name too! Can you imagine it? So every new demon and his cohorts and supporters has to be traced down as to who and what and what they want to practice— on and on. My supervisor grows understandably weary and disgusted with it all and is sorely tempted to quit and retire, but then he says when he sees our group in there having Bible studies and helping the men he tells God he will labor on as long as He wills.

Please pray for him. Not only is it wearisome and totally obnoxious, but it puts him in varying degrees of liability, for

Habakkuk's prophecy also is now alarmingly fulfilled upon us: "Therefore the law is slacked, and judgment doth never go forth: for the wicked doth compass about the righteous; therefore wrong judgment proceedeth." This prophecy also needs no further fulfillment, does it? Oh, God help us to work while the day lasts!

Let me return back to the observations above regarding the new zeal and awakenings in the classes of late. The enthusiasm and genuine hunger of many is also becoming contagious and the classes are growing in number. This is encouraging indeed, but we are sure Satan is also aware of it and would love to derail the interest and hunger in any way he could. Please pray the covering of the Blood down over these classes until there can be lasting fruit unto holiness out of them. We have often pled the Scripture that "When the enemy shall come in like a flood, the Spirit of the LORD shall lift up a standard against him." That's good, but would it not be appropriate just now to pray that the Spirit of the Lord and the covering of the Blood of Jesus would hold back the enemy from coming in like a flood to start with? We dare not stop short of seeing the power of Jesus and the work of the Holy Spirit, that is evidently at work among them just now, accomplish all that it is sent for. "He shall see of the travail of his soul, and shall be satisfied," is our desire, and nothing short of it. We need not desire any more.

Thank you each one, Brothers and Sisters, for being part of this work by your prayers.

William Cawman

2
Give Us More of These Souls, Lord!

April 1, 2013

IT WAS A VERY MISERABLY raw day in south Jersey. The March wind still had the bite of winter in it combined with the dampness and drizzle of spring. I was walking toward Facilitythree of the prison when my eyes beheld a scene that occupied my thoughts, my heart, and my emotions for a while thereafter. An old, gray-haired man, shuffling behind a decrepit walker with head bent low and back stooped, was painfully making short steps to wherever he was supposed to be going. It was obviously taking all of his concentration to simply navigate himself forward into that raw wind and drizzle.

My mind began to wonder just what offer Satan had made him howsoever many years ago that brought him now as an old man to this pitiful condition. Who was he? Was he someone's daddy? Was he some woman's husband? What had he known of life in better days than this? If there exists somewhere on earth a child born of his body, where are they now, and what would be their feelings should they be able to see what I saw? I thought of my own Dad and couldn't imagine ever for any reason at all being able to continue to function in any frame of life whatever with him in such a condition as this.

Whatever it was that Satan offered him certainly was not what he is now experiencing. And then I thought of the many, many others who are grinding in Satan's prison house of sin's horrible wages. As I pondered these thoughts with pain in my own heart, I thought of the brief stanza from a poet, "The world's great heart is aching; aching fiercely in the night!" And just outside of every aching, crying heart, Jesus stands weeping too, longing for them to open the door and let Him come in and bring rest to their weary, sin-sick soul.

Once inside the building a sixty-year-old man came in to see me for the first time. He took a chair and I asked him how he was making out. He looked into my eyes for a moment and then said, "I'm lost. I'm just lost. I'm lost spiritually; I'm lost emotionally; I'm lost physically. I am just at the end of the road and I don't see any way out."

As he began further to unfold his story it was different from the majority. He had, one might say, lived the American dream. He had a wife and children, he had a home and automobiles and a motor home and boats and vacations and... until it all came to a crashing end inside of a ten by twelve prison cell with a roommate he did not know. He was born and raised a Roman Catholic, but early in life was disillusioned by the corruptions he saw and simply walked away from it and ignored God and religion altogether. But it must be noted that sometimes the Hand of redeeming mercy is pretty rough.

He told me he had tried to pray at times, but he couldn't tell that God was saying anything back to him.

I interjected at that point and let him know that his very sense of being lost was God speaking to him. I suggested he recognize that and go and thank God for helping him to recognize how lost he was instead of letting him go on in a dream. I told him there are many Americans like him who are living their dreams, and enjoying them too, but would spend all eternity in a burning hell.

He looked at me and knit his brow. "Do you mean to say that just living life for the world and not really doing anything wrong is cause to burn in hell? My father was a good man. He went to work, came home and ate the supper my mom fixed for him, was good to us kids, went in after supper and watched TV for a while and then went to bed and got up and did it all again the next day. Is he burning in hell?"

I replied with a story. I said, "Supposing a man has known for a week or two that his brakes are squeaking and that he should replace them, but the family is all excited about a picnic in the mountains and so he ignores what he knows he should do and goes up into the mountains. On the way back down he comes to a long, steep slope in the highway with a sharp curve at the bottom and a lake below it. The car begins picking up speed and he steps on the brakes only to hear a screech of failure as the car with his whole family plunges into the icy water below. I daresay the only thought in his mind is a screaming reminder, 'I knew I should have changed those brakes!'"

I said, "There will be no one in hell asking why they are there and accusing God of unjust punishment, for it will be clear for all eternity that they themselves are the reason they are there. They should have listened to the very same Voice you are hearing right now." He nodded his head in deep thought. He promised to give it some serious consideration and we had prayer. The next night he appeared in Bible study for the first time and listened attentively, though with an expression I couldn't discern. At the close he came up and shook my hand and said, "That was a very good sermon, thank you." He needs your prayers.

I believe God had a very special reason (doesn't He always?) for giving us the account in His Word of Elijah out under the juniper tree feeling that he alone was left of those who loved the Lord. It might be surprising to all of us just how many souls there are, even among those we meet day after day, who really have experienced a genuine relationship with God. Just this month a young man appeared suddenly on the scene and I have had a couple visits with him as well as having him in the classes. He began to tell me with real enthusiasm that he had gotten saved from his sin and is seeking God. He had gotten out of prison and was on parole but then violated the parole. There was a space of eleven months, between his violation and when he was sent back into prison, and not knowing for sure he would be sent back he married. His wife is a Christian girl whose mother is a pastor.

After he came back to prison he sought God and it certainly seems from all appearances that he really got a genuine experience of salvation. He said to me, "I am seeking nothing now but God, and I'm seeking Him passionately! I want my life to be God's." After he came back to prison his wife had a baby which he is looking forward to going home to. Fortunately he has less than a year left on his sentence and I believe if he keeps going as he is, we will not see him again in prison. I'd far rather meet him next in heaven.

Do you remember the ex-military man I wrote about in an earlier letter? His life had spun out of control when he found his wife had been wasting all his living while he was gone. Last week at the close of class he wanted to come up front and say something. He told us that in 2007, I believe it was, he was baptized and when he came up from the water it felt as though a hundred-pound weight fell from him. He began to cry and threw his arms around the minister who baptized him. He told the men that this class had made him feel the same uplift and he wanted to thank all the brothers and us for being there in the class. But now, he said, this would be his last class as he was going home. We all agreed to pray for him. I trust what he heard and felt will not be lost.

Now, to be really fair with the picture of a chaplain's life, let me insert a sample of encounters that are not as rare as one would wish. In my mailbox were three request slips, all from the same inmate. He actually comes from the same town in which the prison is located. One request slip simply stated that he wanted an interview with the chaplain. The other two requested that he be enrolled in all Bible studies and Sunday services, Seventh Day Adventist services, Buddhist services, Jehovah Witness services.

He came in and took his seat and I exchanged a few words of introduction. I then asked him for a bit of clarity on what he really wanted in religious help. I told him that it was against prison policy for us to enroll him in more than one belief system at a time. His prickles immediately went up and he wanted me to give him the supervisor's name so that he and another inmate could write up a grievance against him, because they should be allowed to go to any religious service they wanted to. I told him that rule had nothing to do with the supervisor, but that it was a rule sent down from Trenton and that there was a very valid reason for it.

I asked him under what religion he was classified in the prison system and he said he was a Jew last. I looked up his record and he wasn't presently classified as anything at all. Then he wanted to know why the Rabbi had taken his name off the Jewish list and I told him it was simply because he was not a Jew. He asked for the Rabbi's name so that he could file a grievance against him for taking his name off.

At that point I kindly suggested that he take time to cool off and then go and seek God and ask Him how He wanted him to serve Him. He said, "Do you have any booklets that I can read that will help me?" I happened to have one in my case and so I handed it to him. He looked it over and shoved it back on the desk and got up to leave, saying, "Don't call me down for any more visits." Why doesn't a person realize their misery and turn around?

As I write this I just returned from a very rousing class among the group that is presently the most vibrant and enthusiastic about the way of holiness. Even though we would not want for anything to bruise a broken reed or quench a smoking flax, yet truth is truth and not a bit of it can be held back. For a few weeks we have been discussing all aspects of the thought of our bodies being the temple of the Holy Spirit. Today we launched an attack against the American idol, commercial sports. And what a discussion we had. Scriptures were quoted to try to make at least an allowance to watch the favorite team. Experience was appealed to in the person of a professional athlete who "was a wonderful Christian!"

We listened patiently to each and every squirming loophole, but kept pointing them back to a very clear Scriptural command: "Love not the world, neither the things that are in the world. If any man love the world, the love of the Father is not in him. For all that is in the world, the lust of the flesh, and the lust of the eyes, and the pride of life, is not of the Father, but is of the world." I asked them to take the whole commercial sports program with its idolizing of heroes and the extravagant waste of money, such as 76 million dollars for one man for a single year of doing nothing more profitable than entertaining grown people. Take this along with the total worldly atmosphere at a ball game— just take it all and overlay it on those two verses of Scriptural command. I asked them, "Does it fit?"

"No," resounded through the room. I went on to ask them if a Christian could knowingly disobey the commandments of God. They responded with another "No." I asked them if it was not a Scriptural command that we keep the Lord's Day sacred and holy. They responded that it was. I then brought up the American idol (the professional athlete they mentioned earlier) again and asked how God would see him. Can a man give his Lord's Day away to the world and keep himself and multitudes of others from dwelling upon God on His holy day and be a genuine Christian? Heads went down and one could see the wheels turning. I must tell you that the class time ended with God's presence rich and full, nearly to the shouting point.

I then closed the class with this scenario: I told them that a couple of years ago I came home from the prison one evening and my wife had made a delicious salad for my supper. I began to eat it with relish when she asked, "Do you want anything else?" I said, "No, just more of this." One day I fell in love with Jesus and He is all I want. I am finding Him altogether lovely and satisfying and I would hate to leave Him to go to a ball game or anything else. Light began to dawn in fuller measure with that. Thank God! Keep praying for these men that they will make a complete sacrifice of all they are and have to obtain what is so, so much better! Don't you agree?

On Good Friday evening our church will be going in to hold four services, two at 5:30 and two at 7:30. Then on Sunday evening we will take a few young people in for the Easter services in one of the facilities. We are praying that it will be a time when the Blood of Jesus can be applied to the satisfying of the travail of His soul.

William Cawman

†††

May 1, 2013

A SHORT TIME BACK a young Hispanic man began to come to class at the invitation of his cellmate. He is eager for everything God has for him and it is such a blessing to visit with him. This is the same man we mentioned in the last paragraph on the first page of last month's letter. One day recently he was sitting in class listening as we were simply relating the scenes around Jesus' death and resurrection. Before long he was wiping tears from his eyes with his sleeve and then told us as he went out, "I couldn't keep tears from coming because He is so beautiful and you were talking about Him so beautifully."

A day or so later he came to visit with me and said, "Chaplain, I'm just so hungry for more of Jesus and I spend my time seeking Him and reading His Word, but some of the men are telling me that I am going too fast; that I need to slow down a bit."

I asked, "When you were out in sin and following Satan did anyone ever tell you that you were going too fast?"

"Oh no! I went in no time from two ounces of cocaine to one pound and no one told me I was going too fast."

"Well then," I said, "pay no attention to those voices, for this is far safer than the old path was."

He brightened up and gave me a facial expression that said, "Go after it even more!"

Another young man is also so encouraging. I love to see people excited about their relationship with Jesus. As soon as he came in the room for another visit he said, "Glad you called me down, chaplain. I need to know if this is right— the way I've been feeling. I am seeing so much evil all around me that it disgusts me and I can hardly stand it. Is that the way I should be feeling?"

I began to explain to him how Jesus hates sin but loves the sinner, and that we need to feel the same about it.

"Oh, that's good, that's what I'll do."

Then I suggested that there was a time in his life that he also was a sinner.

"Oh my, chaplain, I've been through some stuff! I've been in fights. I've been tied up and locked in the trunk of a car by some black fellows. I've been burned and left for dead. I fell out of a tree sixty feet to the ground and broke most of the bones in my feet and legs. I shouldn't be alive, but God saw what He was going to do for me. I'm here on a parole violation for just a short time, but I'm glad. It has turned my life around and God saw what was best. I used to want so many things I could never have, like a house and car and family, but now all I want is Jesus."

I said, "If you have Jesus you have all you need."

"I've got Him! I've got Him! Wow! It's wonderful to have Him in my heart!"

What a joy to sit and listen to a soul who has been pulled from the fire and is so happy about it. He is rather rough looking for his thirty-five years, but he is so happy.

Let me insert part of a letter from an inmate who has been moved to another prison:

I was listening to a sermon by Brother Warren [not Rick Warren, mind you] called "Show me thy glory" out of Ex. 33:14-23 and verse 21 stopped me in my tracks: "…a place *by* Me… thou shalt stand upon a *rock!*" The Gospel of Jesus Christ is woven all throughout the scriptures. How else can we be by Him, except by standing upon the Rock that is Christ? Praise God!

I somehow believe you can tell, but just so that you can hear it from me: I am doing better. Thank Jesus. Thank you so much for your Easter letter. It always blesses my heart to hear from you. I look forward to the eternal day when everyone talks like that.

I was thinking about my upbringing recently, and I saw a lot of parallels, spiritually, between my godless and idolatrous upbringing and that of the Canaanites. Most of the brethren in the Holiness church do not know what it is like to be raised in a home given over to worldliness (thank God), but I can tell you from personal experience that it is a miracle of God's grace that Jesus could undo all the damage.

Millions of children are being sacrificed to the fires of hell by godless upbringing. Twenty-four hours a day, three hundred and sixty five days a year (366 on a leap year), children are fed and polluted at Satan's altars. TV, video games, the internet, music, school, and even children's cereal boxes preach Satan's filth. It is the demonic version of God's commandment to teach His Word to our children, in and out of our houses, when we lie down, and when we sit up… (De. 6:6-9)

I do not believe that God could not have sanctified me and kept me all these years, but I can tell you that every fall has found its root in a seed planted in my childhood home. Thank Jesus that the training of a child in the way he should *not* go can be undone. Hallelujah! Greater is He! I pray for His help to spare as many children as possible from the trauma of being raised in sin. I hope the children who are blessed to be raised apart from this wicked world know how blessed they are?

In your Easter letter you asked if we would regret any cost, missing out on the devil's offers, or question the careful life once we are with Him. Dad, I have tasted more of this world and the devil's sin than I care to think about and I can tell you that all of it, every single lie and filthy pleasure is a rottenness in my bones that would make life unbearable if not for Jesus and His grace and mercy. Hate does not seem strong enough, but I am so grateful to God that loving Him is the best way to show my distaste for sin.

Oh the unsearchable riches of the goodness of God in Christ Jesus... No one but God can make life worth living. To think that we too will one day rise and meet Him in the clouds...well, it is heavenly. I love you dad. Thank you for blessing me to see Him in you. In His love —— .

And oh, I must tell you this, for the angels in heaven are rejoicing! A fifty-five-year-old white man came to prison for the first time a few months back. He joined my classes and Bible studies and then desired a visit. We have visited several times now, but at the first one I readily detected a man who was just as much of a heathen as if he had been raised in a pagan land. He had a Roman Catholic beginning, but strayed away and for years has apparently given no thought to God. He has been given to alcohol for twenty-three years; lost his wife over it as well as his daughter. Now in prison he has been sobered up and has been doing some serious thinking.

For the first few visits I tried to acquaint him with what it means to have a relationship with God, but I had to start from base one as he was even totally unfamiliar with the Bible. He asked where to read and I would try to direct him, but he kept saying that God never answered him. The visit before the last one I asked him if he was hearing any-thing from God and he said, "I don't think so. I can't tell that He is answering me."

I encouraged him to turn from every sin and he said he had. I told him to open his heart to Jesus and ask Him to re-veal Himself to him. He would always agree and had the sim-plicity of a child in taking directions. But— at the last visit things changed. His countenance was one of joy and peace and he told me that he had begun reading the Book of Romans and that it caused joy to spring up inside his heart and butterflies in his stomach. He said, "It's wonderful. It's speaking to my heart!"

I asked him again if he was hearing from God and he looked a bit mystified and said, "I can't really say that He has spoken to me, but I have such joy!"

I said, "Don't you realize that is God speaking to you?"

"Oh, really?" And with that even more light broke in on his face. I suggested that he testify to it that afternoon in class. He said, "All right, I will, but I'm afraid I'll break down."

"Go right ahead and break down," I told him, "It takes a man to cry."

That afternoon he got up in front of the class and said, "I have been seeking to find God for some time now, but in the last two weeks I FOUND HIM!" He broke down and so did others. One after another arose to hug him and welcome him into the wonderful family of God. He testified that the power of sin was completely broken.

You see, dear praying readers, God is answering your prayers, so let's pray some more, shall we?

Again I must report that the enthusiastic excitement over the work of holiness is on the rise. Class times are exciting as God reveals more and more of His holy standard for our lives. There are three successive stages in response to truth. All three are spoken of in the Sacred Word of God. First there is the response, "What new doctrine is this?" And right there we find old Simeon's prophecy still being fulfilled: "Behold, this child is set for the fall and rising again of many in Israel..." Peter also prophesied, by quoting Isaiah before him: "Behold, I lay in Sion a chief corner stone, elect, precious: and he that believeth on him shall not be confounded. Unto you therefore which believe he is precious: but unto them which be disobedient, the stone which the builders disallowed, the same is made the head of the corner, And a stone of stumbling, and a rock of offence, even to them which stumble at the word, being disobedient: whereunto also they were appointed." This new doctrine pulls like a magnet on a hungry born-again soul, but to the disobedient it is offensive.

Then the second stage of response is that of a mental assent. The doctrine of heart holiness, if understood properly, is the most intelligent, natural, sensible life that can be lived.

The third stage of response is the only one that begins to have redemptive power in it: a "love of the truth." This is impossible within the carnal mind, but when there has been a rebirth of the divine nature within one, a love of the truth is one of the first glorious birthmarks. It is a failure to receive this love of the truth that we are warned by God's Word will bring on a downward regression into sin and away from Christlikeness that has no limit known to man. Thank God, some of the men here have "received a love of the truth." Now pray that they will be filled with truth, which in turn cleanses from all unrighteousness.

Off and on for years we have mentioned a man who was sanctified by the Blood of Jesus before coming to this prison but who only came into the clear mental understanding of it after sitting under the proper teaching of it. He is a wonderful example of "That ye may be blameless and harmless, the sons of God, without rebuke, in the midst of a crooked and perverse nation, among whom ye shine as lights in the world."

We have told you that he volunteers to go and sit with dying men in the prison hospital and has seen a number of them turn to Jesus in their dying hours. I thank God for him! Recently, he was assigned to the bedside of a Muslim man, and although at first he did not break prison rules by trying to convert him, he freely discussed the Bible and God's grace with other Christian inmates who would come into the room.

After a time the Muslim man asked him to bring him a Bible. He began to read it and asked who Jesus really is. Our brother told him that He is the Son of God and the Muslim man said, "I believe that too." They then began having prayer together.

About that time the prison administration decided to have the news media do a report on the hospice program in the prison, so they chose to bring the reporter to the cell where our brother and the Muslim were. They interviewed them both and during the interview the administrator commented that she really liked the thought that a Christian and a Muslim could pray together. The reporter took it all in and published an article about it in two daily newspapers in the area.

Our brother told me, "I knew they would report it that way, but the real truth is, the Muslim was praying with me because he found Jesus to be who the Bible says he is." Thank God, news reporters cannot change facts! Pray for this brother that he can be used of God to bring many more *sons unto glory!*

In love, William Cawman

June 1, 2013

HOW QUICKLY THE MONTHS are flying by. For those of you who do not have something that occurs every month, such as writing a prayer letter, does time go slower? To anyone who shares with us such repetitive items as these are it seems hardly does a month come than another is here. If a person is building their hopes and dreams on this present life that could become a source of depression indeed, but to those of us who are "looking for a city," it is exciting to realize how rapidly we are approaching that glorious day awaiting the Blood-washed children of God.

We have mentioned before some of the battles we encounter with false prophets and spirits here in the prison. It is not something to be marveled at in one sense, because the Bible clearly warns us that they will multiply in the last days. But it is very, very painful to watch a bright new convert become confused over these false teachings that are so prevalent, then watch as confusion gives way to argument and finally to a spirit that robs them of the joy they found in believing. If that is not enough to make one in love with Jesus hate Satan, I don't know what else would.

The Scripture is so dramatically fulfilled in these words: "The thief cometh not, but for to steal, and to kill, and to destroy…" Isn't it so restful, however, to have those words followed by these: "I am come that they might have life, and that they might have it more abundantly." This battleground— this auction block, one might call it— brings us to a deep appreciation and longing that Jesus' words be fulfilled: "I am the good shepherd: the good shepherd giveth his life for the sheep… I am the good shepherd, and know my sheep, and am known of mine. As the Father knoweth me, even so know I the Father: and I lay down my life for the sheep… But he that entereth in by the door is the shepherd of the sheep… To him the porter openeth; and the sheep hear his voice: and he calleth his own sheep by name, and leadeth them out. And when he putteth forth his own sheep, he goeth before them, and the sheep follow him: for they know his voice. And a stranger will they not follow, but will flee from him: for they know not the voice of strangers."

Now, having said that, let me tell you about a time of the Shepherd's correction to my own soul. Two young men recently found this wonderful Shepherd and Savior. There is no question but what they were new creatures and loving to be so. Within a few weeks of their birth into the family of God, and not yet having "their senses exercised to discern both good and evil," they attended some Bible studies where the primary emphasis was that once saved you would always be saved, and that there was no possibility of ever losing one's salvation.

We have covered this ground over and over, as it keeps being taught and promoted with zealous fervor, but after spending most of that class period endeavoring to combat it once more, I felt a cloud come over my spirit. I felt it was largely a wasted endeavor. Why, pray tell, would anyone make it such a focus of teaching that one cannot lose his salvation instead of teaching dear souls to "earnestly contend for the faith once delivered to the saints?" I felt the Scripture strongly applied to my conscience, "...strive not about words to no profit, but to the subverting of the hearers." And the thought came to me, "If striving to prove one cannot lose his salvation is of no profit, but rather a subversion of the hearers, then striving to disprove it could fall into the same condemnation.

Don't misunderstand me; I am not saying this damnable doctrine hasn't and won't need to be tackled at times, but too much time spent striving over it simply causes the devil to stand back and laugh in glee because he sees we aren't getting to anything more constructive. I want God's help and your prayers that I can know when the Spirit would reprove and when the Spirit would turn to the "weightier matters of the law." I wish these false teachers could be kept away, but since they cannot I do not want to give the devil the satisfaction of having them win the battle by the slippery method of giving too much focus to their undoing. There is a counterfeit, but thank God, there is a real! I am promising God that by His help I will not allow the counterfeits to become a diversion or a distraction, but that we can hold up the real in its true glory!

The following day we had a powerful class time with a record attendance and God gave me great liberty in holding up the real. And it is real! Praise God!

Now I know it's full and free;
Oh the wondrous story;
For I feel it saving me!
Glory, Glory, Glory!

Jesus told us that if He be lifted up He would draw all men unto Him. How often have we seen this demonstrated. Arguing doctrine often leaves the valley full of the same dry bones we found there, but lifting up Jesus brings men's hearts alive with glowing response and hunger. Lamenting and exposing false counterfeits has its place, but O God of glory and virtue, let me see Thy face and then carry that glow among dying souls!

It wasn't Stephen's impeccable theology— fresh from Pentecost— that pierced the hearts of his accusers. It was his shining face as he looked up and saw Jesus standing at the right hand of the Father. Oh, let me see that Face! I somehow feel correct theology will flow out from it quite naturally.

Well, that was intended as a confession, not a sermon— but "what I have written, I have written."

One of the young men mentioned above needs your prayers (not that the other one doesn't). In the last class period he opened up his most honest heart with these words: "Chaplain, I want to ask something. When I first got saved I really felt a lot of God and nothing else mattered to me, but it's not that way now. I am not finding the same joy and everybody around me is bothering me. Is that normal? I don't really like it this way. I want it to be the way it was, but is it normal for it to wear off?"

I thanked him for his honest confession and then assured him that although many do fall victim to that state of affairs, it was most certainly not God's will for him; that God never intends us to look back to better victory over sin than we have right now. I urged him to repent of leaving his first love and to ask God to forgive him and restore that joy and power he had before. He said he would do just that. The poor boy has had so little in his background to help him forward now. He has had a very tumultuously rocky existence in his twenty-some years, with no spiritual influences whatsoever to guide him. Surely he is a perfect candidate for Him who "came not to call the righteous but sinners to repentance."

Please pray that he will so seek after God that he will become a shining example of the restoring redeeming grace that Jesus purchased on Calvary. Don't be concerned just now over the missing teeth and gory tattoos and scars of sin. Jesus can shine through them, too. I've seen it already in others, so it is too late for Satan to tell me it can't be done.

I want to give you an honest assessment, as nearly as I am able, of how the grace of God is working among the men here.

In 2 Cor. 6:1 Paul wrote, "We then, as workers together with him, beseech you also that ye receive not the grace of God in vain." This excludes any grounds for claiming any work of God as the work of some man, whoever and whatever that man may be or not be. We find it a matter of rejoicing and great comfort that God has laid the burden of this ministry to men in prison on the hearts of several in our church. Could I be safe to say that He has laid it upon all of us together?

Then He has also laid it upon many of your hearts as well. To some He has committed the burden of prayer, to others of encouraging words to those ministering, to others the gift of helping those who are released, and to others the burden of giving of their time, when they already have much to do, in order to fill in vacancies in classes, Bible studies, and Sunday services when we ourselves are gone in meetings elsewhere. To each and every one of you we want to say a huge and heart-felt thank you. God is using it all in ways that I would like to try to express to you.

My heart has been warmed again and again in returning from a meeting and being welcomed back with overflowing and enthusiastic love, to hear the men either in testimony or prayer thank God for each one of the volunteers who have ministered to them in our absence by name. It thrills me that unless from some isolated case of egotistical self-righteousness (we have a few of these too), I hear nothing but love and praise for the ones coming in to minister to them.

Now, just in case you might think that this is coming from undiscerning charity, I tell you clearly that these men for the most part know full well that much of what is given to them in other Bible teachings and Sunday services is unscriptural and grievously sparing of the sin that Jesus came to destroy. Some at times relate to us how troubled they are with the teachings of many of these and how satisfying they find what those from our church are teaching them. I am not intending to single out our church as the only church that is teaching any truth, but as I sometimes tell the men, "I do not say that a person must go to our church in order to make it to heaven, but I know why I go there."

New Jersey is a barren land when it comes to the message of heart holiness and living free from sin. Churches are everywhere, but sin is also. It would be a very dangerous thing to make such an assessment as I have just made were it coming from only man's viewpoint, but God Himself prophesied in His Word of the last days, "Now the Spirit speaketh expressly, that in the latter times some shall depart from the faith, giving heed to seducing spirits, and doctrines of devils; Speaking lies in hypocrisy; having their conscience seared with a hot iron..."

Again, Peter warns us, "But there were false prophets also among the people, even as there shall be false teachers among you, who privily shall bring in damnable heresies, even denying the Lord that bought them, and bring upon themselves swift destruction. And many shall follow their pernicious ways; by reason of whom the way of truth shall be evil spoken of." If these prophesies do not refer to the tidal wave of so-called "Christianity" that has pervaded our land with all types of emotional phenomena that allows sin to go on unchecked, then what do they refer to?

I have said all that to point out that we have a good number of men here in prison who have had "their senses exercised to discern both good and evil," and who are receiving the truths brought to them by the volunteers from our church, backed up by your prayers, and are growing steadily. They are not vacillating and up and down, but are growing stronger in the way of holiness with every class and Bible study.

In the fifteen years I have been ministering here in this prison I have never before witnessed such a genuine heart acceptance of the message of true holiness. To all and every worker together with Him, "Thank you" is way too small a thing to say, but Thank you, anyway! I will whisper to you a little secret on the side. When I hear men say, "I love your pastor," I love them and him all the more for it! Thank God for the privilege of simply being "workers together with Him!"

When all of our labors are over, whether in prayer or ministry or support of any kind, we will receive the glorious crown of being but "unprofitable servants" of our glorious Master. I have been on mission fields, in churches, at camps, and have been very conscious that I was merely reaping where others had sowed. The rescue of a soul from sin is often the result of a long chain of circumstances and events. The worker who God uses to put the last link in the chain is often crowned as the "soul winner" in that case, when in reality there may have been many workers before him who put in a link without which the last one would never have been. One of the joys of heaven will be that there will be no big heads, no VIPs, no outstanding personalities, no pat-on-the back favorites— oh, no! All will be bowed in rapturous worship "unto him that loved us, and washed us from our sins in his own blood."

Thank you, fellow-laborers. The best is yet to come! Hallelujah!

Your fellow-servant, William Cawman

3
"Is Anything too Hard for the Lord?"

July 1, 2013

I CANNOT TRUTHFULLY BEGIN this letter with the statement, "as usual." No, it has been very unusual, and that applies to both good and otherwise. It has been a month of very genuine spiritual growth in some, awakening in some others, and also of sad disappointments in others. But that is a very general beginning, so let me go to some specifics.

First of all, I want to thank you again for all the prayers you have been praying for us here in the prison. I am continuously aware that God is hearing them, but one day recently in class I was very conscious that someone was praying for us. I had given the classes, two weeks before, a list of fifteen questions and asked them to write their answers or understandings on typing paper that I had passed out. I did not do it altogether for their benefit, but that I might get a better grasp on whether the teaching had been effective and where we needed to go back and strengthen some concepts.

Question number six was, "Why does a saved person still have a sinful nature?" Almost to a man the answer was that we are still living in a human body. When returning to that question a couple weeks later I told them how many had answered that way and then told them that it was easy to understand why they might think so. The absence of the Divine Nature that we come into the world with has so trained our human body to be its servant by the time we even come to accountability for it that it is easy to think our human body is the source of sin.

As we went on to differentiate our body from the "sin that dwelleth in me" (Paul's terminology), one man in particular felt it necessary to voice how he had been taught and the first half of the class became rather tense with conflict. All of the sudden like a breath from heaven I felt my spirit lifted and anointed and it passed on to them until by the time the class time was finished God was there in power, convincing men of truth. The man who at first was rather contentious came and with a huge genuine smile shook my hand and thanked me and as they passed out the door I could hear them saying to each other, "Wow, what a teaching!" I know full well that heads pitted against heads don't bring that. Intelligence pitted against intelligence doesn't do that. Theologies pitted against theologies don't do that. God does! And He did it because someone or "someones" were praying for us just then. I could consciously feel it. Thank you! And thank God!

Truth is beautiful when applied by the Holy Spirit. Without that, Paul wrote, "the wrath of God is revealed from heaven against all ungodliness and unrighteousness of men *who hold the truth in unrighteousness.*" If we step out from under the Spirit's anointing, even in speaking the truth, it becomes just one more demonstration of "that which is born of the flesh is flesh." I believe it was J.A. Wood who for several years opposed the idea of a second work of grace because he did not understand it. When he finally became convinced of it he said he fought to defend the second work so arduously that he lost the first work over it. God save us from flesh!

Oh, by the way, the next day one of the men in the class came and honestly inquired, "Chaplain, I am not arguing about a second work of grace, I just can't find it clearly in the Bible." As I began to point out the clear teaching of Scripture regarding it, he listened very attentively and then said, "Don't get me wrong, I just wanted to see it from the Bible. If there are five works of grace available, I want them all!" It's not hard to convince a hungry soul, is it?

One afternoon as we assembled for class in Facility 1 I asked a man on the front row who bears all the marks of a new birth (notwithstanding almost complete coverage by tattoos) to pray. He reached out and put his arms around the two brothers beside him and began. "Jesus, You know my heart is heavy right now, but Jesus, I'm coming through with You. Oh, Jesus, these trials are only to purge out the dross and refine the gold. Jesus, I love You with all my heart."

And with that he broke into tears and sobbed. He continued praying but there was pathos in his voice that spoke volumes he could not speak with his lips. It was evident that he meant every word he was praying. He was not praying to impress anyone or to be heard of men, but he was pouring out his soul to God. When he finished there was such a Presence in the room that, not knowing why his heart was heavy, I felt the men desired to support him and so I just suggested it was time for a group hug. After they had joyously accomplished that, and with arms still about each other all over the room, I said, "Now brothers, let's all tell him in unison, 'We love you brother!'" In such atmosphere it is sometimes difficult to know what we ought to do next.

After the class the brother took me aside and whispered to me that he has twin girls who are now fourteen years old and that one of them had been raped. He went on to say that his old self would have wanted to really hurt the perpetrator, but every bit of that was gone from his heart. He said, "While my heart is hurting, I have nothing but forgiveness for the man who sinned against her, and I don't ever want anything else to be there." I say again, this only the marvelous grace of God can accomplish. I told him that the trials of life will reveal if there is anything left in our hearts that is unlike Jesus or they will prove to us that there is not. His face beamed as he said, "Thank you, man, I needed that!"

This class has now outgrown the room we are meeting in. The fire code only allows thirty-six men including the teacher in the classroom. Will you help us pray that we can get our chapels back so we will not have to turn any away? This past week the officer had to send the last three or four that came down back to their units because the room was full. It is God who is drawing these men to come, so will you pray that this same God will provide a bigger room for us? We could have worse problems, couldn't we? It is always a wonderful problem when the church overflows. This group of men are for the present the most lively and responsive group in the prison. They are not contending against the truth, they are welcoming it and walking in it and I know God is working deeply in their hearts.

Do you remember the young man who had been so emotionally trashed in the conflict in Iraq? He had gotten out but is back for a short time and my heart goes out to him. He expresses the fact that he really wants his life to be right but that most of the time he just feels so weak that it is easier to just give up and let the devil run over him. He needs prayer.

Last month I told you about the class where such a contention had come up over eternal security. One young convert who I really believe was genuine has been under that teaching by another instructor and lacking both foundation and discernment has been bombarded by that instructor with Scripture after Scripture that "proves" that you cannot lose your salvation. He came down for a visit with his guns loaded and his list of Scriptural artillery all in place to straighten me out and prove to me that once you are saved you are always saved. The brightness and joy and clearness he had a few weeks ago when he first got saved has now given place to a countenance that is sadly disfigured.

I saw immediately what he was up to and stopped him and

said, "Listen to me. Put that list away because we are not going to even talk about that. I want to know, how is your love for Jesus? How is your communion with Him?"

"Oh, it's good." But he was so full of vinegar over eternal security that he could not bring himself to give up. I again refused to go in that direction and tried to point him to something more important— what he should be doing to not lose the joy of the Lord. Oh, how sad to see this young bright convert so led astray and drug back into darkness over the "doctrines of devils." Satan himself knows better than the doctrines he teaches. He knows full well he has lost his salvation and will never see heaven again. What a liar! He doesn't simply lie; he is a lie.

In one Bible study recently among almost the same group in Facility 1 that is so on the move, one of the good brothers asked if he could say a word. He began to tell the men that he could not disobey God in a word that He had given him and began to urge them to quit playing around with God and sin at the same time and get right. He said, "I'm not pointing fingers, I'm not calling names, but some of you are not living outside of church what you are professing in church. If that is you, why don't you just come right on up front and ask God to get this right?" One man on the front row immediately jumped up with his hands in the air and said, "That's me, brother." Several others followed and we had a good time of prayer with them. I do believe God was in it, for it certainly produced good results.

The sixty-year-old man I wrote about who is so confused has been so worried over his much beloved wife that I cannot at present really get him to concentrate on anything else. He has not heard from her since March and she had been so faithful in writing. They seem to be deeply in love, which is good. He told me he has been having terrible dreams that she has passed or she would write to him. When I saw how distressed he was I feared that he was about to go into deep anxiety and so I contacted the social services and they placed a phone call to his wife. She had been busy with her sister who had suffered a stroke and she said she was well and would write to him. That evening I told him and what a relief came over him. He said he would sleep a lot better that night. Please pray that he will seriously consider his eternal welfare and seek God in spite of all his lifetime of disappointments over having Him misrepresented.

And then let me update you on the fifty-seven-year-old who was a drunkard until the last few years in prison. He is absolutely a child in spiritual understanding and every time I meet with him I have to help him find his way through a new battleground. But in spite of it, he listens and agrees and God is helping him. He said, "Chaplain, I feel so good when I'm with you. You help me so much." Perhaps he is like Ephraim of whom God said, "I taught Ephraim also to go, taking them by their arms." It seems some just need that, so we will continue to do our best to help him.

Having just returned from a camp meeting I want to express my heartfelt gratitude to each one of you who remember us from time to time, and even faithfully, in your prayers. So many times when I am away, brothers and sisters in the Lord come and tell me how much they enjoy the letters and how they are praying for us. That is exactly why there are new victories to write about— God answers prayer. How aware I am that God did not call us into this work alone. He has also laid the burden on many of your hearts, and that is so precious. We are workers together with Him. The battle is His; the work is His; the victories are His— we are but unprofitable servants. But He has chosen to do His work through us and every one of you who sends a prayer up to heaven for us is just as much a part of the ministry among these men as we are.

Not only does that encourage and warm my heart, but it binds us together as one in this little sector of God's great harvest field. "Thank you" seems so small an expression for the part you are doing, but God will have to fill in the rest, and I know He will. Someday in heaven would you mind if a former inmate of a New Jersey state prison comes to you and says, "My dear brother/sister, it was you who prayed a prayer that helped me through all that I was facing until I touched the hand of Jesus. Could I thank you for it now, since we didn't know each other then?"

I believe just this will happen, but for now— Thank you!

In Him, William Cawman

August 1, 2013

Isn't it a wonderful blessing that God has not appointed a single one of us to select candidates for His grace? He gave us a most powerful Book containing all that we need to make it from earth to heaven, but He closed it with this simple condition: "And the Spirit and the bride say, Come. And let him that heareth say, Come. And let him that is athirst come. And whosoever will, let him take the water of life freely." God and God alone has the accurate record of every individual soul in this present world that is coming and taking of that "water of life." Every so often He lets us in on a part of His secret, but without a doubt there are many more that we never meet here on earth.

If you or I would go into a Sunday night service in the prison (one of the eight held each Sunday night) and look over the men while they are seated in the chapel, we would probably pick out an outstanding face here and there and conclude like Samuel, "Surely the Lord's anointed is before him," but we might also hear God whisper to us, "the Lord seeth not as man seeth; for man looketh on the outward appearance, but the Lord looketh on the heart." Consequently it continues to amaze and thrill us to discover among all the many just who it is next that God is working on.

And so…

He is well into his fifties, we would guess; bears the unmistakable features of a Roman Italian; walks very stiffly with the help of a cane; and is suffering from bladder cancer. He just began coming to classes and Bible studies a few months ago, but is growing like a weed. We have him in class or Bible study but two hours or so a week, but from all observations God has him in His school around the clock, and he is demonstrating clearly the Scriptural truth, "though our outward man perish, yet the inward man is renewed day by day." Whether he will ever last long enough to get out of prison, who would know, but he is happy in God's grace that he is finding in richer measures all the time. He does not look a bit well physically, but he surely does spiritually. Is he the natural make up that one would readily pick out and expect God to make a saint out of? I couldn't say Yes to that, but I am not God and so glad of it. "The Lord looketh on the heart."

And then let me give you an update on our dear brother whose prayer in class we told you about last month. He came in the door recently to class and came up to us with such a warm hug and said, "Brother, I'm finding it easier and easier to obey God." Do you remember how we told you that he had prayed, "Jesus, I love You with all my heart," even while his heart was heavy with sad news from home? Well, are you putting the two together? Love made perfect renders easy obedience, doesn't it?

It is so glorious to watch the Biblical graces grow in gardens that would appear outwardly so non-conducive. Demonstrations such as this give no foundation whatsoever to a thought of, "What shall we say then? Shall we continue in sin, that grace may abound?" No! Rather, such growth in such unfertile and unlikely soil just magnifies the wonderful grace of Calvary's cleansing fountain. It has been more than sufficiently demonstrated that He is "able to save to the uttermost!" There is not a tragic wreck of Satan that Calvary cannot restore. Let all controversy over that cease!

The class in Facility 1 continues to grow and vibrate with the beauty of God's holiness as taught in His own Word. Thank you for praying. Starting with the first class in August, we will be moving to a larger room where we can put all the men that we had to move to a waiting list back on the appointment sheet. Please continue to pray that these men will allow the truth of holiness to so cleanse and fill them that they will not only be convinced and hearers of the word, but will obtain pure hearts that will stand whatever lies ahead for them. Pray that more of them will get genuinely sanctified. Pray that they can shed off some grave clothes— for some, the teachings of an insufficient Christ; for some, the lingering remnants of Charismatic teachings; for others, the shackles of undisciplined living so easily developed in this present age. God is able for all of these needs and more, isn't He?

Then let me give you an update and prayer request for the sixty-year-old man that we also told you about, who hadn't heard from his wife and was so beaten up with anxiety over it. His whole countenance has softened and changed since he has heard from her and she is doing well. I sat down with him and began to press the thought that God hasn't allowed all this to happen for him to stop here. He listened very attentively as I tried to point out that even though he has lost everything he had (and he was living the American dream— $400,000 house, motor home, boat, vacations, etc.), if this means spending eternity in heaven instead of in hell, he would thank God for it for all eternity. He then said, "I hear that and I know God has my attention. I promise I will seek Him further." He was raised a Catholic, but early saw the inconsistency of all that and since early adulthood has simply lived for this present life. But "The Good Life" or "Life is Good" slogan found on bumper stickers can end in hell just as effectively as the bottom rung of the social ladder can. I do want so much to see this man really find a living relationship with God.

I will update you also on the fifty-seven-year-old recovered drunkard from last month's letter as well. As I already said, he reminds me of what God said concerning Ephraim: "I taught Ephraim also to go, taking them by their arms…" This dear man has no spiritual military training whatsoever, but I trust he is learning. He comes in with a cloud over his countenance and begins to tell me about the warfare he is in with Satan. As soon as I try to explain to him that this battle is not to be marveled at but that here is what he needs to do, his face becomes bright again and he is ever so willing to pledge himself to do it. I will stand by him, but oh, how much I want to see him learn the secret of going to Jesus and finding victory in his conflicts. God was patient with me— pity on me if I cannot be so with him.

And this brings me to something else that was made freshly real to me this month. It was said of Jesus by the Prophet Isaiah and quoted in Matthew's Gospel, "A bruised reed shall he not break, and smoking flax shall he not quench, till he send forth judgment unto victory." So often in teaching men from various religious backgrounds we confront those errors that they have been previously taught. It is easy to become too hasty in counteracting these errors and bruise a tender soul who is not yet ready to have his foundation crumble, for he has not yet developed another. Oh, how much we need the anointing and wisdom from above that can guide us in leading, as under-shepherds, these wounded sheep back to the way of pure truth. As you hold these men up in prayer, do please also hold up those of us who are endeavoring to bring them into the knowledge of the truth. If we were building houses and made a mistake, we might be able to correct our error, but when dealing with souls, damaging them is a very serious thing. Oh, the value of each and every soul that is behind prison walls. Lord, lay it more deeply than ever on our hearts!

You would enjoy and probably be amused, as I also am, at one of our dear Hispanic brothers. He has been in classes and Bible studies for several years now. Just how much discernment he has between the various doctrines being taught I really could not say, for his English/Spanish handicap is fairly significant. Notwithstanding that, he really enjoys his studies and his Bible and is as faithful as the clock and calendar. He always gives a slight bow and smile and handshake when entering the room to be taught. Several years ago I can remember how much he loved his Bible, and over the years (I can't remember how many now) his Bible has had many papers stuffed in it and it has been read many times and marked much, and as all this attention is given it, the pages have swelled fatter and fatter until today it is probably almost three times its original thickness. When it breaks apart in the binding, he secures it with another layer of clear tape and this has been repeated so many times that the back spine has a thick layer of translucent tape binding it where the original material is about non-existent. I sometimes pick it up and show it to the class and they get amused while he just grins with love for it.

The other day he came into class and gave his little bow, his smile, and his greeting of handshake and then went to his desk and sat down. While waiting for the others he opened for the who-would-know-how-manyeth (excuse me, computer— that's the way I want to spell it!) time, and then after reading a bit looked up at me with a very satisfying smile and pointed to something in his Bible and then made the finger symbol for perfection. Then he pointed to it again and then laid his hand over his heart, and his smile grew even bigger. I have a feeling that he will be satisfied when he sees for the first time the Living Word face to face. He will be no stranger to Him then, for he is growing so acquainted with Him now.

Some of you have asked how things are going with the Muslim chaplain who was gaining such a foothold in the institution. Well, you prayed, didn't you? He was suddenly exchanged with a much younger Imam from another prison, and while we don't know for sure that it will be permanent, it has given us a real breather for a good while now. The younger man has only been a chaplain for four years, but was educated in Saudi Arabia. He wears the entire Muslim garb, but is very friendly and open to greetings and is a refreshing change from the utterly negative atmosphere the other one created wherever he went. It is also a relief because he does not have all the inside connections as the former one. You might remember in prayer that God will continue to keep this whole transition under His control for as long as He has work for us to do.

My supervisor becomes very discouraged at times with all the politics of the system, but he does an excellent job of holding the doors open to us, and he also needs and wants your prayers. It is not an easy or comfortable position in present America to be a supervisory chaplain in a state prison. There seems to be no end to the many cults and so-called religious beliefs that are coming up and wanting to spread their "whatever" within the prisons.

It used to be that in order to be recognized as a "religion" a belief would at least have to have some Biblical foundations. Not so anymore. The most bizarre perversions of truth and common sense can ask and gain governmental approval to propagate themselves while evangelical Christianity is being shoved further and further into the realm of "dangerous." Little wonder, if you have read your Bible even once. Shall we give up the battle? Never! God is still bringing souls to Himself in spite of it all, and we will carry on with love and joy until He comes. We will be so glad then that the last sheaf was not left behind. What if that one were you?

As you remember us in prayer, please don't forget the volunteers from our church who fill in so faithfully when I have to be away at meetings throughout the year. It is an absolute blessing that they are so willing to go in and take the classes and Bible studies and church services, because it is not just a single voice stemming the tide against all the other doctrines that are taught. I thank God for such a willing and precious team of helpers. Even though I am not allowed to put personal names in these letters for security's sake, they certainly desire your prayers also.

With love and gratitude, William Cawman

September 1, 2013

GOD ASKED A QUESTION OF Abraham and Sarah when Abraham was one hundred years old and Sarah was ninety: "Is anything too hard for the Lord?" We know well the history— it wasn't. Sarah gave birth to a son at the ripe old age of ninety. Seventeen or eighteen hundred years went by and the Angel Gabriel made a proclamation to the Virgin Mary: "For with God nothing shall be impossible." Should not this settle all doubts concerning God's almighty power?

I was reminded and quickened as well just a couple of days ago concerning God's omnipotence as I listened to a modern-day miracle. The man I am referring to has been mentioned a few other times in the last few months, but this visit was especially precious and heart-stirring. I thought it good to have another one-on-one visit with him so put him on the list. I knew from his looks that he had experienced plenty of the devil's wares and wages. He is of a very dark complexion, which is added to by intense tattoos just about everywhere they would fit. Over the past year I have watched this man grow in grace and in humility and in power over sin and it has been precious to behold.

But now he began to unfold the pit from which he came. I will not be indiscreet in this letter except to give you a glimpse into who he was so that you can appreciate and magnify the grace of Jesus Christ and His atoning, re-creating Blood. This previously reckless soul was so hardened by sin and degradation that it is almost unbelievable. Forgive, if you can, this exposure from his past, but he actually brutally murdered one woman in his life with a hammer, and says that he didn't even feel bad about it. He was so spaced out on drugs and alcohol and abandonment to Satan that he just plunged recklessly and rough-shod over the feelings of anyone, so long as he could obtain the next promised pleasure for self.

Had you met this poor wreck of Satan on the street a few years ago you would have run the opposite direction. His facial appearance and large physical frame would have been more frightening than any Halloween mask has ever been. Furthermore, this life-style went on for a long time (he is now fifty years old) and he was clever enough to evade capture over and over.

Could I suggest right here that God's decree, "and be sure your sin will find you out," is actually a part of His infinite mercy, notwithstanding it being often viewed as a threat? Anyway, after spending some time in prison, he was finally arrested by the Supreme Judge and began to seek the Lord. Has the grace of our Savior taken away his tattoos and scars and all the bodily suffering he is now enduring because of the treatment of his physical? No. He is still afflicted with stomach pains almost continuously because one of the women in his life tried to poison his food numerous times. She choked to death on a piece of meat since he has been incarcerated.

But one day about a year and a half ago as he began to listen to the drawing of the mercy of God, a tear came into his eye for the first time for the woman he had so brutally murdered. He asked God to break his heart and He did. He came in deep repentance and is now serving God just as violently as he served the devil. As I sat and listened to far more than I have told you (and, by the way, there was not a hint of glorying in this awful past, but rather deep regret) I couldn't help but say to him, "Brother, I can see clearly the marks of what you used to be, but shining through it all I see such a tender love for Jesus and your brethren that were I to meet you on a dark street at night I would feel perfectly safe to run into your arms." With a soft and tender smile he said, "And you would be safe there, too! Chaplain, thank you so much for calling me down for this visit. This has been such a blessing to me, it has made my day!" It made mine too!

"Is anything too hard for the Lord?"

The next day I was visiting again with a gloriously sanctified man who I also have written about several times over the years past. There is no letup in his walk with God. He glows with victory and clearly states that his prayer closet is the source of it all; that is of course, the God he meets with in his prayer closet. He is the one who sits with dying men in the prison hospital and has seen a number of them come to Jesus in their last hour. He was telling me of the suffering he has been passing through by seeing so many go into eternity with no clear witness of being ready for that. He said that two men he had worked with died the same day recently and he couldn't feel that either of them had made their peace with God. He was struggling with how a soul can know full well they are going into eternity and seem so unconcerned about having no assurance that they are ready for heaven. I told him that it is impossible to live close to the heart of Jesus and not feel that pain, because He feels it. Yet at the same time he said there is peace and joy and rejoicing in the Lord along with the suffering.

I then pointed out to him two statements from the Apostle Paul. "Rejoice evermore." And then, "I say the truth in Christ, I lie not, my conscience also bearing me witness in the Holy Ghost, That I have great heaviness and continual sorrow in my heart. For I could wish that myself were accursed from Christ for my brethren, my kinsmen according to the flesh." We talked about how nothing other than the living presence of Jesus within us could have both of these emotions at white heat and at the same time. Then I said to him, "Bro. ———, certainly, as you know, God did not put you in this prison, but now that you are here, He is using you to His glory and purpose, for you are doing a work none of us can do." Please pray for this dear brother of ours. He is God's man through and through and is reaping a harvest where you and I cannot go. Pray for continued anointing on his life and testimony.

Some time back we wrote about a man from Sierra Leone who got saved during a Bible study that our pastor was holding in the prison. From that time, he has not turned back to his old life. For some time now he has been in another prison in the state, but just a week or so ago was moved back here. He immediately sent word through other inmates that he wanted to see me and join again in the Christian classes. When he is finally finished with his sentence he will undoubtedly be deported back to Sierra Leone and he wants to be prepared to be a missionary to his people. I am looking forward to meeting with him again, but it will have to be next week after this letter is already printed, so I will have to let you know the outcome next time. In the meantime, please pray for him. He is naturally a very quiet and meek person, but as far as I can tell has been very steady with the Lord from that day God saved him.

Not every visit with these men is uplifting such as the first one I told you about in this letter. Yesterday I had a written request from a man I did not recognize by name and so had no idea what he wanted. You see, by state rules we are obligated to respond to an inmate's request to be seen, but often this means entering into a dialogue with a man with no time to prepare or ponder what he is about to ask or tell one. For instance, one day in responding to a request I was confronted with a twenty-seven-year-old who was desperate for me to tell the Department of Corrections to give him the female hormones he wanted so that he could become a woman. He said he was a woman trapped in a man's body.

I suggested that since he was actually male by birth he request hormones to make him content to be a man, but he refused that suggestion and said he didn't want to be a man. I told him I could not help him and that was the end of that interview.

Well, back to the man we are now talking about: he presented himself a twenty-three-year-old with a very juvenile look, a pleasant smile and soft voice and eyes. He got right to the point: he announced that he was a Luciferian and wanted a vegetarian diet. He also wanted to obtain a Black Book (forbidden by the prison— so far) and a book of Luciferian magic.

I ignored the request for the time and began to probe into his past, for my whole heart was crying, "What is wrong here and how did this boy get so far out at sea so early?" I asked him about his family and he basically has none. He has a twin brother who is doing thirty-some years. He has three other siblings that he did not want to talk about.

His mother and father never wanted or loved him and he wants nothing to do with them. His grandfather raised him but didn't care what he did. He committed his first murder at the age of eleven. He joined the gangs and literally wasted his precious youth in hell on earth. I asked him why he had joined the gangs and why he now wanted to follow Luciferianism. He dropped his head and thought for a moment and said, "I needed love." I asked him if he had ever tried coming to Jesus and he said, "Yes, I tried that, but it didn't work for me. I pray to the angels and they make me feel good."

Then he began to ramble on and on about how he believes and what it does for him, etc. I said, "Where did you come in contact with all this and learn about it?" He said, "On the internet." I said, "You couldn't have done that in here." He said that it was before he came into prison while still at home, whatever he was calling "home." By the way, this thankfully is one professed "religion" that the prison system does not recognize as anything but a cult, so I have not known them to allow any materials for it to come in. Could I ask the question that comes to me— How lost is lost?

Our fifty-some-year-old man, who we have mentioned to you who is coming from twenty-three years of drunkenness to seek after God, is still struggling with his long-entwined grave clothes. He knows no better than to allow every piece of bad news from home to discourage him and depress him and that causes his cry to God to be nothing more than a pitiful wail of hopeless helplessness. I am trying to point out to him that God wants him to come into a state of mutual indwelling with the Spirit of Jesus until no matter what the storms from the outside, he can experience the peace of God on the inside.

It all sounds good to him and he readily agrees to seek after that, but he is a case that can only be described by Psalm 130:1, "Out of the depths have I cried unto thee, O Lord." Oh, that he would pray from his heart the verses that follow: "Lord, hear my voice: let thine ears be attentive to the voice of my supplications." "If thou, Lord, shouldest mark iniquities, O Lord, who shall stand? But there is forgiveness with thee, that thou mayest be feared."

Thank you so much, dear friends, for your prayers for us. God answers prayer and it can be plainly seen right here inside these prison walls. In spite of all the opposition and the devil's rage, God is drawing men to Himself and some are yielding to the pull. Thank you!

With Christian love, William Cawman

4
JESUS, TAKE US DEEPER!

October 1, 2013

G REETINGS TO EACH of you again in love and appreciation for all you are doing to help men who have never had the opportunities some of us have had. The thought occurs to me often as I listen to another story of a broken life, or look into the face of a life that has been shaken to bits just as Satan desired to do to Simon son of Jonas, What would my life be just now had I been raised in their shoes, their home or lack thereof, their environment, their sense of values? Is there anything so inherently above average about me that I would have attained any more functional and meaningful life than they have?

If the wonderful father God in mercy allowed me to have, had been absent from my life would I understand or value a father image any more than they do? Had my mother been caught in drugs, or cigarettes, or multiple men, or in all the traits of the carnal heart that I never saw manifested in my precious mother, would I have grown up through my adolescent years with any more tenderness of heart than they did? If instead of parental training in the fear of God that curbed not only the violent expressions of selfishness that could have developed, but also that instilled a sense of honor and honesty in early life, I had been left to give vent to every passionate outburst of the roots of sin that I was born with, would I now be struggling with giants and demons within me like they are?

If my loyalties, my admirations, my aspirations had been focused on TV stars and Hollywood actors and sports idols instead of on old-fashioned saints and preachers and missionaries, would I have aspired to reach some goal such as they present— failed, given up and slumped into dysfunctional street behavior as they did? If instead of having been given from first grade through college a Christian school and Christian teachers and faculty and classmates, and instead been shoved along on the rolling and tumultuous tide of the public school system with all its evils, would I have become an outlaw or a criminal? What is the appropriate answer to these questions? Who am I without God and those He placed in my life?

Why did I say all this? I will tell you something I have never told before in these letters, which are about men in prison. I take no credit for the wonderful upbringing God and my father and mother gave me. I will take no credit for the privilege I had of sitting from my earliest recollections under men of God and truth on fire. I was not the one who chose for me to attend a Christian school all my days. But notwithstanding my intense and sincere gratitude for all these blessings, they left me with an undeveloped area in my personal philosophies— I had no sympathy for a man who was bound in chains of sin. I am not proud of that; in fact, I am ashamed of it now, but it was definitely so.

Having been nurtured under all the graces of clean living and spiritual values, I lacked the quality of Jesus' heart that caused Him to stoop to a woman taken in the very act of adultery and say to her, "Neither do I condemn thee: go, and sin no more." Whenever I would see a drunkard or a man all decorated with tattoos or a bizarre hairdo, or filthy garments from his many nights on the street, my attitude was, "Why don't you get a hold of yourself, man, and snap out of that?" It breaks my heart now to remember that I was ever that way, but I was. Under such self-righteous bigotry it would never have entered my mind or heart that someday I would love these men from the bottom rung up, but I do. And so I continue the story of how it happened. You have a right to know, even though it will not be with comfort that I tell you.

God gave me a precious wife of which I was not worthy. I thank God for that wonderful gift for over forty-one years. Never will anyone convince me that God does not give His best to those who leave the choice with Him. My wife, however, did not grow up in a home like mine. Her father was a drunkard long before she was born and was burned to death in a tavern fire when she was only seven years old. She had a precious mother who loved God and never wavered from that until the day she passed away just two years before her daughter. She did her best to provide a home, a living, and a church for her two children. I thank God for her. But her son, about three years older than my wife, very early in life followed the path of his father and uncles and was drinking heavily before he even graduated from high school. He proved just as truly the Scripture which says, "the way of transgressors is hard," as my wife proved the other Scripture which says, "For the Lord God is a sun and shield: the Lord will give grace and glory: no good thing will he withhold from them that walk uprightly." They couldn't understand each other from childhood up; they were taking different pathways.

God works in so many multiple ways all at the same time, doesn't He? "…there is no searching of His understanding." For the last few years of my brother-in-law's life, God providentially placed him all the way from the west coast back to the east coast to be nearby our family. He loved his sister, but he was addicted to alcohol beyond his control. When his sister was just about to go into the operating room with slim hope that she would recover, he came up to see her on the stretcher with evident agitation and tears. "Sis, I don't know what I'll do without you. Why is God doing this? Why doesn't He take me instead? I'm no good to anybody. Your family needs you. You have lived such a good clean life and look at me. I don't understand it." And he walked out in tears.

When the surgeon announced after a long surgery that he didn't know if she'd make it, he knew only one way to drown his sorrow— back to the tavern. Shortly before that he had said to his sister, "You know all those stories of miracles in the Bible? Have you ever seen a miracle?" She replied that it was a miracle that Jesus had forgiven her sins. He said, "Oh, I know that, but I'm talking about a miracle." Her surgery was on a Friday night while her children were having their school program one week before Christmas. It was almost more than they could bear to try to take part in that program while their mother was on the operating table. The outcome was grim, while for two days my own heart was torn beyond description. I laid her on the altar over and over during those two days.

"But God!" And God has a family and I love them. By Sunday night prayer was going up nearly around the world, and Monday morning when I walked into the intensive care unit she looked up through all the tubing and with a white face said, "Jesus has been here. He's touched me." God gave her back to me for nineteen precious years, and her brother never questioned God's miracle working power again.

Only about a year later he was suffering with sickness. We could see he was going downhill, but was chained by the power of drink. Did God bring him back to be near us for his sake? I will return to that, but that is not all. God brought him into my life for my sake and to prepare me to hurt with hurting men, to understand them, to feel for them, like I had been unable to up until then. As I watched a broken man struggle with the monster of addiction I came to realize that he was to be pitied, not castigated. The chains were stronger than he was.

I talked to him as tenderly as I could. I told him I could see he was bound by drink. He said with uplifted eyebrows, "Do you think I am?" It went straight to my heart. Never again could I look at a man like that and feel or say, "Snap out of it, man!" He was a pathetic slave to the master he had chosen. God used my brother-in-law to melt the hard core of self-righteousness in me that could never have worked among men such as I now love and count my brothers. Don't even be tempted to give any laurels to the man who has been writing these letters for thirteen years; God will take the minutest pains to prepare the most unlikely vessel for the task He has for him.

One night about a year after my wife had been most graciously restored to my arms and my love by a most loving God and His loving family, we heard that her brother was sick. By this time he was living in the upstairs of a very dilapidated two room apartment overtop of an old woman who raised chicks in her bedroom, and all he had to his name was a used car and a wooden leg. His wife was long divorced, his wages had all been drunk up, his self-esteem was shattered except when at a certain level of intoxication, his friends were only his sister's family and a few buddies from the tavern.

After prayer meeting on Wednesday evening my wife said, "I feel like we need to go over and see David." We went to his little apartment, went up the stairs and found him just crawling back into bed from the bathroom. His heart was thumping violently and I could see he was very low. I said, "David, let me take you to the hospital, you're really sick." "No, I don't have any money." "David, that's not a point right now, you need to go, let me take you." "No, don't take me." "David, would you like us to pray with you?" "No, that's all right." "Is it all right if we pray for you then?" "Yes, you can do that."

We left with misgivings and the next morning he was found on the floor between his bed and the dresser with signs of an evident struggle before death took him. That night his employer's wife, a good Christian woman, was awakened in the night with a burden for him. She got up and prayed until that burden lifted. At the same time a pastor in PA was awakened with a burden for him and prayed until the burden lifted. At the same time a Christian woman clear out in WA his home state was awakened with a burden for him and not even knowing he was sick prayed until the burden lifted. What his final choice was that night as he grappled with the grim monster and last enemy, Death, God only knows until eternity, but this much is certain: God never gave up on him until the last breath.

Jesus Himself announced, "They that are whole have no need of the physician, but they that are sick: I came not to call the righteous, but sinners to repentance." He said that to the self-righteous all around Him; He had to teach me that also. I am humbled by it. I am broken by it. But I disdain the man I used to be before that breaking. Will you forgive me just as Jesus has? I never want a trace of that indifferent, insensitive, self-righteous, un-Christ-likeness to come back into my heart or affections, and because you, my dear partners in this little corner of the harvest field are praying, God is keeping my heart sensitive and loving to these men. God only knows what they might have been had they had the vineyard privileges that were given to me.

Charles Wesley wrote,

> I want a principle within, a jealous godly fear;
> A sensibility to sin, a pain to feel it near…

I want also not only a sensitivity to sin, but a deeper sensitivity to the sinner himself; a pain for his pain; a care for his soul. As you continue to pray for these precious men (and thank you so much for it) please also pray for me, that God will deepen the passion of compassion He Himself feels for them.

When I sat down to write this letter I had no idea what was coming out. I had no plans to say what I said, but it is said now and I will just send it to you as it came out. You do have a right to know how God brought all this into being to start with, I reckon. Thank you each one again from my heart.

Your fellow laborer, William Cawman

November 1, 2013

HOW MY HEART AGREES WITH the line of song, "Oh it is wonderful to be a Christian; Oh it is wonderful to be God's child!" There are so many glorious benefits to belonging to the family of God that they never cease to amaze and warm my heart, and even if there were no heaven or hell in the life beyond, I can say without a flicker of doubt that I would still want to be a child of God. This past month and part of the next we have been called away from the prison for about six weeks all in one stretch. We try not to do this, but it seemed duties were calling and with the good team of volunteers to carry on the work until we return, we submitted to it for this time. When we return on Thanksgiving week we are scheduled then to be at home and in the prison for six weeks, which will be a change from what has been for quite some time also.

But the reason for the explosion of gratitude at the beginning of the letter is not simply because it is the time of year for thankfulness (for that is all year, isn't it?) but it is because as we travel here and there we realize with a melted heart just how united and loving God's family is. Now if you care to focus on problems and things which divide, I would have to give you a loving wave and then go a different direction, for I am finding that God's true children love one another just as Jesus told us to in His great and final commandment, "A new commandment I give unto you, That ye love one another; as I have loved you, that ye also love one another." I believe that if Christ is truly dwelling in one's heart, this commandment is the automatic response of that love "shed abroad in our hearts."

On October 22, we embarked for our twenty-fifth trip to

Guatemala and brethren and sisters that we have grown to dearly love there. Among the many expressions of gratitude and love for us for coming to them, they over and over express their desire to send their love to the men in the prison. When we tell the men in the prison how God is helping in Guatemala and other parts of the world, they immediately and wholeheartedly express their desire to pray for them, and so you see God's family really does care about one another, just as Jesus told them to.

Where could you go among the mindsets of Satan's followers to find compassion and desire to pray for men who have been locked up because of their crimes against society? Where could you even find appreciation for the change that grace brings into hearts that have long been the slaves of sin and Satan? But God's family cares about these men, and these men care about them; and I find that heartwarming and worth carrying on for. So the next time you pray for these men in prison, just remember that if they knew who you were they would be praying for you, too.

And now let me tell you about another prison minister here in Guatemala. Just shortly before we came to Guatemala the first time in 1998, a woman by the name of Feliciana (we'll break the rules about giving names, since they are out of the country) who had been a very famous and successful witch doctor, became convicted of her sinful practice and gave her heart to the Lord. She did not stop with a halfway commitment, either. She sought and found not only forgiveness for her sinful life, but cleansing through the precious Blood of Jesus from all sin, and God sanctified her heart.

Among her sons was one by the name of Ramiro, who at the time of her conversion was out in the gangs and going deeper and deeper into that horrible lifestyle. His mother began praying for her lost son and God heard her prayers and began to convict him deeply. Several years ago he beckoned us to him as he knelt at an altar of prayer, seeking God. As we knelt down before him he said, "Some time back I got on my knees and told Satan he could have everything there was of me. The months that followed that were horrible beyond words, but tonight I have told Jesus He can have everything there is of me, and joy has come into my heart."

And he did give Jesus everything and he has not taken it back. Shortly after that he attended Bible school and studied for the ministry and then God began to lay on his heart the lost souls of his former gang members. He started going into the prisons in Guatemala to tell them what God had done for him and what He wanted to do for them, and several of them began also to seek God. But there were also members of opposing gangs and they would threaten him, telling him that the gang would be waiting outside the gate for him. He would simply reply that such could only happen if it was God's will and that he wasn't afraid.

Once several years ago I had made plans to go in with him, but when the mechanic on the mission station heard of it he said, "Absolutely not!" He said that many of them were very angry at the USA and would not hesitate to take out their anger on me because they just simply open the gate and let you in with several hundred of them and do not even watch what they do. They go into prison with knives, machetes, and even guns. Ramiro, while holding service for some of the men in there, has heard guns fired and saw a man run past the door with a bloody dagger. I did not go, but he continues to do so. Please pray for him; not only for his safety, but that God will give him the souls of many of those men.

At the age of twenty-five he began praying that God would give him a good wife if it was according to His will. Sometime before that in a Friday night service God had come in mighty power in the very first moments of the service. The altar crowded with young people seeking God, among whom was a row of six young ladies all kneeling at the same altar rail. As I walked back and forth on the platform praying for them I would go to the young men's side and pray but kept feeling a strong pull toward that row of young ladies.

All of the sudden the one on the end began to grow desperate in her seeking and one could feel the power of God drawing near. Just then I saw Feliciana get out of her seat near the back of the church and start slowly up the aisle. I slipped down around the altar rail and asked her what these young ladies were seeking and she replied that they were seeking to be sanctified. I returned to the front and began praying again, when suddenly it could be felt that the Holy Spirit was right there. Feliciana slipped up behind that girl and placed her hands on her head and the girl sprang to her feet and began praising God just as violently as she had been seeking Him. The second girl launched out in earnest and before long she too prayed through to a clean heart. I do not remember if it happened in order as they were kneeling, but I do know that all six of those girls crossed the Jordan into the Canaan of Perfect Love that night.

Now let me interject something here. As my heart was rejoicing over these precious victories I was also thanking God because He had let me see something that night that answered almost a life-long question in my mind. The question was this: "Why did God allow the early believers to receive the Holy Spirit with the laying on of the Apostles' hands?" The answer I saw was this: "The Apostles almost two thousand years ago, and Feliciana the former witch doctor, were so in tune with the Holy Spirit that they were moving in one accord with Him." I came home from that meeting praying, "Lord, get my heart into greater harmony with Thine!" I have since had opportunity to watch some of those girls grow in grace. One of these is the girl that God placed into the heart of Ramiro.

On Wednesday night, October 23, we drove up to the little church on the outskirts of Guatemala City where Ramiro is now pastor. He was waiting on the front steps of the church with his second child, a little girl of two years, in his arms, with a most winning smile all over his face. As soon as I could hear, he called out, "Here's your little granddaughter!" What a change grace can bring! The first message sent over telegraph wires was this: "What hath God wrought!" That was nothing compared to the change God has wrought in Ramiro. Someone remarked after the service, "Who could ever believe that the face we were looking on could have one day been that of a gang member, deep in sin?" Glory to the Lamb of God Who taketh away the sin of the world!

Our classes and Bible studies continue to grow in the prison, but we are so desirous to see not simply numbers but transformed lives just as we have described. Thank God for the few we do see. Every one of them is a miracle Satan never wanted to happen, but we want to see more because God does.

Just before we left for this six-week stretch, we were having Bible study and a man asked if he could testify. He is a man from India, a former Hindu, who had owned two or three dollar stores in this country. What he did to merit prison I have not inquired, but he has definitely found the true God and is vibrantly happy about it. He came up and began to testify in very broken English and got so excited and overwhelmed that I think some of the time he slipped into his native language, but it didn't matter, God was anointing his testimony and drawing nearer and nearer. Tears welled up in his eyes as he told how precious Jesus is to him and how He has transformed his life from the old Hindu religion. He kept saying with great emphasis and passion, "He has changed me!" By the time he had finished everyone was sensing God's blessing and I stopped him and asked, "Hinduism never gave you peace like this, did it?" "No, Jesus!" he emphatically answered.

With that another man asked if he could also testify. Just then I realized that these men have been taking in and taking in and perhaps have not had enough opportunity to let out what they have been taking in. I right there decided to let it be a testimony meeting if that was what God wanted that night. The lesson could be laid aside.

The second man— an older black man from Trinidad, if I remember correctly— began also to thank and praise God for the change he was experiencing. He had been a drunkard and a great sinner, but God now had control of him and he got so excited and overwhelmed that part of the time we could hardly understand him either, but he was not hurting the spirit of the service at all. By the time he finished God was so overwhelmingly present that I just asked the men to stand and go to prayer again. A good brother led out in prayer and after thanking God for all He was doing said, "God, we want to see revival right here in this prison!"

I have been (forgive me now) in some churches who would proclaim less than what we had already had that night to be revival, but these men are wanting "revival!" Will you help us pray that God will grant the desire of their hearts? I'm not sure, to be honest, just what the prison authorities would do with an all-out, sin-revealing, sin-slaying, sin-cleansing revival, but I verily would love to find out.

Please pray for the continuing protection and covering of the Blood over these men and our efforts there. No doubt Satan is furious about it and we ought not think it strange if he comes at us from even unthought-of sources. But if God will be pleased to pour out of His Spirit in a state prison He is surely big enough to take care of all the repercussions felt by it. Isaiah cried out in a dark and famished day such as ours, "Oh that thou wouldest rend the heavens, that thou wouldest come down, that the mountains might flow down at thy presence..." And then he said, "When thou didst terrible things which we looked not for, thou camest down, the mountains flowed down at thy presence." Have we limited God to that which we looked for? Oh God, do those "terrible things which we looked not for," and then help us to have no fear, for when God comes down He brings His armies with Him. I am sure that all of the volunteers would whole-heartedly agree that we welcome, we pray for, a deep revival that we have not yet seen. Please help us pray. I know you will, and we love you for it.

Your fellow servant, William Cawman

December 1, 2013

"CHAPLAIN, MY SPIRIT HAS BEEN really heavy since Sunday night. We need you here. The minister that came in on Sunday night preached to us that we all know we are going to sin this next week, so we may as well admit it. Some of us know better than that and still hate to hear it, but so many among us haven't yet experienced God's power to keep us from sin, and we are so grieved that men have to listen to that." Now this was just yesterday afternoon, the day before Thanksgiving. And so before we have even had prayer we send a quick prayer up to God for His help and then—

"Now my dear men, let me say that if you have any degree of the love of Jesus in you, such things will certainly grieve your spirit deeply, and rightly so. It is a tragedy when a man stands behind the sacred desk and flatly contradicts the written word of God. It is a mark of spiritual health that such a statement is repulsive to you. But the Bible tells us, "Fret not thyself because of evildoers…' The angel speaking to the Church of Ephesus said, 'I know thy works, and thy labour, and thy patience, and how thou canst not bear them which are evil: and thou hast tried them which say they are apostles, and are not, and hast found them liars: And hast borne, and hast patience, and for my name's sake hast laboured, and hast not fainted. Nevertheless I have somewhat against thee, because thou hast left thy first love.' The angel did not condemn them for their spiritual discernment, but he did condemn them for losing their love over it. You must ever live so close to Jesus that Satan's lies grieve and repulse you, but you must not lose your love while doing it.

"Now, let me go on with this and address something you all need to know. When a man stands before others and teaches that we cannot but continue in sin, we know that to be completely unscriptural; but before we discard that man while discarding his doctrine, we need to know what it is that he is calling 'sin.' Some men erroneously teach that every evil thought that enters the mind, every shortcoming, every temptation, every human error is sin. If that is what they mean, then we would have to agree with their position, but not their definition of sin, for it is not the Biblical one. Scripture plainly defines sin: 'Sin is the transgression of the law.' Before we can teach that we can, by the grace of God, live without sin in our lives, we must use the Scriptural definition of sin. If we use the definition they are using, then Jesus Himself sinned, for He too was tempted! So when you hear things like that preached, pray for the preacher that God will lead him into the truth, and pray for the untutored souls listening, that they will not hear to their destruction."

Now we were ready to have prayer and go on with the class, and what a wonderful class it was. As we went back over a review of what we had been learning together, it shone all the brighter, and it was more evident than ever before that we have here a class of men, most of whom are fully persuaded that there is a Savior who "is able also to save them to the uttermost that come unto God by Him." Have they all experienced it? That's what we want to tell you next.

I don't remember how long it was after working with men in prison that it began to dawn on me what a difference there is in these men from those who have grown up with the teaching of heart holiness. I have witnessed many who, knowing that they need to be pure in heart in order to please God and go to heaven, seek for the blessing, and when they have found it they seem to feel that the cap and gown moment has now been attained— period. These men are not so. They know they need God; they know they need a whole new everything. They seek after God earnestly and when they enter into the complete inner cleansing of their moral nature, it seems only to add fuel to the fire of their passionate desire to live for Him. I will never be guilty of trying to take the Holy Spirit's place in witnessing to the cleansing of the Blood, but I do know the rapturous witness when spirit answers to spirit within the hearts of men. Now let me describe what I am witnessing just now—

There are a few men who are claiming with a clear countenance that the Blood of Jesus cleanses them from all sin and that they are living completely free from it in its actions as well as in its nature. Then I have watched with inner delight as they go on to experience the continual sanctification of the earthen vessel. Grave clothes are not all inherently sinful, but they have been developed because of years of indwelling sin. What a joy to watch those same grave clothes fall off while Christ is formed in them.

When a man develops a continuous crescendo of self-promotion in a desire to teach others, clouds begin to develop over his love for Jesus. When just the opposite continuously happens and a man gets quieter and quieter, and at the same time shines brighter and brighter, there settles around him a glorious aroma of godliness that is precious beyond words. Such is happening in a few of the men. Their hunger and thirst after righteousness is far louder than their profession of attainment, and I confess that I somehow way down deep inside have developed a preference for goods without glaring labels versus flashy facades minus the dynamic glow.

It is distressing to witness a person professing to be made whole in Christ, yet without any visible signs of growth in godliness and virtue. It is equally gratifying to watch a person who leaves no footprints behind that would mar his testimony become continuously more and more like Jesus. Please forgive a personal shout just now— I have chosen beyond controversy to run the race with these who are becoming more conformed to His image. It pulls the heart out of me! I do not see or feel any inclination to set up camp with the others. Canaan Land is too glorious to simply settle for the almanac and picture show. Its mountain peaks demand reaching the next one, even though enemy valleys lie in between. Hallelujah! I had better return to my letter now.

Do you remember the man I wrote about who was so hard and sin-calloused that he beat a woman to death with a hammer and felt no remorse? He is now one who fits the description just above, and I don't mean the description of stagnation either. After an absence of six weeks from the prison (the longest ever in fifteen years, and no plans to do it again) there are many to see and much catch up work to do. As he left the Bible study he gave me a bear hug (he towers over me) and said, "I need a visit with you; and— I got rid of my television! It's gone! Nowhere in the room!" and his face glowed like he had just gotten a long-awaited Christmas present. We will visit! Would you like to visit him too? He would love you if you love Jesus.

Yesterday on my way into the prison I stopped by the hospital as I had heard there were two dying men there, which is not unusual. One of them was gone on a medical trip, so I went to the cell of the other one. When I opened the door I was greeted by our good Brother A——— and another of the inmates who volunteer to do hospice work. The sick man was immediately so happy to see me. Until he became so sick he had been very faithful in attending the services we have at 5:30 each Sunday night in the hospital. What a smile of contentment and peace was shining from his face as he told me that he had the witness bright and clear that all his sins are forgiven and he is ready for heaven.

We had a good visit and then had prayer together and then as I left he said, "Thank you, Chaplain, I needed that today!" Bro. A——— then said to me, "What a difference there is in this room from many I sit with. With many it is so dark and hopeless, but not here!" I think I told you in a recent letter how Bro. A——— had expressed to me how heavy his heart was for the many that go into eternity with no hope. Here is a man who could be boasting in the number of men he has seen come to Jesus in their last moments, but instead he is carrying a heavy burden for the ones who don't. If you remember, pray for Bro. A——— as he gives his time and devotion to these wretched dying men.

Now let's go back to our observations regarding men who are conspicuously growing in the Lord. In that same class and Bible study we have a fifty-some-year-old Italian man who is in extremely poor health. He has bladder cancer and walks with a cane. He has to leave the room every little bit to use the restroom because of his condition. A few months ago he came into class with hardly any concept of the true God except a few distorted teachings from his Roman Catholic background. Over these few months I have watched him grow in a knowledge of God that cannot come from anywhere except the greatest Teacher of all— the promised Holy Spirit.

I do not really know what the true condition of his heart is in the sight of God, but I do know that he has a bright and open reception to the truth and is grasping it whole-heartedly. Yesterday in class we were discussing the continuing work of holiness in its effects on the earthen vessel with all its appetites and emotions and behaviors. He suddenly said, "Doesn't the Bible say, 'Having therefore these promises, dearly beloved, let us cleanse ourselves from all filthiness of the flesh and spirit, perfecting holiness in the fear of God'?" "Indeed that is what it says," I answered him, "and that is just exactly what we are talking about. It does not say that we are to cleanse our own hearts, but that we are to perfect the holiness of our hearts by cleansing 'ourselves from all filthiness of the flesh and spirit.' There is a continuing work of holiness for the rest of our lives whereby we are to become more and more like Jesus in every part of our flesh and spirit— in all our appetites and emotions and responses and lifestyle— until we see Him in heaven above." Were these words distasteful to these men? Absolutely the opposite! They were audibly rejoicing and digesting it with satisfaction.

Would you like to join us for Christmas Eve services in the prison? If you can't, would you join us in prayer for that evening? We want Jesus to be lifted up and some souls to let Him come into their hearts. Christmas is probably one of the hardest days for men in prison. By Christmas night one could walk into cellblocks and hear grown men crying bitterly out loud. In spite of all the opposition and antipathy hell has flung against Jesus Christ for years, His day still carries an aura of sacredness and fond memories that men cannot ignore. Pray for these men this Christmas!

Here is one more prayer request. A man who was in this prison and doing so well spiritually was moved to a northern prison as an administrative move. Since then he has battled severely with the false teachings all around him there, but has off and on seemed to really pray through and walk with God for a while. In a recent letter he writes, "I feel terrible right now, but in a good way. I just keep messing things up dad; I can't get past this deceitful heart. I find the desire to be like Jesus, but not the power. I can walk for a time w/o sinning, but failure is not far behind. All my efforts fail and I do not know what to do. I know that Jesus is able, but I do not know how to let Him. What a sad state I am in. I'm not giving up on Jesus, I just need the strength to hold on long enough to let go and let Jesus. Dad, I'm tired. I'm tired of messing up. I'm tired of failing. I'm tired of myself. Sigh… I wish I knew what's missing." Please help him pray clear through to deliverance once for all!

Thank you for all your prayers this year, William Cawman

5
ANOTHER YEAR OF MERCY

January 1, 2014

Happy New Year! During the closing month of the year just passed I have been very conscious of the promise, "And let us not be weary in well doing: for in due season we shall reap, if we faint not." We have told you from time to time of how God has been moving during the year, and awakening the men to the truth of heart holiness and the desire for it. The atmosphere in Facility 1 has been one of increasing inspiration and anointing. These men have been doing what God's Word admonishes, "But ye, beloved, building up yourselves on your most holy faith, praying in the Holy Ghost, Keep yourselves in the love of God, looking for the mercy of our Lord Jesus Christ unto eternal life." Now, having been home for the whole month we have taken time with many of the men, one on one, to hear from their own hearts what God is doing for them. How our heart has rejoiced with what we have heard. Would you like us to share some of it with you? After all, much of it is in answer to your prayers!

The man we have told you some about— who was so obdurate and hardened in sin in his former life that he could murder without conscience but who is now transformed by the grace of God into a loving, tender devout servant of Jesus — came for a visit. From his spirit and his testimony previously I had begun to wonder if he has entered into the fullness of the blessing and so I began to ask him some questions. It went something like this: "Understanding that we will never in this life be free from temptations to our physical appetites and emotions, do you ever find within your heart a kickback or resistance to God's further workings on you, or do you ever feel a desire to have your own way when He speaks to you about something?" "Oh, NO! Never anymore! That's gone!" I couldn't keep my face straight. I encouraged him to just plunge on into the transforming of his mind, and he was more than ready for that.

Then I began talking to him about living a life free from sin. I told him that we still have human appetites and emotions which Satan can appeal to, but that God would make very clear to him whether there was still anything within from whence they were coming or whether they were fiery darts from without. He was listening very intently and suddenly began to get all excited. "Chaplain, I am hearing you! I am hearing you! Wow! I'm getting goose bumps all over me! I see it now! Oh, thank you and thank God!"

A few days later he wanted to talk to me again. He referred to my asking him about a year ago if he wanted to take a good course of holiness study that some of the men are taking, and he said yes and started it, but then brought it back. Now he wanted to apologize. He said, "I was not ready at that time, and instead I enrolled in the Bible Institute. [This is a course another man is teaching here in the prison which is extremely Calvinistic and full of endorsement to continue in sin, for you cannot lose your salvation anyway.] To be honest I was lazy and thinking of my own comfort and so I chose to take that course, but I have found it more and more contrary to truth and it has become very troublesome to my spirit. I only have a short way to go to complete it, but I felt so heavy over it that

I asked one of the other brothers and he said I needed to quit it. Chaplain, I'm sorry. Could you find it in your heart to forgive me and let me enroll in that good course?" Of course you know what my answer was.

Then I went to Facility 3 where a like case was developing and asked the same questions and got the very same answers. I was not surprised to hear what they testified to because their lives were already bearing witness to it. Now let me tell you why cases like this are so thrilling. John said in his precious first epistle, "But if we walk in the light, as he is in the light, we have fellowship one with another, and the blood of Jesus Christ his Son cleanseth us from all sin." Fellowship one with another? That has been precious for some time, but what does this Scripture say will happen "if we walk in the light, as He is in the light?" This is exactly what has happened in the hearts of these men.

Some of us grew up under holiness teaching and truth and we have expectations, and rightly so. These men have never heard of holiness of heart until coming to this prison, but they have been walking in the light! Oh, how glorious to watch a soul walk in the light and walk right into holiness of heart, and then have someone explain to them what has taken place. And what a thrill to watch them as they discover what to call the grace they have received. Years ago on the western plains a dear old grandma who was living all alone fell in love with her Bible and with Jesus. She prayed and walked in the light until one day as she was sitting in her rocking chair God cleansed her heart from all sin. Sometime later she had visitors who were testifying to her of how God had sanctified them. "Oh," Grandma exclaimed, "that's what I've called my rocking chair experience!" Isn't it better that correct terminology follow correct heart experience than correct terminology taking the place of correct heart experience? I think so!

Then there is another man that I have been watching for some time. He is very vibrantly zealous about his walk with God, but it was evident a year ago that there was a lot of self and pride in his walk. A year later, that is gone and he is a quiet, different individual. He testified to me for about forty-five minutes and in short this is what he said: "When I first came here I did love Jesus, but now I see I was so full of pride and self-love. Some of my brethren pointed it out to me and it really hurt. I went down before God in fasting and prayer and God began to show me my heart. Chaplain, it made me so sick I hated myself! I asked myself what right I had to try to be helping others when I was so vile and full of sin myself. The more I opened up the more God showed me until I could not bear it anymore. Then God cleansed it out, and it is gone! I am so happy to be rid of all that self and sinfulness!"

Now perhaps you remember us telling at times of a large Italian young man who was gloriously and vibrantly saved some time back. He has been eagerly taking in all the teaching we and the volunteers from our church have been giving. If you remember, he is the one who became for a little while very confused over the erroneous teachings from the same source mentioned above by the other man, but who came out again into the clear light as we simply took him through Scriptures showing the way of truth.

Well, now it is his turn for a visit. Beaming with joy, he begins: "Chaplain, it has been a while since we talked, but I have something to tell you. On August 13, at 10:15 in the morning, God sanctified my heart in shower number 5! Ever since then I've been having wonderful times of communion in that shower stall." I couldn't help thinking of the line of song: "I remember the time, I can tell you the place..." If you, like myself, enjoy definite testimonies, there you have one!

So, you see God has been answering your prayers! I say this very humbly, but I do believe I may know a wee bit of what Jesus felt when He prayed to His Father, "I have given unto them the words which thou gavest me; and they have received them." Oh, thank God for receiving hearts! Would God they would all receive. Some are still much like Agrippa: "Almost thou persuadest me to be a Christian."

Then there is a good brother from Haiti who has been walking in the light for several years now. When he is finished with his sentence in the near future he will undoubtedly be deported back to Haiti. In class the other day he said, "God is continuing to purge my heart, and I want Him to do it. The other day God reminded me of something I haven't thought of for a long time. I was standing in a welfare line waiting my turn and I noticed that the woman's handbag in front of me was open and there were food coupons in it. I slipped them out and used them myself. Now I feel so terrible about it but I don't have any way of finding her or knowing who she was, so I can't confess it to her and neither can I walk around here with any secret sins in my heart, so I'm just confessing it here. As I think back on it, maybe her children had to go without food because of my selfishness and sin. I feel terrible that I was that way." Then he broke down and cried out loud before the class and then continued, "I've asked the Lord to forgive me and I know He heard me, but I just had to get it out."

There is another man who was in prison a few years ago, got out and is now back for a second time. While out he became involved with a woman in her seventies with Lupus (he is in his fifties) who has been supplying him with one hundred dollars a month. He has been struggling with this ever since he came back. He knows this romantic relationship is wrong, for he has been married before, but the money has a grip on him as well as his friendship with her. I have had several meetings with him and been very bluntly truthful that he needs to stop this relationship if he wants God's smile. He said several times that he would pray about it. I told him he need not pray as he already knows what God has said in His Word about it.

Finally one day in class I was speaking about trying to be right with God but at the same time holding onto something we want for ourselves. Suddenly I noticed his face showing evident conviction and he said, "Chaplain, that's exactly what I'm doing." In a day or two he came in to see me and as I talked with him about the seriousness of losing his soul for all eternity over this he suddenly said, "Can we pray?" He bowed his head on the other side of the desk from me and I poured out my heart to God for him and then asked him to pray. He began to weep and sob out his heart with deep emotion. After a time he prayed through and came up saying, "Now I feel the power inside to say No to Satan and Yes to God." Pray for him that he will go all the way through with God and never turn back again.

About a year ago an Italian man, something around sixty years of age, started coming to the classes and Bible studies, but he was obviously not a well man. He had a cane to help him with his worn out knees and he had cancer of the bladder. For a time he spiraled downhill quite conspicuously in the physical, but at the same time seemed to be really catching on and growing spiritually. Then it seemed he took a turn for the better and now says that God has cured his cancer and he is free of it. He also broke out with a terrible rash and asked God to take that away and it disappeared. He looks much better and has good color again in his face. He is scheduled for knee replacement and I hope will find relief from the pain he endures. But with all of that, he seems so hungry for more of God. He told me he was married for sixteen years and then they divorced. They have been divorced for thirty-two years and now they are planning to renew their vows and get back together. God Himself asked this question: "Is anything too hard for the Lord?" Isn't it wonderful to watch God put back together what Satan thought he had as a finished product?

A month or two ago a man was brought into the prison hospital from one of the northern prisons. He has been known in the prison system, along with his brother, to be a very violent and dangerous man. Our dear brother who goes over to sit with dying men did not know what to expect as the man's reputation preceded him, but when he went into his room he found a very docile and friendly man who told him he was forgiven and ready to die. At his death bed a person from his church was standing beside him singing to him and his death was very peaceful. Again the devil was defeated.

The men really appreciated the group from our church who went in and had six services for different groups of them on Christmas Eve. Christmas Day is a very difficult time for men in prison. In fact, the first service time was held up a bit because of an inmate threatening suicide and they had to take care of that before releasing the rest.

As we enter another year, we are so conscious of the longsuffering of God that gives it to us. Let's work while the day is, for night is coming fast. Thank you each one again for all you are doing.

Your Brother, William Cawman

┼┼┼

February 1, 2014

To all of you who are faithfully praying for the men in prison, I so much wish I could take you with me into a one-on-one visit with some of the answers to your prayers! You would not have to wait until you meet them in heaven to reap some of your reward. But let me tell you first about a one-on-two visit just a couple of days ago. I put two of our good, recently sanctified men on the list at the same time. Why? Well, I just felt it on my heart to do so. When they came in I said, "You two won't fight if I put you together, will you?" They laughed vigorously and said, "We sure will, we'll fight the good fight of faith!"

Then I opened our visit by asking, "Have you brethren found by any chance, that the life of holiness is a battleground?" They immediately broke into a knowing grin, looked at each other and then at me and said, "Oh, yes, have we ever! But we're not going back!" Then I began to just talk to them about the beauty of living the sanctified life— the glorious walk with the abiding presence of the Holy Spirit, the beauty of being tempted without a flicker of yielding to it, the battles and pressures with no remaining enemy within to give us trouble behind the lines, etc. They were drinking it in and every little bit would look at each other and then hit their fists together to say, "This is just the way it is!" Oh, thank God for true holiness! It works in church, it works in prison, it works and works and works, and never fails to work! Isn't it glorious? And when another heart has truly found it, there is a ring in the testimony that bears witness like nothing else can.

All the while several of these men have been gaining ground in Canaan and enjoying its fruits and learning its lessons, there is another man who goes along with it all and is very vocally active and always gives me a huge hug and loving words. But somehow there is not the ring that there is in the others. He spent a number of years in a Texas prison and is finishing out his sentence here, for whatever reason I have forgotten now. He is literally a walking concordance.

The other Sunday night as I was preaching to this group a man raised his hand and asked where a certain Scripture I had referred to was. This man immediately had the chapter and verse, and he nearly always does. But there is just not that ring. Well, come to find out, he is making plans to marry a divorced woman when he is released from prison. Some of the good brothers found this out and they were very burdened about it. They went to him and began to point out in the Scriptures how unpleased God is with what He plainly and clearly forbids. They did it lovingly and with tenderness, but he refused to listen to them, saying there was more to it than that.

The two men I was visiting with told me about it with deep concern for him and one of them said, "I am in that condition. I was married and am divorced, and I have told God that I will never think of another woman unless somehow He brings my wife back to me and we can walk together. I am not running a risk of missing heaven!"

Then he just opened up with deep emotion and began to tell me of the unfathomable mercy of God to his heart and life. He is the man I have written before about, who in his days of deep sin bludgeoned a woman to death with a hammer and felt no remorse. He said, "Chaplain, I was hopeless! I tried rehabs but they did me no good. I tried programs, but they were powerless. I was out of control! But oh, the mercy of God that He never gave up on me. He's got me now! I'm not turning back! I am not that man anymore. I don't care what it costs me, I am going to heaven!" Finally I said, "Brothers, I don't know how much longer it will be that I will be able to be free to preach this glorious truth, for I may soon be locked up with you for doing it, and then we can just visit and visit, but I'm afraid our time is up for now."

With hugs of Christian love we parted physically, but they are getting deeper and deeper into my heart. Jesus has made us one.

And then in another facility there is a man who I believe with all my heart has entered into the experience of heart holiness, but he does not have a support group around him like the others do. Sometimes I wish I could move him over with the others, but God knows where He needs him and he is certainly not flickering in his quest after more of God.

I asked him the other day what his past has been and he began to relate one more account of the mercy of God. He was raised on a farm in South Carolina, but left home at the age of seventeen and went to a city in the Midwest. He married and had two children, developed his own trucking firm with three trucks and was doing well, but without any time for God. Then he began to squander his life away in drugs and lost everything. He left his family and came back to his family farm for a short time and was then planning to visit his older sister in New Jersey. His father warned him not to have anything to do with her, but he thought he could handle anything and did not need to listen to anyone, so he came up to New Jersey and to make a long story short ended up committing two murders as directed by his sister.

At the time of his arrest he was sleeping in his pickup truck by the side of the road. That night he found himself in a lonely jail cell in a county prison. As he restlessly spent the night a Voice said to him, "Tell the truth and the truth will set you free." It was so strong and persuasive that the next day he simply confessed all before the judge and when he got back to his cell a great burden lifted from him and the Voice said, "Now give it all to Me." He confessed before God and was wonderfully saved and has not lost it for twenty-seven years.

When he heard us preaching and teaching the way of holiness, he never questioned or hesitated for a moment, but walked right into it. Now he is discovering with delight just what all God has really done for him. He sits in class and with a radiant face thrusts a hand up in the air every so often and one knows he just got another bit of light from heaven. Oh, how delightful to teach men like this!

Then there is another man that I have written about some time back, who simply was a man of this world, living the American dream— autos, motor home, boat, nice house, vacations in the mountains, etc. On coming to prison a couple of years ago he was broken almost to the point of despair, but little by little he has begun to really think seriously and has been opening up more and more. Finally the other day he wanted to visit and asked just how he could really have the genuine thing we have been talking about. We encouraged him to turn from every known sin and simply ask Jesus to come into his heart, promising Him that he would obey Him in everything. He seemed very willing for that and also wanted someone from the church to visit his wife, which we said we would see to. Pray for him. He has had his good things, but now he is facing his senior years and he absolutely does not want to lose his soul for all eternity.

Several months ago we requested prayer for the situation with our Muslim chaplain. Let me give you a brief review of him. He is a Nigerian and his father is the high priest of Islam in Nigeria. One of either nineteen or twenty-one sons, Nigeria did not have a place for them all so he ended up coming to

USA and at the Nigerian government's expense taking degrees from several universities. Then he became a chaplain and was in this prison from its very beginning, even a little while before I came. Over the years he has worked his way into a support group among some of the officers and a couple of the lieutenants (nobody knows why) and has done everything he could to uproot our supervisor to get his position.

Now to look at the situation from his perspective; here he is, the Islamic Imam over approximately 450 inmates, and his supervisor is a white Christian. That does not fit the image he desires even in the slightest. But furthermore, he is obsessed with lust for power. He is anything but a pleasant man to be around— very negative and moody and cynical, so much that any effort to be pleasant to him is much the same as firing a BB gun into a rotten pumpkin. At the time we requested prayer things were very tense around him and his agenda, and then all of the sudden a much younger Imam from a nearby prison had an altercation with the custody and was immediately traded for ours. We all liked the younger man; very pleasant and easy to get along with and without the slightest trace of animosity toward our supervisor. The inmates liked him so much better and all was going smoothly for the past number of months. But the replaced Imam we had was seething with what he felt to be injustice. The prison he was sent to was smaller, there was not nearly as much work for him to do, his pay was the same, but he hadn't finished his ambitions at this prison, and so he was agitating to get back.

He filed a grievance against our supervisor and the prison system and so had a hearing on Jan. 8. He gave the prison system twenty days to have him back where he felt he belonged. During that twenty days, which ended today (February 28) there were several very conspicuous attempts on the part of the officers and lieutenants that are supporting him to set up both our supervisor and the younger Imam in order to try to create an incident whereby they could get what they wanted. They failed to get the reaction that they were expecting. Today the younger Imam was called to Trenton and told he must go back to the other prison and that our former Imam would be returning to our prison.

At 12:30 when I went to have my afternoon class the officer told me they had to lock everything down and report to center. I decided there was no use staying if all was to be in lockdown, so on the way out I joined a large group of officers heading up toward center. I asked a sergeant what was going on and he said they had orders to move a large number of inmates down to the other prison and bring a group of them up here. When I got up front I called my supervisor and told him and immediately we both knew what it was all about. This man that everyone is afraid to handle or cross up (if they do, they immediately get a call from the Nigerian embassy in Washington, DC) just to gratify his personal lust for power, has the whole prison system in an upheaval. They have to move any inmates who were involved in the altercation of the other Imam with custody in the other prison up to this prison so that they will not have another incident down there.

My afternoon class as well as all other classes and my evening Bible studies had to be cancelled over the personal politics of this man, all in the name of religion! We dread his coming back, for now he will feel his strong arm more powerfully than ever. No one seems to be able to handle him or tell him to back off.

Now I did not tell you all that just to "air off" or to get sympathy. I hope I do not get in trouble for putting it in print. But we do need your prayers in it all. God has allowed it— or has God been asked to leave as in many other departments of our society today? Whichever way, we will not fret ourselves because of evildoers nor will we faint in the battle. Just when God is moving in greater ways than we have ever seen before in this prison, all this is taking place. Is it just an attack of Satan? If so, do we not have the promise that the gates of hell will not prevail against the inroads of the church? And God has surely been making some inroads, bless His name! So we commit the battle to God and rejoice in each new victory and we will carry on till God says it is enough. Will you help us pray that this Imam will get saved? "Is any thing too hard for the LORD?"

Your Brother in Jesus, William Cawman

March 1, 2014

THERE IS GOOD NEWS this month! God is still sitting on the throne of His holiness! He is not nervous regarding the outcome of this present evil age. He is not hindered by Satan. He is not shaken by false doctrines. He is not in confusion over the smorgasbord of religions. "Behold, the LORD's hand is not shortened, that it cannot save; neither his ear heavy, that it cannot hear." His purpose concerning man's heart condition has never changed nor has His power to change that heart suffered harm. One day very soon, simply by the Word of His mouth, He will set all things right again and expunge this entire universe of all that has ever risen up against Him. Isn't it a glorious thought that while men and devils have just about invented every conceivable misconception about Him, He still sits as ever upon the throne of His holiness?

And now, some more good news! The Church of Jesus Christ is alive and well! The gates of hell have never, nor will ever, prevail against her. She stands against all the background of devils, dirt, and evil men, pure and spotless, without one dirty smudge print of this old world on her. She is not pessimistic. She is not looking down a dark rat hole wringing her hands. She is not faultfinding or critical of those who are throwing mud at her. She has not become a victim of Babylon or Sodom, either one. She is not trifling with her affections. She is not compromising with sin or with anything that is in the least way short of complete holiness of heart and life. She is keeping her garments, her ethics, her associations, her character, her love-life, her attitudes, her priorities and all else pure and spotless and centered on Jesus her Lover and soon coming Bridegroom.

And among that glorious Blood-washed Bride are some of our brethren in prison who once were willing slaves to sin and Satan. Are they sub-standard members of His Bride? Are they less valuable to Him than you are? Does their past dim the light of their present relationship to Jesus? Do you understand forgiveness? Are you sure you do? Scripture tells us, "which things the angels desire to look into..." Why? They never needed such forgiveness. They stand absolutely in awe of a God who can take a dirty lost sinner and so clean him up that His Son is not ashamed to take him as a brother and a bride. Gabriel said to Zachariah, "I am Gabriel, that stand in the presence of God," and yet he marvels at the scope of God's forgiveness. Perhaps you, too, stand in awe of the God who forgave all of your sin, but you cannot fully comprehend the forgiveness that reached depths of sin and shame that are by God's prevenient grace beyond where you went.

Now this being the case, Jesus tells us concerning the sinner woman who anointed Him with ointment, "Her sins, which are many, are forgiven; for she loved much: but to whom little is forgiven, the same loveth little." Is it safe to conclude from this that perhaps some of these men you are praying for have a love for Jesus that is more fervent than mine or yours? This much I can tell you: they are not one-hour-a-morning Christians; they are not Sunday Christians only; they are not taken up with the things of this world; they are not immersed in television nor technology; they are living every moment of every day to get closer to Jesus.

We sing, perhaps often almost thoughtlessly, "Is this vile world a friend to grace, to help me on to God?" They are living as though they believe that. We sing: "Take this world but give me Jesus!" They live as though they mean that. "Oh, yes," you say, "they have no other options." Then what about the rest of 3500 men in the same prison? Sometimes I feel like putting out my hand to some of them and saying, "All I ask is that as you pass me up in the race, you put out your hand for me— I'm coming!"

Now, lest you think that we are floating in the clouds in this particular ministry, let me bring to light some of the battlefronts we are facing. First, we are facing the alarming advance of Islam right within the prison system. Its voice and presence are pressing hard. Several years ago we were required to attend a seminar on gang awareness. A national detective was heading up the teaching and during one of the breaks he came directly over to where I was standing. Noticing that I was a chaplain, he opened up what was easy to detect as a boiling disgruntlement, before which he was willing to be totally politically incorrect. "Chaplain, do you know what is really bugging me? One of the worst gangs in our country is one that we cannot touch, because it goes under the name of religion. It is the Muslims." It has gotten far worse since that statement.

Secondly we are facing almost a tidal wave of bizarre philosophies under the name of religion. Buddhism, Native American, Odinists, Santa Maria, Pagans, Jehovah Witnesses, Seventh Day Adventists, Arians, worship of dark angels, and others that do not come to mind at the moment. None of these were heard of fifteen years ago, but now they are each one in turn and out of turn demanding their individual rights, days, and symbols. Then inmates who claim to be Jewish and are not keep the waters troubled. And the State moves over and makes provision for each and every one of them. Meanwhile the powers that be totally ignore our blessed Savior Jesus Christ. Truly we are fast approaching the complete takeover of him who is anti-nothing except Jesus, the One who died for us and who alone can mend all man's problems.

Thirdly and lastly for now, but definitely at the top of the list of opposing forces to true holiness of heart, is Calvinism. This doctrine is vicious in its attack against full deliverance from sin. Here is one verbatim statement made right here in this prison by a "Bible teacher" of this doctrine: "We all know that after we are born again, we continue to sin." Here is a verbatim quote from the inspired Word of God: "We know that whosoever is born of God sinneth not; but he that is begotten of God keepeth himself, and that wicked one toucheth him not." On that great day when all stand before the Great White Throne, who will be the judge, this "Bible teacher" or the forever settled Word of God?

One of the major teachings that is thrown at us over and over is that we cannot lose our salvation. We have seen men who really received a genuine touch of God and started well, fall into the influence of this teaching and by it become arrogant and completely untouchable. If it is true that we cannot lose our salvation, why bother to teach it? What point is there in teaching that you can't do what you can't do? "Oh," but they say, "once a son, always a son. That settles it beyond all controversy." We would reply, "Yes, it settles it beyond all controversy on a very grim prospect, namely, we were all sons of Satan, so we will forever remain so, if what you are teaching is true."

Much more could be said, but that is enough. The carnal mind is inveterate enmity against God, and it is determined to remain so with sadistic fervor. And so this battle will rage on as long as Satan is allowed to move among the realm of men. We have learned over the years that there is little advantage ground gained by arguing against their arguments. There is seldom a person caught in this deception who has any ear to hear; they are all mouth to give. Therefore we find it so much better to simply present the better way— to lift up a Savior from all sin, to exalt the Blood as an all-sufficient cure for a deadly disease. If He is not an all-redeeming Savior, then an all-depraving disease is more powerful than He is, and Satan is the victor. Hallelujah, he is not!

Every now and then this element of opposition crops up all over again with strength and ugliness. There have been a few times when I or one of the volunteers have actually felt we have been in hand-to-hand combat with the powers of evil and darkness. It is astounding to witness and feel the anti-Christ spirit that can emanate out of human flesh. And that is exactly what it is— anti-Christ. It makes Calvary a joke, the death of Jesus a futility, the Resurrection of no use whatsoever. Here is what Paul himself said concerning it: "Christ is become of no effect unto you… Christ shall profit you nothing."

Now, thank God that through all of this religious opposition, not to speak of the filth of outright sin and gang activity and unsympathetic guards, etc., we have a few men who are finding abundant grace and power to live above it all. Let's pause and thank God and the grace of our Lord Jesus Christ for the real thing— the cleansing purifying Blood of Jesus. To the Blood-washed Church of Jesus is promised that the gates of hell will not prevail against it, and here are a few members of that Church who are proving it day by day.

On Feb. 24 we took on a new Catholic chaplain since the previous one retired. He is a man from Nigeria who spent his first twenty-one years there and then came to this country. I would like to ask you to pray for him. He is fifty-four years old and has a wife and three girls. He is not a priest, but a deacon. He is very friendly and has a likable disposition, which is a very great asset.

My supervisor asked him as part of his orientation to sit in on a class of each of the other chaplains, so this past Tuesday he sat in on my Christian Living class. I let him introduce himself to the men and then I silently prayed, "Lord, You know this chance I may not have again, so please help me." I then took advantage of the hour and a half to come from every angle I could regarding real salvation, and a Savior who forgives our sins, and a real relationship with the Lord, etc. At the close of the class I asked him to pray and he prayed very well and closed in the Name of Jesus. Then he turned to me and told me how much he enjoyed it. Afterwards I asked the men to pray that we could have a saved and sanctified Catholic chaplain. Was that all right?

Would you be able to join us in that prayer? He does evidence a spiritual desire and just what light he has had I would not know.

Meanwhile, in my last letter I told you that the previous Islamic chaplain was returning and to please pray for God's check upon him. Thank you for praying! Since returning he seems like a different person. He is friendly and helpful and much more cooperative— marvelous! While we are praying for the Catholic chaplain, why not pray for the Islamic one, too? I wonder just how it would be perceived if every chaplain of every "faith" would bow before the Cross and be born again from above? Believe me, I'd be willing to find out!

Oh, what a joy it is to see and hear and feel these men (the prisoners, that is) growing in their walk with and understanding of God. One of them yesterday stood in front of me at the beginning of the class and was literally bouncing with the thrill of what he is finding in his walk with God. This is no avocation with him; it is his life! He is literally standing in awe of the grace of heart holiness at work within him.

And then another one today that I was visiting with was feeling the same thrill, and they are in two different sections of the prison and cannot communicate with each other, so I know it is not borrowed from each other. Both of these men are enrolled in college theological courses from one of our holiness Bible schools and at their age it was difficult at first. Both of them told me that the Holy Spirit is just opening up the studies to them like they never knew He would when they started. They are so thankful to be at the Master's feet, like Mary.

Thank you again for your prayers, William Cawman

6
POLES APART

April 1, 2014

BOTH OF THESE VISITS were held in the same afternoon, but so very different. Why doesn't everyone want to give their all to Jesus? If you have, it is hard to understand why anyone would want to try to make it on their own. So here below I will undertake to give you the contrasting atmospheres of two visits, one after the other.

Man number one: "How are you getting along with Jesus?" "Great, everything's good." "Are you finding a real living response from Him in the place of prayer?" "Of course." "Well, don't be content with just a little of Him in your life, for you really need Him to come in and completely cleanse out all that Satan put within you." "Oh, of course." "When do you expect to be released?" "I should be going home in about three weeks now." "I'd advise you to spend that time really seeking after God and getting as much of His presence in your heart as you can." "Oh, of course." "Do you really feel He has changed all that got you into trouble in your life?" "Oh, of course. I'll be all right." My feelings are sinking lower and lower and my heart is crying, "No, you won't be all right. You

are too cocksure of your own ability. You will not be all right."
I am looking into the face of a very good-looking young man,
thirty-four years of age, who has not yet begun to learn that
he cannot live without God. I fear for him, but his only response to probing questions is, "Of course!"

Man number two: "How are you and Jesus getting along?"
"Oh, chaplain, do you know what? That verse you were dwelling on two days ago in class really got to me. You see, I was
saved in the county jail in 2011 and for a while I was living on
top of everything. I was walking around with a smile and so
happy, but when I came to prison here in 2012 I lost that. Ever
since I have been trying and trying to live the Christian life,
but it just wasn't working. I could not conquer sin in my life.
But Tuesday when you talked about those verses in the first
part of Romans chapter eight, it started really getting into me.
You talked about Christ taking on our flesh and condemning
sin in the flesh and that if He condemned sin in the flesh and
the same Scripture tells us that there is no condemnation to
them in Christ Jesus, then Christ coming into us stops what
brings condemnation. By the time class was up I couldn't stand
it any longer. My heart was burning with the reality of what I
was seeing in that and I ran as quick as I could to my cell and
threw my laundry bag on the floor and knelt on it and began
to ask God to come in and give me that power. Instantly I felt
it happen. Now it's not me doing it but the power of God
within. It was so wonderful that when my cellmate came in
the room I just kept right on kneeling there and praying. This
is wonderful!"

The man I told you about who was a firm believer in the
doctrine of holiness, but was also so proud and self-promot-
ing and yet now is wondrously delivered from all of that, was
visiting with me. He is taking classes from one of our Bible
colleges and enjoying it so much, and several other hungry
men around him were asking him questions that he had just
been studying about. He wanted to help them, but was so
afraid that old pride would get a hold of him again that he

battled over it for some time. Finally he committed it to God and asked Him if He saw him getting anywhere near the way he used to be again to knock him down or do anything to keep him from ever taking that back into his heart.

He and a couple of other men started having a Bible study each Sunday morning and through it another young man has become so hungry that he is on a hot trail after it. When he tells me how God is revealing himself to him it rings a bell down deep inside of me for I know he is not far from a pure heart.

But back to the first man— as he also talked of the things God is helping him with in his personal walk I just marveled at it. He is understanding with the inner man the deeper things of God. It is so wonderful to watch men not even take a break after crossing into the Promised Land, but to see them only double up their efforts more to know God in deeper ways. As he studies the work from the college he is making a list of books referred to that he wants to read as soon as he finishes the prescribed work.

One day recently I went a few minutes early to my 12:30 class. Just at class time a couple of officers came by the door on a rapid mission and shut the door to the classroom behind them. I had a feeling something was happening out of order. No announcement was made that I heard regarding a code, but the officers did not return for some time and so I went down the hall to the outside windows to see if I could ascertain what the holdup was. As I did so I passed by the barbershop and the officer that would have been in charge of our class was sitting in there in a barber chair with two inmates handcuffed and also sitting in barber chairs. He hollered out to me that he couldn't come as he had to watch those two men.

I went on back to the room and after a while he came and said that he was released to send the two men back, but no one else could move as a sergeant had found a bag of heroine lying openly on an inmate's locker. That held things up for about forty-five minutes and just as they were clearing the compound for movement another inmate was discovered lying on the floor of his cell jerking his head and bleeding out of his mouth. He said he was having a seizure, but the officers did not know whether it was that or whether someone had punched him in the mouth and he didn't want to tell for fear of repercussion. That investigation took another fifteen minutes of our time so that it was now 1:30 and the class only goes to 2:30. Just then an announcement came over the intercom that all activities were cancelled for the afternoon, but I asked the officer to call in and tell them to announce that Christian Living Class would meet. He did and most of the men came down.

We had prayer and roll call and then this brother I have been telling you about raised his hand and asked if he could say something. I gave permission and he came up front and apologized to me but said he felt the Lord was asking him to give his testimony. Without fear or hesitation I told him to go ahead and oh, how I wish you all could have heard it. It went something like this: He had been from his youth what they call on the street a "gang banger." I suppose that means he was zealous and very active for the gangs.

He is not a large man at all, but he had no fear of anyone or anything, and woe be unto anyone who would get in his way. He was not telling these things with any sense of pride or glory, but he was telling it in street language that they could all relate to. Once he got caught and went to prison he continued to "gang bang" in the prison and was not afraid to tackle an officer or anyone else... "But God!"

He is now conscious that all of this time God was trailing after him, trying to get his attention. Finally he threw up his hands and yielded and God saved him. What followed after that he never understood until he finally came to this prison and heard us teaching the doctrine of holiness. From the very first that he heard it, he grasped onto it and believed it because a while after he had been saved he had sought to go deeper in the love of God and God had showed him the evil in his heart and he believes he was truly sanctified, even though he did not know then what to call it. With very little light and encouragement and teaching he lost that glorious relationship with God, but continued to tell others they needed it.

Realizing he had lost something he came back in repentance and God again restored his heart. About that time is when he came to this prison. Now these are his own words: "I didn't know better and I was gang banging for Jesus!" He was trying to tell and teach others, but he was full of pride and couldn't see himself. I remember so well that for the first while he was in the class and Bible study he was always ready with an answer and actually ran over with self and pride. One day several of the brothers on his tier cornered him in the courtyard and told him that his teachings were good, but he was himself full of pride. He went to his cell deeply hurt (I told you this part I believe last month) and began to pray.

God came down and tore the cover off of his pride until he became so sick of himself that he could not eat or enjoy anything. He fasted and prayed and God came in and delivered him from it all. Before I had ever had a chance to hear him declare publicly that God had sanctified him I knew something had definitely happened to him. He was now quiet and teachable and humble. Now you see why it is that he wanted nothing to do with ever getting near that old proud self again, and I don't believe he will.

Last month I told you that a new Catholic chaplain had just started. Right after I wrote about him attending my class and saying he loved it I had another chance to be with him. The supervisor asked me to go with him into one of the four Jumah prayer services held by the Muslims to show him what we have to do there. You see, the Muslims have no heart for volunteering and we only have one Muslim chaplain, so when four Muslim services have to be held all at the same time, the chaplain cannot be in all four at once, yet the prison rules require that a staff member or volunteer has to be present whenever inmates meet together.

So I went in with him and we sat down to wait for the Muslims to come in. He immediately started, "I was looking on the schedule for when some more of your classes would be. I'd like to hear more of that. My, I can see God's spirit shining all over you. I love it!" So I started to testify to him of things God has done for me and he was thrilled to hear it. Then I asked him when it was that he had first come into a consciousness of God. He said that he grew up in the terrible war days of Nigeria and it so deeply affected everyone— as in missing family members, etc.— that it made everyone think about God. He said he never got over that and has always wanted to belong to God.

He came to this country and attended several of our universities as well as a seminary. While in seminary he saw the other young men going out for dates with various girls and having relationships with them and in his heart he cried out to God, "Oh God, I don't want to do that. I want to give You a pure life. Please, You choose a wife for me." He married and has a family, but he has told his wife that someday he really wanted to give all of his time to God. Now he says he is finally where he can do that and he loves it.

I really believe this man has a hungry heart and may even have times of connection with God. There seems to be not a speck of resistance to truth or to God's presence in him. I told you in the last letter that I would love to see a saved and sanctified Catholic chaplain here in the prison. I want it even more now. I will strike an agreement with you, if you will accept it: If you will pray that this Catholic chaplain will get thoroughly saved, if he is not, I will let you know as soon as he does! Let's gang up on him and pray him into the Kingdom. Can I hear you asking what God will do about his "Catholic?" I don't know. I'm not God and never have been, but I promise I'll let you know about that, too, at no extra charge.

How precious it is to have these men come and tell me with great excitement all that God is still doing for them subsequent to their obtaining a holy heart. We believe in a second work of grace subsequent to the first; what about the subsequent continued washing of the Word after that? These men are not dodging that, they are enjoying it! "...now being made free from sin, and become servants to God, ye have your fruit unto holiness..."

W. Cawman

May 1, 2014

IT'S TIME FOR class again. The third man in the door is coming fresh from the biblical experience of "they took knowledge of them, that they had been with Jesus." His face is aglow with a radiance that is coming from deep within. I doubt if he ever heard the Sunday School song, "It's bubbling; it's bubbling; it's bubbling in my heart..." but there is no doubt he has found that "well of water springing up into everlasting life." I just had to call on him to pray, and pray he did; not to be heard of men, but to pour out the river flowing deep within. When he had finished and we sat down, with no motive of drawing attention he just sat there still glowing and saying softly, "Hallelujah! Hallelujah!" Then we began to sing, "To be like Jesus..." Some eyes were closed, some hands were up, some hands were over heart, and there was a hallowed atmosphere that paved the way so beautifully to teach the way of holiness. How inspiring!

A man recently arrived here in the prison and it is his first offense. He is quite young and his family originated in Colombia although he was born in this country. He wanted to know about getting into some of the Christian services as he has been totally foreign to anything of that nature it seems. As I asked him what his past had been he said, "I've heard people say about being born again. What's that about?" I began to explain as simply as I knew how what it means to be born again and I had not gotten beyond a sentence or two when he began wiping tears from his eyes. There is one more reminder that among all the people we meet on the walks of life about us, there are empty reaching souls that are so lost in the night. Oh, Jesus, help us to find them and lead them to Thee! Is there any other reason to be living in this age?

Another man that I feel so sorry for has just recently arrived also. He hadn't been here long when he got word that his teenage daughter had been struck by a car and instantly killed. She was a very beautiful and talented young girl who was very active in her church. Her father is all torn apart and came to see me right from the psychiatrist. I did my best to steer him away from the fast developing anger at God and tell him that he must for his own sake and God's look away from his emotions and use intelligence. His face immediately softened and he said, "I see that. I will do my best." He needs prayer, too.

The young man that I told you about who has been on a hot trail after holiness seemed to get stalled for a bit. I called him in and he said, "The other brothers are telling me I need to open up to you and ask you something."

I invited him to go ahead and he began to tell me the incidents surrounding why he is in prison. I will not relate them here in this letter, but suffice it to say that sin will get you into trouble beyond what you had in mind and its wages are merciless. He was wanting to know whether he should try to bring his case back to trial to get a more fair judgment on it or not.

I said, "Now let me tell you just what is happening here. You were really seeking to be sanctified weren't you?" "Yes, I was." "Well, Satan saw that and the last thing he wants is for you to be pure in heart and him lose his ally within you, so he is trying to sidetrack you and get your focus on your case instead of on getting sanctified. You need to lay all that aside and pursue a holy heart until you know that you have found it. Then the Holy Spirit Himself will guide you as to whether you should do something about your case or just let it go." I saw the light come back into his face. "That's exactly what I'm going to do." He left the room with his face in the right direction and I believe victory is not far off.

It is so heartbreaking to see men pass by one opportunity after another and still go on so spiritually bankrupt. Way back in the earliest of these prayer letters we told you often about a man that at that time we named C——— . I have a letter in my hand that I will share with you after I brief you in again on his history. He was born roughly fifty years ago to a mother that did not want him. He never knew his father. His mother dumped him into a household of lesbians who raised him and hid nothing from him.

At the age of seven his mother would come and get him and put him out on the street to sell drugs for her. He would sit by her couch and inject the drugs into her arm and watch her carefully until just the right amount went into her and no more. Often he wondered, "Why am I doing this?" But she was his mother.

When about eight years of age, he was in an empty apartment room with his mother and brother and cousin, with nothing much but a bare mattress on the floor. Suddenly the door came crashing in and a huge black man from whom she had taken some jewelry for drugs grabbed her and slammed her into the wall and with one blow of his fist knocked every tooth she had out of her mouth.

When he was seventeen, he and his mother were arrested in a stolen car and both sent to prison. Four days after they got out he made a drug deal and his mother took the drug and overdosed and died. From there on he was in and out of prison until now. One day around twelve or thirteen years ago, maybe even more, he stopped me in the hall and asked me if he could talk to me. We stepped into the chapel area and he told me that even though he had become a paralegal and was free to move about in the prison, he had been a steady user of heroine for over twenty years. One day, two months before, he became so sick of his life that he went into his cell and shut the door and began to read his Bible. He read for several days and it suddenly dawned on him that all desire for heroine was gone. He asked me, "Chaplain, am I right to think that God did that for me?" He then began to earnestly study the Bible and come to my classes and Bible studies. After several years he got out and for a time came to our church, but I had a feeling he was back into drugs again, even though he denied it. He went back into the prison system again and tried to commit suicide by slitting his wrist, but it failed. He got out and again went into drugs and was back again. This has been his history in brief up to the date of this letter, March 30, 2014.

Dear Chaplain Cawman,

Please let it not come as a surprise that I am again now a number in the city of New York. I hope all is well with you and the true family of God in your church. You once said to me, "C———, God will never allow you to enjoy sin!" Those words continue to haunt me as I know how powerful and wicked men of the world can be towards those who continue to know the truth; however not yield to the Lord's gift of love and salvation.

Please brace yourself for what I am about to share with you. But also know that I believe there may be hope that our merciful, loving, God and Father of our Lord Jesus Christ, may extend His loving kindness and tender mercies once again to me. Also, know that I am not speaking as a man sorry for being in jail again, but a man whose spirit is now finally broken to the point of crying in my despair and suffering, pleading with God to not take my life in my sin. I was truly terrified of dying without God in me.

I was released from ——— 5-16-13… within a week I was injecting heroin and smoking crack to a point of 30 bags of heroin a day and several grams of crack. From then and by that time in July of 13 to February 2014, I was drinking 5 pints of Vodka a day, injecting crack cocaine by breaking it down with lemon juice, injecting heroin and on 80 milligrams of methadone for 5 months straight until Feb 23, 2014, the day of my arrest.

I know not a single person in this world who could handle

what we "junkies" call "a ton" like that. I didn't even know
who I was and can't believe that God didn't take me out of this
world. I do thank Him for this arrest. I pray every day for God,
through Christ, to please give me just one more chance. Please,
please, I am begging for prayers for me to bring this madness to
an end. In June of 2013 I had a terrible episode of pericarditis
that led to a heart attack. That was terrifying! I've been home-
less and lived in the street throughout all of this. Without
thought or reason I was doing so many bad things.

I arrived here at ——— 2-23-14. I've been targeted and attacked five times just because I'm white, down to 148 lbs and
very weak. A man punched in the face so hard that I was almost out on my feet. But by the grace of Him who is all powerful, I was able to lay him down and wrestle another man off me
just a few days later. They simply wanted what little I had. I
live in fear every day. The main reason that I am sending you
this letter is to please ask you to send me any old King James
Bible and some paperback holiness books. My heart is burning
to hear the true words of God and drown myself in His Word
stronger than I ever had. I need to "dig in" as you used to say.

I know how and why I continue to fail; it's because I give up
digging in after a few weeks and somehow convince myself
that has condemned me. This was the most dangerous sickening and craziest 10 months of my life on the street. God knows
that I still can't believe that I'm alive.

I'm currently regaining weight and digging in with such force
that I have promised myself to never give up. I was always
afraid to promise or vow to God never to use again. After this—
the most horrible time of my life in and out of jail— I took a leap
of faith and vowed to never touch heroin or cocaine again. And,
if God so wills that I serve Him again, I will flood the prisons
that I have to now go to with the beauty and salvation offered
by God through holiness. Please just some of those precious
paper backs on holiness and an old, soft cover King James and I
will not fail.

Again, don't feel let down because of my life. I almost died

twice and have had two bloody fights and lived in the street.
But because I survived by the grace of God, I'm going to fight for
my salvation. Believe me, I have some years to face in the
country's most dangerous prisons in New York. I may be sent
to a mental hospital for life but that's okay too. I'll go with the
booklets and Bible you send me and do His will. What I couldn't
do while in society, I'll do in the only home I've ever known,
prison. Amen.

Dear praying friends, can you hear this pitiful wail? There
is an old song that says,

> *To be lost in the night;*
> *In eternity's night;*
>   *To sink in despair and in woe—*
> *But such is thy doom*
> *If thou turn from the light,*
>   *Refusing God's mercy to know.*

That is unthinkably sad, but what about living in that state
this side of eternity as well?

We who have been raised in a Christian home, a Christian
society, with Christian privileges and benefits, cannot possibly climb inside of a man like this and look out through his
windows. Another old song says,

> *Dark the stain that soiled man's nature;*
>   *Long the distance that he fell…*

Is it too far? Is it hopeless? Listen to the Word of God: "But
if from *thence* thou shalt seek the LORD thy God, thou shalt
find him, if thou seek him with all thy heart and with all thy
soul." Has he gone beyond *thence*?

The Bible as requested has been sent. The booklets will follow. Would you join us in prayer that someday he can join us
in singing with deep, unworthy gratitude:

> *Just look out yonder, where I have been;*
> *Oh, I thank God, He brought me in!*

Thank you again for all your prayers.

Your fellow laborer, William Cawman

June 1, 2014

LAST MONTH WE SENT you a letter from a very pitiful life of failure in every way. Thank God, not all are that way, and so we would like to send another with a much better story this month. The man writing this letter we have known well for about fifteen years. When he came to our prison, just that long ago, he was in a state of spiritual and emotional turmoil almost beyond description.

He had already been in prison for seven years before that and had left behind a wife and two little girls. When he got out after seven years he said a demon entered into him and he just hit the streets for thirty days and caught a fresh sentence. He had not even gone home to see his wife and children. He was weeping bitterly over himself as he told us about it all and said that he just felt so guilty and mean, as his wife had told him, "All I wanted was for you to come home to me." For perhaps two years we tried steadily to help him to look to Jesus for a change of heart, but he was so wrecked emotionally that it seemed he could not forgive himself.

Then for about the next four years or so he would come to all of our Bible studies and classes and seemed to enjoy them, but would also read all of the New Age literature and listen to the TV evangelists and almost find comfort in his failure and disobedience because of all the confusion. One day he came to me and said with a resolute face, "Chaplain, I am tired of this life. I know what the truth is and I'm going after it." He did. God graciously gave him new life and he went right on and let God fully sanctify him.

After another year or a little more he was released again on parole, and immediately started coming to our church. For several months he was a real blessing, entering into the services wholeheartedly and wanting to see others get in. Part of his parole stipulation was to obtain employment (what a dismal chance of survival to require this of a man with every strike against him) and finally he did find a job at a recycling plant. It was outside work in the bitterness of winter cold and ten-hour days. He wasn't used to that strenuous schedule and began to wear down. He began to neglect his morning devotions as he was so tired.

One week it seemed he felt so drained, and the old devil, just waiting around the corner, saw his chance. He began telling him that he didn't have any grace because of the way he felt. By Friday night the devil had his ear and so whispered to him that he was so cold and tired that night and because it had been so long since he had taken a drink of alcohol, and therefore would not still be addicted, he could just get one drink on the way home and feel so much better.

What a lesson! Let discouragement have your ear and it will open the door and let all the rest of Satan's brood in behind it! He took a drink. All the old demons rushed right in behind it and before the night was over he had committed three robberies. "When he came to himself," he came back to the church and confessed to us with a wail in his voice that was heart wrenching beyond description. The men of the church gathered in and prayed with him, and after a while he felt that God had forgiven him. He asked what he should do then? We told him that there was only one thing he could do and that was to go to the parole officer and confess the robberies.

On Monday morning the pastor took him to the parole office and he walked in with his Thompson Chain Reference Bible under his arm and did not come back out. We gathered in prayer meeting at the church and felt worse than any funeral we had ever attended. We prayed that God would minimize the damage and give him another chance. Another man we were also working with in the prison, and who had gotten out about the same time, committed the same thing. They gave him twenty years on a new sentence; they gave our brother five. He did about three of those and was again released on parole. We watched as he wavered back and forth. Satan was determined; so was Jesus. A gracious brother and sister in a neighboring state took him in and did their best to give him an environment in which he could get his feet down, but in spite of it all he began cheating on God and getting into trouble with robberies again and finally was caught and imprisoned in that state.

But oh, the mercy of our God! He would not let him go, and once again he repented to the bottom and then sought earnestly until God purified his heart once more. Now, serving we know not yet how much time in that state, he writes this letter of victory through the Blood of Jesus to us.

Before we go any further, you might be tempted to wonder if after all of the above the present state of victory can be genuine. Can we have confidence in one who has failed so many times, that he will now go forward and not fall again? I humbly beseech you for this son in the gospel. I, who he views as his spiritual father, also floundered and failed and made miserable shipwreck of my faith for so many years that you could have wondered about me the same. Of course it was not robbing stores and homes, it was robbing God. Which is worse? But I am happy to tell you that by the faithful mercies of God I have been delivered from the shackles of the past. My wilderness night is over, my chains of spiritual bondage and disobedience are broken, and I have had more years in victory over it all than the years in the house of bondage. Blessed be the Lamb of God "which taketh away the sin of the world!" Please forgive a bit of digression from the purpose of this letter. I cannot help it. If you are a struggling victim of spiritual failure, give it to Jesus and walk away from it! I stand a living witness that the chains of chronic spiritual failure can be broken, never to be bound by them again!

And so now his letter:

Dear Bro. Cawman,

The Lord is so faithful and merciful to us. The Lord is certainly turning what the devil meant for evil into good. You're truly loved and missed. God has placed such a love in my heart for these men and for the body of Christ. I'm so glad God spared my life; there is a desperation in my soul to depend upon Him solely.

I cannot express in words my thankfulness to Jesus, but it is my chief desire to exalt Him and please Him in all things. The walk with the King of Kings is precious and with each passing day a greater urgency to tell others what Jesus has/is doing for my soul.

The other day God granted me the blessed privilege of witnessing to 3 men at one time while we were waiting to be arraigned on charges. I marvel at His love and kindness to me. There is no doubt I'm the most incorrigible man in this prison, yet God has given me a pure heart to tell all that they can be delivered from the prison house of sin. The opportunities arise daily to tell detectives, prison guards, officers, nursing staff doctors, classification personnel, and public defenders, how the Blood of Jesus can make the vilest sinner whole. "smile"

My precious brother, and I do mean that; do you realize that this is the longest period of time that God has/is keeping me walking in the beauty of holiness? The only time I've ever been happy was when I was pleasing God and doing His will. Life is wonderful here in prison and many would say I've lost touch with reality, but they called Jesus "mad." However, "...for what is highly esteemed among men is an abomination in the sigh t of God" (Lk 16:15). Life is so empty and miserable when we're living unto ourselves (Ro 14:7). How I ask the Lord to keep me humble; confessing that I'm a little child and depend on Him to lead me daily and to fight my battles. I ask continually for His divine love to love everyone I come in contact with, and for godly fear to stay true to Him.

I know after planting and watering I can only say "...we are unprofitable servants. We have done what was our duty..."

(Lk 17:10). Sometimes I can only weep after the Lord has allowed me to partake in this ministry of reconciliation. I'm dependent upon the Holy Spirit for Him to help me talk to everyone.

What carefulness there is to guard this treasure and to walk circumspectly with God. The exciting benefit I receive is when a soul yields to Jesus. Even when some are not so receptive, commit them into God's hands. God is faithful to give the increase as long as we plant and water. Walking in obedience we can have confidence that the petitions we ask He grants because we're pleasing Him.

I recently read: "In Christ Seeking the Lost" autobiography by R. G. Flexon. What a precious saint this man was and his wife too. They labored and God supplied all their needs. How my heart broke as I read the book, realizing I don't know nothing of suffering for the cause of Christ…

I'm using this time to prepare for what God would have me to do. I'm reading the Bible thru for the 9th time since May of 2013. It's a joy how the Lord talks to me while I read. It's a new Book now that obedience is enjoined. Hallelujah to the Lamb of God who takes away the sins of the world! I love Him today Bro. Cawman, and I've asked Him to epoxy my hands to His omnipotent hands "smile." He does want to do exceedingly abundantly above all that we ask or think,… (Eph 3:20)…

I know the Lord will help me make every bit of restitution so I can be totally clear with God and man. "smile" What a day that will be!! Everything made right. I get excited thinking about making restitution.

Bro. Cawman, I can hardly wait to see what the Lord has planned all along, now that He has saved me and sanctified me, I'll see His plan unfold and I'll shout the praises of God as He does . "smile"…

I do want you to know it's great to be back in Father's house and I'm enjoying Him thoroughly. Life is full when He reigns in the heart!… Bro. Cawman I'm so amazed at God's mercy and gentleness towards me. I cannot fully comprehend God's love to me especially because all my rebellion in the past… you're loved and missed. Thank you for all your help over the years. I'm certainly indebted to you in this earthly existence. Please do give me advice and please pray for me… I'm praying for you and the multitudes you speak to.

Abiding in Christ, ——— .

Isn't that just like our Jesus? Do pray for him as Satan has lost a soul he thought he had, and he doesn't give up easily. Thank God He has promised to heal our backslidings! Pray that God will use him as a light in the darkness of the prison where he is, for there are more— they're not all in yet!

Your fellow servant, William Cawman

7
FEAR OF THE LORD, OR...?

July 1, 2014

P ERMIT ME TO QUOTE a chain of Scripture that would read as follows:
"And unto man he said, Behold, the fear of the Lord, that is wisdom; and to depart from evil is understanding."

"The fear of the LORD is clean, enduring for ever: the judgments of the LORD are true and righteous altogether."

"The fear of the LORD is the beginning of wisdom..."

"The fear of the LORD is the beginning of knowledge..."

"The fear of the LORD is to hate evil..."

"The fear of the LORD is the beginning of wisdom: and the knowledge of the holy is understanding."

"The fear of the LORD is a fountain of life, to depart from the snares of death."

"The fear of the LORD is the instruction of wisdom; and before honour is humility."

"And the spirit of the LORD shall rest upon him, the spirit of wisdom and understanding, the spirit of counsel and might, the spirit of knowledge and of the fear of the LORD; And shall make him of quick understanding in the fear of the LORD..."

"And wisdom and knowledge shall be the stability of thy times, and strength of salvation: the fear of the LORD is his treasure."

Would it not easily follow that without the fear of the Lord there is an utter void of understanding and wisdom and knowledge? We once asked a Jewish rabbi what the ancient rabbis taught regarding the "image of God" in which man was created. He replied, "They taught that it consisted of two things, the power or capacity of moral choice and intelligence." As we thought about that it dawned on us that history and our present age has well demonstrated that if a man or nation uses that God-given power of moral choice to choose against God, then intelligence goes right out the window behind it.

And so, given that scenario, our nation is now facing a dilemma in which intelligence seems to have no part, and that is this: we have ever so many men and women in our prisons for the use and sale of drugs, and now several states have legalized the drugs. Can you imagine what is going to be the outcome when a national panel of morally defunct minds who are presently reviewing this inconsistency come out with a solution to an embarrassing predicament? It might well be said that sin is nowhere more preposterous than when it tries to handle sin. It is very possible that many individuals who are now in prison will have their sentences shortened or aborted because of the awkward inconsistency we have backed ourselves into.

But, turning from such disheartening scenes as this, God is still moving in heart-warming ways among the men here in prison. One dear man we have written about a few times is just ever so thrilled with what God is doing in his heart and in his daily living, that he almost lives in awe and wonder day by day. Do you realize that while as sinful and carnal as a wrong self-love is, there is also a healthy and glorious side to self-love?

Before you throw me out over that let me illustrate it this way: Some time back there was a man in the minimum security camp outside the wall who had not finished the third grade in school, and very possibly did not have the capacity to have finished it. Notwithstanding that, he sat for several weeks in Bible study and listened with a furrowed brow until one day after the class he came to the front and said, "Chaplain, would you pray with me? I want Jesus to come into my heart." We did pray, but time running out by the call to lock in, I was not really satisfied that he had found what he was seeking for.

That evening there was to be a volunteer appreciation banquet held in the visit hall of the minimum camp and so I said to my wife that I wanted to go to it early and go upstairs and talk and pray with this man some more. We did, and as I tried to explain to him what it really means to be forgiven and saved, he listened very attentively and then we prayed again. That time I had no question but what he had found the Prize he was seeking. The next day I met him and there was a very deep look of distress on his face as he said, "Chaplain, Satan's fighting me! The other men are throwing pornography on my bed and turning on TV programs that I don't want to watch. Satan's fighting me!"

I said to him, "J——— , did you think that Satan was just going to walk away from you with a wave of his hand and tell you it was nice knowing you? He of course will fight to get you back, and you must fight by pleading the Blood of Jesus against him."

"Oh, all right," he said in his simplicity. Two or three days later I met him again and this time his face was all smiles as he said, "Chaplain, it's working!"

Several weeks went by and one day as I was teaching them a Bible study, he was sitting directly in front of me but I could tell he was not with me at all. He was lost in his own thoughts, but by the look on his face they were something he was really enjoying. His face quite resembled a little boy with a great big chocolate chip cookie. All of the sudden he put up his hand. I stopped and recognized him and he said, "Chaplain, I just love this new man God is making out of me!" Let Jesus have

His way in you and you will like yourself better, too! That's the proper side of self-love— loving the "new creature" that grace produces. Isn't it wonderful?

So please understand when we say that some of these men are loving what they are finding in themselves, for it is not of themselves. To find Christ being formed in them as opposed to the horrible results of indwelling sin is indeed something loveable! I love it too!

The last week of May and the first week of June found us, for the fifth time in the past eight years, in Africa. Let me tell you that God's great family is so full of love for one another that it's hard to imagine the atmosphere that will be in heaven when they all get home. On Sunday morning, June 1, I asked the little congregation who were in the little brick church in the village of Jahle if they would like to send their love and greetings to the men in the prison in New Jersey. Let me show you how they did. Can you tell that they really meant it? How I wish I could take them in to meet the men in prison; it would immediately form a bond even greater than they already feel— and how do I know? Because I can't help but love these dear people myself. I think I would be right to say that we who have so much have so little love for each other compared to how these people love.

Now you may wonder how much the people in Malawi understand about prison life? Well, in the town of Mangochi, which is the nearest town of any significance near where my daughter is living, there is a prison with both men and women in it. It is a very un-prison looking edifice with a fence made of chicken wire around the compound where the prisoners grow vegetables for themselves. Certainly they know nothing of a "lifer," a person with a life sentence, nor would they even be familiar with such terms as "maximum security" or "detention center" or "administrative segregation." Most prison terms there would be short termed and perhaps there would not even be that much concern if one of them got away. So how much they can really understand what some of our men here are facing would be dubious. Nevertheless, they were very enthusiastic about sending their greetings to them.

And it is mutual, for the men here are always very eager to hear about a trip over there, and of course they want to see pictures and they ask many questions about it all. However, they did not really seem impressed when I told them that my daughter's work crew of seven full time men cost her a payroll of $100 per month. Why would it when they are making about $1.50 a day?

It seems that throughout the prison there is a rising animosity, or at least uncooperativeness, among a number of the officers when it comes to the men getting to the classes and Bible studies. I do thank God for all the professing Christian officers, and certainly the problem doesn't come from them, but not all of them are anything close to Christians. Sometimes only about half of a class arrives and they say that unless the officer hears the specific class called out he will not let them out, or in other cases he just won't open their cell doors to let them out.

And so while I have reported the situation to my superiors, I have also been telling the men that it is a wonderful opportunity to be Christians. I remind them that Jesus told us we would have persecution, and that in Iraq and Nigeria and now southern Mexico, Christians are being killed simply for being identified as Christians. The inconveniences that we are encountering here are very minor compared to what others are enduring. One man today came down late and said that the officer on his tier hates him personally because he tried to witness to him and so he refuses to let him out of his cell to come to Christian Living Class. As he told that in front of the whole class I reminded him in front of the class that it seems he has a perfect opportunity to "leap for joy." A chorus of approval erupted with that thought.

Very soon now, as soon as some appointed one in Saudi Arabia spots the moon, Ramadan will be on again. It always causes disruptions in our prison schedule as the Muslims must fast until the sun goes down which then brings their meal to them after all the others have eaten. Often this meal movement impacts our Bible study times and evening services, but at least it only lasts for a month. Another thing about it that I have noticed over the years is that the Muslim chaplain becomes more and more irritable as the fast progresses. One would think a spiritual fast would improve one's spirit, but it seems quite obvious that neither Allah nor his prophet Mohammed have anything to offer those who worship them. They do not even offer hope of eternal life or happiness; one must just hope that Allah will be merciful to him at the final judgment, for if not they preach it is hell fire, and they talk about that with no more feeling than the hope of paradise. Thank God we have been privileged to hear the truth! Don't ever take that for granted, for both now and hereafter only the Truth will set us free.

With love and appreciation, William Cawman

August 1, 2014

HOW QUICKLY the summer is slipping by. With so many camps to attend and then jumping back into prison between them, it hardly seems summer lasted but a week or so. Now that statement didn't sound very wonderful, did it? Going back to prison between every camp meeting? Oh, what a display of fervent charity I find among my most dearly beloved Christian family, that they continue to demonstrate brotherly love to such as I. I don't know what I would do without you all, my dear praying friends.

We had the privilege this month of having our Bolivian mission director and his wife and daughter with us for a few days and so locked them up, too. I love to lock people up, but only good people. Now you are really wondering about me, aren't you? Oh yes, the more like Jesus someone is, the more delight I have in getting them locked up! Anyway, it was so good to have them give a fresh report of the work in Bolivia to the men first hand.

I have never really conducted a survey among the men in my classes as to what the majority of them are in prison for. There are statistics available for the prison population overall, but just what the most common sin is of men who either have been religious to a degree or become so after they are in prison, I don't know that I could say.

But this I have discovered on various occasions: when addressing things that can lead a person into sinful ways, I do not hesitate to tell them that television is no friend to a spiritual life and that I have never had one in my home. That comment, could I estimate, finds reception with perhaps ten percent of the men. After all, some of them spend much time with it as it is all they have in prison. However, if I mention having the Internet in their homes there is a resounding recognition that it is a direct cause of many of their problems. One man was plain enough in his uncovering of his past to tell me that with the Internet so easily at his disposal he could just go online and get a woman for the night whenever he wanted one.

Where do most of the ideas and the know-how and the emotional disquietude that it takes to walk into a school and begin shooting children come from? It comes directly through the medium of the Internet in a young man's room. Where has the total moral breakdown in our present society had its roots? What Elvis Presley and the Beatles left undone the Internet porn has brought to completion. I cringe down deep inside whenever I hear a person make objection to faithful men of God who have blown the trumpet from Zion's wall about this evil in the home. Perhaps they would do well to listen to the woeful tales of those sitting in our prison cells who once thought it just as harmless as they do.

When I tell the men that I do not have it in my home or on my phone and never intend to have it there, they immediately acknowledge that I am doing the right thing. I'm not sure just how much credibility I would lose before men in prison if I should take it into my home. As I indicated, I do not know how many of their crimes are related to it, but they are certainly not ignorant of the fact that it is far more detrimental than the television.

For some time now a very bright man of sixty-two years has been coming to the class and Bible study and yesterday I had a visit with him. He was very deeply involved in ministry— senior pastor of a fairly large church as well as bishop over about one hundred churches, with a very active food kitchen and community helping program. He is very grounded in the Biblical view of marriage and yet his church was in a town that was very pro same-sex marriage, and so when the town went up for a vote for such he and his people lobbied very strongly against it, thus making many enemies.

Tensions increased and finally one of his own secretaries accused him of inappropriate contact with a little girl. The case went from bad to worse even though his entire family and church community stood firmly behind him and not one shred of evidence was found to substantiate the accusation. Before the trial the judge said to the attorney, "This is a setup." They were sure of a favorable outcome, but it did not come; the jury pronounced him guilty and now he is in prison.

However, I cannot sense one drop of bitterness or unforgiveness in him. He says that since God allowed it to happen there has to be a purpose in it and he has forgiven everyone involved. He has been reading way ahead in the book we are using for class— *The Holy Way*— and he says he loves what he is reading. He promised me he is searching his heart and life with the help of God to know what God might say to him next.

The whole thing is a clarion call of warning as to the age we are living in. One CANNOT be too careful! Had he endorsed same-sex marriages in his community and church he could probably have done far more than he did and never been called into question, but this world order is fast closing in on any semblance of righteousness whatsoever. Habakkuk had only written a few words of his prophecy when he uttered these words: "Therefore the law is slacked, and judgment doth never go forth: for the wicked doth compass about the righteous; therefore wrong judgment proceedeth." It is imperative that each of us, ministers and laymen alike, pray that we can so live as to have at all times the covering of the Blood of Jesus.

And then following that I had a visit with one of the precious brethren who are exploring with joy the precious Land of Canaan. As he spoke to me of what God is continuing to do in his life I could see every mark of love perfected working in him and helping him to grow in the grace of heart holiness. He testified to me that he has been reading John Wesley's booklet entitled, *A Plain Account of Christian Perfection.* He is loving it and it rings a bell within him.

He told me that actually God led him down the death route to self and sin before he knew that such existed or what to call it. Once again let me emphasize this keystone Scripture: "But if we walk in the light, as he is in the light, we have fellowship one with another, and the blood of Jesus Christ his Son cleanseth us from all sin." It all hinges upon that powerful little word "if." If we do what it says, He does what He says, and it's just that simple. No wonder the Bible tells us that "an highway shall be there, and a way, and it shall be called The way of holiness; the unclean shall not pass over it; but it shall be for those: the wayfaring men, though fools, shall not err therein."

Now he went on to testify that God is leading him out of his comfort zone. He has always been a loner by nature and just desires to be alone away from the crowd, but God has been putting His thumb in his back and moving him out of his cell to speak to other men, and as soon as he does it he finds a joy and delight in it and feels so rewarded for telling others what Jesus can do for them. He named one of the other men who has been walking in the same Light and said that when they first met they clashed, even in their thoughts about God, but now they are provoking each other to love and good works. Isn't it wonderful what grace can do?

I would like to give you a special prayer request, and a very important one, too. When the Lord first led me into prison ministry I had no idea just how it was all to come about. All I knew was that God had put a passionate love for men in prison into my heart and I was drawn irresistibly toward them. That has never changed by the grace of God and your prayers and the answers to them. For the first year and a half I volunteered all the time I put in and even though I knew I was in the center of God's will, the financial picture grew pretty grave. Volunteers' paychecks are nothing to write home about.

After that period of time in which I was cast upon the keeping power of God and had to trust Him for every need, the head of Chaplaincy for the State of New Jersey walked into my office and said, "Are you ready? You're going on the payroll today." By that time God had made it pretty clear that this was not a full time occupation (long story) but that He was also leading into calls for evangelistic meetings. Through the years since, I have tried to seek out God's will and balance between keeping up with the prison needs along with answering the call to other meetings.

For those first several years, whenever I was gone in a meeting I would just have to cancel the classes and Bible studies until I returned. Along with that, there was a sentiment floating about in the prison that what I was teaching was just "Chaplain Cawman's" theology, for no one else was preaching that we could be completely delivered from sin. (Isn't that strange, since that is exactly what Jesus came to do?)

A few years ago my pastor as well as a few other men from the church began to volunteer to fill in the vacancies whenever I would leave. The first glorious benefit to that was that the men began to see that it was not one man's theology, but that others were preaching and teaching the same thing. Then as we were able also to take various evangelists in to preach to them they began to see that it was not even just our church that believed that way. What a blessing that has been. But in addition to that blessing, it has been so good that rarely does a class or Bible study have to be cancelled because of no one available to take it. The other brethren in the church have stepped into this vacancy with a wonderful sense of dedication and a love for the men in prison that has been a blessing indeed.

This now brings us to the prayer request: these brethren already have busy schedules. They are not men who have nothing else to do. They already had a full plate when this opening presented itself. But they are gladly sacrificing family time and time that they could, and sometimes need to, give to other things in order to keep the fire burning in the prison. They need your prayers that God can continually renew their strength and above all reward them as only He can for what they are doing. Will you please do that?

Even though I am not allowed to print their names in these letters, that should not hinder the effectiveness of your prayers. Pray that God will give them wisdom, anointing, and emotional and physical strength for this extra load they are carrying. In so doing, you are not only praying for them, but for the effectiveness of the ministry of the Word to the men in prison. What they are doing is invaluable and no one is more conscious of that than I am. I love my brethren and I love what they are doing for our brothers in prison. And the men in prison love them too. I hear nothing but good about what they are doing.

Do you remember the pathetic letter from a man we put part of in the May letter? I just received another from him and let me just put a bit in here:

> Dad, and I definitely truly mean that. You are as close as a father that I've ever had...You repeatedly told me that "God has His finger on something(s) that you will not let go." Well the truth is— and I carefully traced it back— I still kept company with the wicked. I still held to worldliness, TV, Radio, smoking

and the old man of being a hustler. Thank God for His mercy!!! Now I pray on my face and knees and have let the world go!

I'm grateful to God for opening my eyes to have another opportunity to once for all "dig in" and get through to that wonderful power from glory to cleanse a nature that has been too long in me. There's no doubting or confusion now for I know what I must do. Praise Him, love and adore Him, and hold to that Blessed Trinity, Father, Son, and Holy Ghost! Wow!!

We won't give up, will we? He, too, has his name written on Jesus' hands.

In His love, William Cawman

✝✝✝

September 1, 2014

ARE YOU STILL praying for our Catholic Chaplain? I hope so, and I will give you an update. I have wanted to have more time to visit with him, but there are so many needs among the inmates. It had not happened until one morning when I was scheduled for some interviews in Facility 1 I found it shut down due to a code. I thought, "All right, this is the opportune time since his office is in this facility. I will go down and visit with him." I went to his office and he was not there. I went up front to the administration office and found an empty office and had just started catching up on some recording of attendances and scheduling of visits when he walked by.

I motioned to him and he readily came in. I asked if he had some time and of course he did. He sat down and I said, "I've wanted to tell you some more about what God has done for me. We work here together and you have a right to know what I am and what I believe and I just want to share with you how God has worked in my life."

He almost bounced on his chair and welcomed me to go for it. I went back into my whole journey with God, even sharing with him the years that I have repented of so many times when

I was by far less than what I ought to have been, but how God had brought me out of that and into such a satisfying and victorious walk with Him for these more than thirty years. He listened very intently and then said, "Oh my, I am so glad I was here with you today. God ordered this because I needed it. I want that, too. I am struggling. Every time I see you I see God all over you and I want more of that."

Subsequently he has asked for the address to our church and he says he is going to come soon. Believe it or not, we have a great big welcome mat out in front of our church for a Catholic chaplain, or any other Catholic for that matter. I most ardently love our dear church family!

At the beginning of August the men who are enrolled in a theological course in one of our Bible Colleges had the privilege once again for the fifth year of spending a week on the mount with the president and his wife teaching them morning and afternoon for five successive days. These times are monumental in these men's lives, and that is why I termed it "on the mount." It is precious in many ways:

(1) They get to be with each other and see that they are not alone in this walk of heart holiness. That is the only time in the year that the men from different facilities get to see each other and fellowship together. God even worked a miracle for them this year. Two of the men enrolled had been moved outside the main perimeter to the minimum security camp. I asked if they could be brought back in for the classes and doubts were expressed as to whether that would be allowed. I put them on the appointment sheet anyway to see what would happen.

The first day they did not show up, nor the second day. I went out to see about it and they said they had not been put on the appointment sheet. I went back into the main prison and went to see the secretary who makes up the appointment sheets for the minimum camp. She apologized that she had seen them and did not know what the "college classes" were and so removed them. She immediately called the sergeant in the camp and he said he would find them and send them.

Thanks be to our great God Who is still in complete control, even of state prisons. They attended all the rest of the classes. They as well as the men on the inside were rejoicing in God for working this miracle.

(2) They get to spend a week shut away from all the prison culture and lack thereof and just enjoy the presence of God and learn of Him. I might comment that to walk into that classroom is as different an atmosphere from that in one of the housing unit dayrooms as can be imagined. It was nothing short of glorious to see the men walking back to their respective units after a class let out, enjoying God and each other's fellowship with no thought of hiding or putting their lamps, all freshly ignited, under a bushel. It was as different from most groups of inmates walking the same pathway as could be.

(3) They get to see that there is perfect unity of teaching between someone from the outside and the chaplain and volunteers from our church who are ministering to them week after week. As you can imagine, there is NOT that unity in many of the others who come in to teach whatever!

While on that note, I will relate something else to you. There is another teacher who has been coming for a few years and it seems from what I hear that all he teaches is that you cannot lose your salvation. Perhaps indeed he is teaching the truth, for one cannot lose what one does not have to begin with. However that might be, he teaches such with a passion and with an anathema for anyone who would contradict him.

I felt the Lord lay a burden on my heart and so in the Sunday night services that I had this month, I preached to the men from the Great White Throne Judgment. I told them that I recognized that they were hearing many different and contradictory doctrines from over the same pulpit. I then asked them if they would permit me as a state chaplain to apologize and ask their forgiveness for them having to wade through all that confusion. I told them that if they were on the outside they could choose for themselves what they wanted to listen to, but they did not have that privilege but were being spoon-fed many different diets.

I then began to point them to what really matters— were they that moment ready, if they should not wake up the next morning, to face that Great White Throne and give an account of themselves? I asked them if they really wanted to be arguing over whether or not they could lose their salvation when Jesus came and called for them. I pointed out that when they heard someone telling them they could not lose their salvation, that was either true or false. If true, why bother to teach it or worry about it. If false, let's do what the Bible tells us to do in order not to lose it!

Then I said to them, "I am glad for every man in this prison who has settled it and is walking with God in all the light He has given him, but some of you are still playing around about this. Is that where you want to be when Jesus comes back for His bride? Let's get serious about where we are going to spend eternity instead of thrashing back and forth over winds of doctrine." Please do pray for them. Thank God there is still a clear Shepherd's voice and a shining way of holiness that leads gloriously through to heaven and leaves no question marks behind!

But with all of this positive news, for which we humbly bow and thank our God, so many are still "struggling Christians." Did you notice that I put that in quotes? One day recently I sat with two men in a row who admittedly were struggling terribly in their endeavor to live a Christian life. My heart goes out to them so keenly because I have been through those struggles and I know how disappointing it is. If I could somehow reach down inside of them and make the radical choice for them that they need to make, I would do it without a bit of hesitation, but only they can do that. I just hate to see souls struggling when there is such power in the Blood of Jesus. If they only knew, as Jesus told the woman of Samaria, Who it is that bids them come to Him!

And then thank God, some have committed the struggle to God and are growing remarkably in grace. Follow us this very day into the room where we are visiting with a few men who have and are finding perfect peace and victory through the power of the Blood. We have spoken of these men at different times before, but are happy to tell you that there is not a trace of letting up in the race with them.

And so the first one tells us that he has just been through a hand-to-hand combat with Satan himself, but by the power of God he came through with complete victory. He says that he doesn't want to leave any particle of his consecration to God off the altar, and so he has been reading again very carefully such books as John Wesley's *Plain Account of Christian Perfection, The Holy Way* by Dale Yocum, *The Way of Holiness* by Samuel Logan Brengle, etc.

He says that he is seeing everything more clearly than ever before and that Satan's accusations are falling helpless at his side. His heart is burning with the reality of the abiding Comforter and it is nothing short of rapturous to sit and listen to how the Spirit is guiding him into all truth. There is no slackening of his pace, no ground left for the devil to catch his ear, no trace of spiritual indolence. He is on a journey with the Holy Spirit and loving it more and more. And this is the man who a few years ago was so hard and feeling-less that he bludgeoned a woman to death with a hammer and felt no remorse over it. Oh, what a washing is in the Blood that flowed from the pierced side of our Redeemer! Yes, Zechariah, that Fountain that was opened in the house of David was and is indeed for ALL sin and ALL uncleanness!

Man number two is the one who was sanctified at 10:15 a.m. in shower stall number 5, if I remember the number correctly. He is now out in the minimum camp and encountering a whole new set of battles than before. While behind the wall, as they call it, he had plenty of time to be alone with God in his cell, but now he is in a dormitory room with eleven other inmates, most of whom are totally unsympathetic with the way he has chosen.

He went to God and asked Him to open a door whereby he could have time with Him and God opened the way for him to work in the library where much of the time he is alone, and when he is not he is able to witness to those who come in for help. He leaves his well-marked Bible lying open beside him and it sparks many inquiries and opens many doors for him to tell others about his wonderful Savior.

And then, listen carefully to him and try to place yourself in his position and ask your heart how you would compare in your response. He goes over to the sink to brush his teeth. As he is brushing another inmate walks over and leans over the same sink and snorts out the contents of his nostrils into the same sink right beside him. Satan instantly throws a fiery dart of temptation to react to the perfectly normal revulsion he feels over it. Instantly he looks to the fountain of Blood and says, "God, You just gave me another opportunity to grow in grace!"

Friends, these men were not raised in a Christian home by any stretch of the term "Christian." They never attended a day of Bible school nor had a godly Sunday School teacher. But they have the indwelling Holy Spirit who is doing His office work that Jesus promised, and doing it well, too. It is glorious to witness indeed.

Man number three has even more recently moved out to the camp, so I ask how he is finding it. He replies that it has brought a whole new set of things to apply grace to, but he is finding the work of holiness perfectly sufficient for it all. He is in another dorm room with eleven other inmates, and they do not know just what to do with the likes of him, for they have never seen anyone like him. He has arranged a prayer spot with a couple of Tupperware containers where he can kneel and pray, and he hears them making all kinds of remarks behind his back.

One day the officer called him out and said to him, "You

know the guys don't like you." He said to me, "Whatever that means I'm not sure, but I'm just returning all the love I can to them for it."

Then he noticed a man sitting reading a Bible and he asked him if he was a Christian. He said, "I'm a Jehovah's Witness." He said, "Can we talk?" "Sure." To make a long story short the JW was soon in tears and asking God to forgive his sins. Every time he brought up something from the JW, our brother just took him to the Word, and today I had a visit with him as he is now seeking to find all that God has for him.

Thank God for our "fishers of men!"

Thank you too, for your prayers, William Cawman

8
"YE DID RUN WELL..." BUT—

October 1, 2014

How precious it is to live for Jesus! I find this pathway to heaven so wonderful that were there no heaven to gain and no hell to escape, I still would want to live for Jesus! I mean that with all my heart.

Because you pray there is never any lack of things to tell you, so if you want these letters to stop— stop praying! Please don't! I will however, with the opening of this letter, tell you some very, very sad news. For over a year there has been a young man of twenty-six years old who it seemed really got saved and was very enthusiastically seeking to be sanctified. He was faithful in class attendance and Bible studies and would come to visit me and at times it seemed he was not far from a full surrender to God.

Then for a bit it seemed he stalled. He came to see me and I found out why. He was in prison with a charge that was not just. He had been at a party with a number of young people and with their loose morals a young girl enticed him into sin and then another girl did the same thing. One of the girls, while claiming to be eighteen, was only sixteen and after the affair was over she went and turned him in. Someone on his tier had advised him that he should fight his sentence so that he would not have that charge hanging over his life. A couple of the other men who were very much alive spiritually told him that it was a trick of the devil to sidetrack him from getting sanctified.

When he told me this I immediately recognized why he had seemed stalled in his seeking and confirmed to him that it was indeed a trick of the devil. I advised him to lay it aside and put all of his efforts into seeking God and then let God tell him what to do about it. Immediately he agreed and began to seek again. Then he told me he was getting out soon on parole and wanted the address to our church because he wanted to continue to seek God and obey Him. I gave him the address as well as the pastor's phone number.

He was released and having said he would be in church the next Sunday we were looking forward to seeing him there. He did not call and about two weeks went by. Finally he did call and the pastor went and got him and brought him to a prayer meeting. He took it all in with delight and said, "I've hit the jackpot! I want everything you've got!" (Just for clarification, we do not have a jackpot!)

He came back on Sunday and stayed all day long. The following Wednesday he called and said that he was tied up with his parole officer and would not be able to come. Sunday we heard nothing from him. The pastor, as well as two of the men who also have been in prison, tried to call him but got no answer. One of them went to his apartment and did not find him there. Finally after about ten days they got through to him by phone. He said that he was fighting with a demon. He had slept with a girl and was battling. He was not fighting with a demon at all; he was giving in to it. We have not seen him since.

When I returned to the prison I went through the classes, setting aside the lesson as usual and talked to the men straight from my heart about facing forks in the road. I told them what had happened. I said, "Men, that young man had every-thing in his favor. He knew he could come to church and get all the help he needed, find the good path God had for him and spend eternity in heaven. But for a moment of pleasure he took the other fork in the road and if he doesn't turn around will spend a miserable existence here on earth and a burning hell for all eternity."

I felt it so keenly that I spared nothing in preaching to them and warning them that the moment they step out of that prison compound they will stand at a fork of the road. Satan will see to it that a thousand offers come popping up to allure them. I told them that he would try to get them to say, "Oh, I will just go down that path and experience one thrill of pleasure and then I'll cross over to the right fork of the road." But I warned them that many have already fallen by listening to that voice.

I pled with them. I told them, "Men, I love every one of you, I really do. I thank God for every man who has gotten out of prison and is walking in the beauty of God's will and grace, but for the few who have done so, many, many have told me they would be in church the next Sunday, but I've never seen them." No wonder Jesus said, "few there be that find it." But I told them they could be one of the few.

As I was pleading with them that way, one of our good sanc-tified brothers raised his hand. I recognized him and he said, "Chaplain, I just have to say something. What you are saying is right on target, but that is the reason we need what we are studying about. We must get fully sanctified. I thank God that through His mercy He has given me a pure heart and I want others to find it. Men, don't think you can find what the Chap-lain is talking about unless all sin is gone from your heart!" He said much more, but that was the content of it. Thank God for such men as him.

Do you remember that last month I told you that two of the men who have felt they were sanctified had been moved out to the minimum camp? Well, one of them who has really been a diligent seeker and student and who certainly has gone a long way from where he was, came to class looking a bit downcast. He said to me, "Chaplain, I didn't do so well today. I literally had a meltdown."

He then told how an officer had roughed him up because he didn't like him and his religion and he felt he had not responded right. He went back and asked the officer to forgive him, but I could tell he was troubled over it. I told him to get immediately to the Blood and if there was still something in him that was not of God, He would show it to him.

The next time I was with him in Bible study I asked him how he was doing with it. He said, "God has showed me in several ways that there is still work to be done inside of me. I'm after it, too!" Pray that he will not stop short of the full cleansing that was provided in the fountain that has been opened for all sin and all uncleanness.

Another interesting thing happened just recently. Do you remember the occurrences that were responsible for my getting into prison to begin with? Three young men had committed a heinous crime by murdering an elderly couple in their own home in Vineland, NJ, and netted thirty-seven dollars out of it. As I followed the story in the paper I was haunted by the thought of how three young boys (two sixteen and one seventeen) could become so hardened and wasted so soon. I finally could not get away from it until I contacted and began to visit them. The first one I visited got saved and we visited for two or three years before I finally knew where God was leading with this and became a chaplain. When I did that I had to drop being on his visitor list and so for a number of years we had no contact.

Finally— twenty years later— I discovered that he had been moved to the prison here. I called him in for a visit and found him very friendly, but also very much changed. He had used his time in study of law and had also developed his own brand of religion, more or less. As I have visited with him several times I have noticed that as he is about to get out he is very self-confident and I fear for him. I'm afraid he will find out that he cannot handle the world about him but it will handle him. Even though he says he is going to come to our church, he really needs an awakening.

A couple of weeks ago my supervisor called me in and showed me a letter from the outside. He said, "Do you know this inmate?" It was this same one. I said I did and he said that the Department of Public Relations in Trenton had sent a request that someone from the family of the young girl he had killed wanted to have a visit with him and tell him that they forgive him.

I told my supervisor that there must be a mistake, because I had known this inmate from the very time of his crime and it was not a young girl that was killed.

He sent the information back and they insisted that it was indeed this inmate that the family wanted to see and they wanted me to talk to him and ask if he would be willing for it. This time they sent the request letter and when my supervisor gave it to me I then got the straight of it. The one requesting to visit him is the grandson of the couple that were killed. He said in the letter that he is a Christian and loves the Lord and wants this inmate to know that he forgives him and would like to share his faith with him. By the time all this came about the inmate has been moved out to the minimum camp and is to be released very shortly.

I went to him and took the letter and let him read it. He read it through very carefully and every so often would break out in a smile. When he finished he said, "I would be open to this, but I want you to be with me when he visits." I said that would be fine but since he was getting out soon would he rather have the visit in the prison or out of it. He said it could be either way, but that he would prefer it to happen before he gets out.

I told my supervisor and he said it could never be arranged in the short time he has left, but that he would set it up to happen when he gets out and request that they contact me to be present. I am eager to see just what grace this grandson is experiencing and hopefully it will also speak to the inmate to come to a higher level of desire than simply human goodness. At any rate it is a real prayer request.

After writing some of the above part of this letter I went to the minimum camp today and the inmate I told about who had felt some wrong stirrings and responses in his heart asked if he could testify. He got up and told in brief the whole story of how God brought him into the understanding and grace of holiness, but then went on to tell about what had happened and where he had gotten into trouble again. We had just been studying about how Solomon had started out so well, but had then taken the gifts of God to his own advantage and had lost his early dependence on God and ended up so tragically.

Our brother said that after he had been walking in victory for some time he did the same thing. He became self-confident and began to rely on his own understanding of the way and the fire and glory had departed from him, although he didn't recognize it at first. When all of the sudden something arose within that instantly grieved and overwhelmed him he wasted no time in humbling himself and going back to God in earnest prayer and seeking. He said it was there that God showed him just what he had allowed to happen and then helped him repent of it and find complete restoration again.

After the class he lingered back and told me that Satan was really fighting him saying all that, but he knew he needed to. I encouraged him that we do not belong to Satan and that it is always safe to yield to the faithfulness of God in anything He reveals to us. One thing I have noticed about this brother and that is a violent refusal to live on any known background spiritually. He is dead in earnest about being right with God. I love that for it rings a bell in my own heart!

Thank you for praying for the man I wrote you about who is now in the New York prison system. He will undoubtedly be there for a very long time, but God is really helping him after all he did to dispose of himself under Satan's wrath. What a merciful God we have! Please keep praying for him as I have never heard him speak so sincerely before in all the years I have known him. I believe better days are ahead for him.

Your Brother in Jesus, William Cawman

November 1, 2014

MANY YEARS AGO THERE WAS a family with a very chubby boy attending our church and this boy was obviously a very ardent lover of good things to eat. One evening two families went together to the ice cream stand and the man who was not the father of the above described boy went to the serving window and asked them to stack ice cream on a cone as high as it would stack.

With such in hand he smilingly took it to the chubby boy who without reluctance took it from him, eyes popping with excitement and anticipation. The first lick on the top of the stack of ice cream sent the whole stack plummeting to the parking lot, leaving the empty cone in his hand. Seldom is such grief shown on a human face. The man who had gotten it laughed and went back to the window for a replacement. When he returned with the second one, the boy was just finishing the pile of ice cream, gravel stones and all, which he had retrieved from the pavement. He was more than ready for the second one.

Now you may wonder why I told you that in a prison prayer letter, so I will tell you. We have a grown man, once a murderer, now a Blood-washed happy pilgrim, who is relishing the grace of God with no less zeal than the chubby boy did his ice cream. I wish you could have a visit with him. Yesterday as we shared "ice cream" together he was nearly exploding with excitement over what he is finding as he is growing in grace. Then as I shared a few things with him regarding the deeper life in holiness, he just shook his head and with a grin said, "Oh, you're just dropping diamonds on my plate!"

Paul prayed for the Galatian believers, "My little children, of whom I travail in birth again until Christ be formed in you…" To be honest I would have to say that I am gloriously thrilled to watch "Christ being formed in [him]." There is no teacher so absolutely gifted and talented to impart the things of God as the indwelling Spirit of Jesus Christ.

And the work of God is going deeper in some other men, too. Do you remember the man who felt he was sanctified in shower stall number five? He has since been moved out to the minimum camp and since his job there is to oversee the law library, he has much opportunity to witness to others. His Bible lies open on his desk at all times.

Yesterday I went out and called him for a visit. I noticed something different about his approach from before and as soon as he sat down he said, "Chaplain, I am stunned. I'm so glad you came to see me just now. Something just happened to me. I was trying to witness to another man about the two works of grace and how God can deliver us from all sin and he became very argumentative and did not want to receive it. I pressed the truth on him and suddenly discovered that the thing I was telling him he could be delivered from was coming up in me! Just then you called for me. As soon as I leave this visit I am going to ask his forgiveness, but God showed me something still in my heart that needs to come out." Thank God for the faithful "Hound of heaven" that came to reprove the world of sin! I don't believe this brother will linger long under the revelation. He is on the dead run to find deliverance from it all.

Now let me tell you about another visit. The dear man who has been so alone in his facility was recently moved to another where he now has some other good brothers to fellowship with. He came in a few days ago to visit with me and as soon as I asked him how he was doing he said, with evident joy in his voice, "I have a problem; my face is sore from smiling so much!"

"Oh, really? Wonderful! I have just one bit of advice for you: don't take any pain meds for it."

"Oh no, not at all. God is so good. He is so good. All is good; everyone here is good. I'm just having a wonderful time. I just love everybody around here."

What a refreshing change from all the complaints I hear from so many others. In speaking briefly of the many false doctrines that are taught he simply said, "Oh yes, I just let them go in one ear and out the other." This, believe me, is no false pretense or false victory or imaginary fantasy. This man is experiencing constant victory through the Blood of Jesus. As he left the room and walked down the hall past the open doorways of social workers and mental health doctors he was saying to himself out loud but unconscious of anyone else, "Oh, glory to God! Hallelujah!"

He met another man coming down the hall the other direction to see me. Thank God this one was just as happy and just as glowing as the first, one very black and the other very white. Isn't the grace of God just wonderful in its ability to so gloriously fit whosoever will? I sometimes get blessed thinking what Jesus sees as He looks down on these who once were what they were, but are now washed in His precious Blood and enjoying His presence so deeply. "For the LORD taketh pleasure in his people: he will beautify the meek with salvation."

There was a time in Jesus' ministry when He lowered the plow of truth to those who were following Him. They were happy to hang around while He was breaking bread and fish, but when the truth began to touch the hidden idols of their hearts, we read, "From that time many of his disciples went back, and walked no more with Him." Last year about this time the class in Facility 1 was growing and thriving and many were embracing the truth, and some the experience, of full heart holiness.

By the same time this year, the class has almost dropped in half. Some of the men told me that numbers of the men became angry and put out because the volunteers and myself teaching the class were telling them that they could be fully delivered from sin. I began to try to rationalize that, and I will share some of my reflections with you.

First of all, why are these men in prison? Would there be one in a thousand that is there suffering for righteousness' sake? So where is any rationale to be found in getting angry at a man who would tell you that you can be delivered from the thing that sent you to prison? Isn't sin ridiculous?

Then, where is any sound reasoning to be found in believing fully that Satan made perfect sinners out of them but refusing to believe that Jesus Christ cannot make them fully righteous? This is basically what the Bible itself calls "doctrines of devils," for it attributes to Satan just exactly what he professes himself— to be god. It renders the cure insufficient for the disease. I said to the men, "Either there is a deliverance from all sin or there is not. If there is not and you ask for it, what have you lost? If there is and you do not ask for it, you have lost everything worthwhile here and hereafter!"

But the sad fact is that if there are men who only come to criticize and find fault with the truth, the class is healthier without them. And thank God, we have a number who are fully persuaded that the Blood of Jesus Christ cleanses from all sin.

This remains a very vibrant group of men to teach. They are not there to mark time or just get off their tier. They come down to class at times with a few fingers already in their Bibles at various places. It doesn't take a controversial subject in order to have a lot of discussion.

However, every once in a while I am awakened anew to how the confusing doctrines so prevalently taught today completely intermesh our human body with sin, and how difficult it is to conceive of being free from sin when in the body. This past week I just interrupted our normal vein of study to try to bring some clarity to this very issue. One of the first things I point out to them is that Paul clearly stated, "Now then it is no more I that do it, but sin that dwelleth in me." God made our body, but He did not make sin, so to say that our body is inherently sinful is to blame God for the whole mess. We didn't finish last week in Facility 1!

Let me follow up to date on the incident I told you about last month of the family of the victims wanting to contact and forgive the boys who had committed the crime that got my attention and led me into this ministry twenty years ago. When I responded back to the department in Trenton who requested my visiting with the inmate, they said that it was probably too near his release to arrange a visit within the institution, but they said the family would like to talk with me. They suggested that I do it from the prison so that my private phone was kept out of it and so I agreed.

I called and talked to the mother of the grandson who wanted to visit with the inmate. She was the daughter of the elderly couple that had been murdered twenty years ago. We had a very good visit for about an hour and she told me that the whole family had forgiven all three of the boys and wanted them to know it and that all they wanted was for the boys to do the right thing from here on. As I talked to her about my visits with the boys over the past twenty years she said, "You are an answer to our prayers! These are questions we have had for years."

They do not live in the area but she said that next time she is nearby she would like to visit our church. Please do pray for the young man who now has been released. He has said he will come to church, too, but I fear he is way too self-confident to escape some severe disappointments. It is entirely possible to repeat a Rip Van Winkle experience after twenty years in a state prison.

And then I want to renew a prayer request for another man that I have written about a few times. He is the one who, at almost sixty years of age, had been living the American lifestyle when one indiscretion brought him to a crashing halt and landed him in prison. After a couple of years in prison he lost absolutely everything he had accumulated in life and his long standing common law wife (?) had been reduced to a low income housing arrangement. He was very concerned about her as they did seem to really love each other and she was all he had left.

At one time he had asked if someone could visit her and show her some support and so our pastor and his wife had paid her a visit. She really seemed to appreciate it and wanted them to come again. Then our pastor received a phone call from her sister that she had suddenly passed away. She wanted the husband to know it, but wanted someone else to notify him. This becomes a very touchy scenario when a couple is not lawfully married. Social services would not inform him and my supervisor felt reluctant to do so until social services had done it. This situation went on for almost a month.

Finally my supervisor told me to try to tell him without telling him. Whatever and however that is to be done, I did tell him and immediately he was very devastated. He began to cry, saying, "She was all I had." I directly tried to comfort him and let him know that I knew all about it; that I, too, had lost my precious wife three years ago and I knew how he felt, but I begged him not to become angry at God, for that would not help him or anyone else. I followed the visit up with frequent ones and I must say that God is really working and knocking loudly at his door. I have seen it bring him into a much more serious frame of mind regarding his future and his soul's condition.

However, he really needs prayer as he is battling with all the lies that today's religious teachings cover a man's conscience with. Up until he was stopped in his tracks and came to prison, it seems he gave little thought to God or his soul. Now he is struggling with, "But Chaplain, I've never been a Christian. I see others who are and I want that, but how can I ever be worthy to be like they are? And now that I'm seeking to know God my past is coming back to haunt me— the things I said to my parents that I can never make right now. Everyone is gone out of my life and I have done so much wrong. I feel so guilty. And how can I ever stop sinning anyway? I've always sinned and my body is sinful. I do want to live right and have God in my life and go to heaven, but where do I begin?"

Will that help you to know how to pray for him? Not all heathen are across the ocean. We have all around us men and women and young people and children who are total strangers to the God we love so well. Their concepts are so warped and their hopes are so dim. O God, have mercy on the poor souls of America the Beautiful!

On Saturday morning, October 4, I went in to the prison specifically to sit with the few sons of Abraham and a few who thought they were, while they went through the holy day of Yom Kippur. How very sad. My heart always goes out to them as I watch them struggle behind the willful veil, beyond which stands the God of their fathers longing to embrace them in the love of His Son. Aren't we glad for our Jesus?

Thank you for your prayers, William Cawman

December 1, 2014

WOULD YOU SAY AN "AMEN" to this prayer, prayed at the opening of a class by a brother who is literally charging into his Canaan inheritance with a zeal seldom seen: "O Lord, let every one of us be on this death route." While many in our churches today are trying to steer away from such "abrasive" terminology, this brother is delighting in it!

Now it seems that just about the time my heart gets under a burden that more of the men aren't finding what this man and a few others are, God sends along an encouraging token. Another brother who has been in class now for about two or three years came to visit with me. I had noticed that his face was all aglow most of the time in class and Bible study and now he was prepared to tell me why.

He told me that his heart has been walking in the light and that it is settled that he is going with God no matter what. He is not struggling any longer with reluctance or rebellion or disobedience, but is on God's hands completely. He is thirty-four years of age and his wife is wanting to get a divorce. Her parents don't want her to and neither does he, but he realizes that she has a will of her own. He said he told her that he would never sign a divorce and that he would beg her to give him another chance, but that he has settled it to mind God. He then went on to say that he knows what the Bible says about it and that if she leaves him he is determined to stay pure and single and just give himself more fully than ever to God.

Do pray for this man. I wouldn't be at all surprised to find that God has fully sanctified him. Once again, "…if we walk in the light, as he is in the light, we have fellowship one with another, and the blood of Jesus Christ his Son cleanseth us from all sin." God means what He says, doesn't He? Not only does He mean what He says regarding sin and its conse-quences, but He means what He says about our obedience to Him as well. Bless His name!

Last month I told you about the dear man with sore face muscles from smiling so much. Do you want to hear more? I was visiting with another man from his tier and as soon as I mentioned our brother's name he brightened up and said, "Oh my, what a dear brother. He just walks around with his face shining. I wonder if that's what Moses looked like? You know men on the tier are coming up to him all the time and asking what it is about him that makes him so happy like that. He is a blessing to everyone!" A little while later the brother came in that we are talking about and his opening words were, "Chap-lain, I want more of Jesus! I want revival! I just want more of Jesus. He has been telling me that I have been asking to see His hand, but He wants me to ask to see His face. Oh, I just want to have more of Him in every part of my life."

He will find more of Him too, for our Heavenly Father can-not turn away a request like that. After Moses came down with the shining face he asked God to show him His glory. God showed him just as much as a physical man could bear, then finished answering the request 1526 years later on the Mount of Transfiguration when He showed him the One who is "the brightness of his glory, and the express image of his person." I am eager to behold what God is going to do yet for our dear brother in a state prison.

John in his first chapter tells us, "That was the true Light, which lighteth every man that cometh into the world." Every once in a while I have to stand in awe at the truth of that observation. Again today as I talked to several new men, for the first time to visit them one on one, I found in at least two of them very good evidence that they are truly recipients of that Light. With confidence they declared that they are loving Jesus with all their heart and keeping His commandments.

Then nearly every man I have ever visited with can point to a time somewhere down life's journey where Jesus the Savior of sinners came to them and brought His light into their hearts. With some it did not last long, but they definitely know what it is and where and when they received it. What a faithful Witness is the Blessed Holy Spirit. Scripture and human testimony bear witness that He is not willing that any should perish. Oh, how that should pull our hearts out of us to be clean channels through which He can shine that light.

Coming back to the prison after a revival meeting in which several of you dear people had told me that you pray for these men in prison, I told the men at the beginning of a class what a precious family of praying people they had that they didn't even know. One of the men said very feelingly, "Could we pray right now for those people who are praying for us?" Of course we could, and they did too. To some of these men it is a brand new concept that they have a loving family. They are total strangers— this is hard for some of us to conceive— to anything whatsoever related to a family.

And I am not speaking of only a few here and there. Satan has done a dastardly deed in the destruction of home and family such as many of us grew up knowing. I hate Satan! I mean to say, I hate Satan! Not one good thing comes from him, and yet the world is blinded by his lies and multitudes are following him in a stupor that will send them into hell for all eternity. I think of the words of the old song: "The world's great heart is aching; aching fiercely in the night!" And again,

The curfew tolls the knell of parting day;
Oh children, 'tis the last, last hour!
The work that centuries might have done
Must crowd the hour of setting sun.

One of our good sanctified men who is making such glorious progress in the sanctified life missed the Bible study last Friday night. I happened to have the service Sunday night that he was in and when he came in the door he apologized about missing Friday night and said it was his fault, he just wasn't alert when they called it out. I said, "Well, Brother, just don't let that happen when the Rapture takes place!" He looked at me and said, "Whew— no, that would be terrible."

We went on with the service and one of the men called for the song, "Pass Me Not." After we had sung it I exhorted a bit on that thought and no sooner had I finished than our dear brother waved his hand and stood up. "Chaplain, I love you, man." Then he told the men about missing the Friday Bible study and what I had said to him when he apologized. Then he continued on, "I want to thank you for that reproof. I needed that. Whew! I don't want to miss that. Thank you, Chaplain, I really love you and thank you for that reproof!" I don't think this man is going to miss the Rapture.

Today I had a visit with him and he began to tell me in detail just how God is still molding and forming him out of his old self and into the new man, and the whole testimony was absolutely picture perfect when held up in the mirror of God's Word. I confess that I couldn't help but think how much farther along many who have had this truth all their lives would be if they would just as humbly and eagerly allow God to transform them into His image as this man is. I love to watch men grow in grace! And I love to do it myself. Carry on, con-quering Savior!

And with that let me give you a couple fresh prayer requests. Last night in one of the Bible studies a man who had come for the first time came up to my desk at the close and said, "Chap-lain, I wish I could talk to you. I've tried all my life to be into the Lord, but it seems I always fall out again and I don't know how to stay with Him."

I said, "Give me your name and number and I will put you on the list for a visit next week."

"Oh, thanks! That will be good."

In that same Bible study I noticed also for the first time a young looking man who very obviously had already been through Satan's sifting process and come out for the very worst. He was heavily tattooed and marked up and his ears had been pierced and stretched until the holes in them were big enough to hold a quarter. So far I have had a visit with the second of these two men. He is twenty-six years old and I'm happy to tell you that after visiting with him I believe there are better days ahead for him.

At the age of seven his father died, causing him to go wild on the inside and outside. He began to drink and drug and get into trouble in and out of prisons and finally joined the Bloods, hence many of the tattoos. He also got into sa-tanic rituals and worship and has a very heavy satanic sym-bol tattooed into his forehead and then many very vivid tattoos elsewhere. His mother was addicted to drugs and thus was no help to him in staying out of trouble at all. He had one grandmother on his mother's side who was a church woman and tried at times to steer him right, but it had little impact on him.

When he was sixteen, his father's mother died while he was holding her hand, pleading for God not to take her. This caused him to turn wilder yet, simply giving himself over to alcohol and marijuana and cigarettes. Then two close friends (?) (Blood gang members) were killed. The one was shot in the head and died in his arms; the other was shot in the face and also died while he was holding him. He explained to me that when a man has teardrops tattooed at the corner of his eye and they are not filled in, it means he has killed someone. If they are filled in solid it just means someone dear to him has died.

By the time he came to prison this term he was wasted down to eighty-five pounds and was little more than a skeleton. Then he met Jesus! He turned his back on all before and served notice to the gang that he was finished. He is searching, but already feels a sense of God's forgiveness and a communion with him that he doesn't want to lose. I will visit with him again soon. "Hallelujah, what a Savior, who can take a poor lost sinner; lift him from the miry clay and set him free!" Can you understand why the angels themselves stand in awe and wonder at the power of Jesus' redemption that can lift such wrecks of Satan and so wash them in the cleansing Blood that He will make them His bride for all eternity? "And without controversy great is the mystery of godliness..."

There is another church that holds two Bible studies on Tuesday evenings and the Tuesday before Thanksgiving they called out. My supervisor asked me if I would fill in for them and maybe give a Thanksgiving service. I readily agreed and after we had prayed and sung a chorus I gave them a few things that I was thankful for, one of them being the men in the Bible study, and then asked them to tell us something they were thankful for. The time went by quickly as one after another gave thanks. I want to tell you especially about two of them.

For a number of years I have mentioned at times a man who was a double murderer but is now a sanctified blessing. He said he wanted to thank the Lord for something very special to him and that is that every morning since his life is wholly the Lord's, he wakes up with a sense of purpose. Life is more than an existence in a prison; he is living and working for the Lord. He recently changed tasks and is now in what is called the Shadow Program. He goes for hours every day to the unit where the special needs men are housed and helps them with anything they need. He feels it to be a wide-open opportunity to help them find the Lord.

The other man was in the same group and even though I have seen him around he is not in my classes so I don't know much about him. He got up and began to tell how his life had been wasted on drugs and the street life and prisons and that for twenty-one years he had even tried everything in prison, but nothing would bring him satisfaction. Then one day (I think he meant recently) it dawned on him that he had never confessed his sins. He said he began to confess his sins to God and— then he broke down, then continued— "and Jesus came into my life. Now I have found what life is about." It was attended by that witness that only God gives to testimonies like that and it really touched the men.

Please help us pray for our upcoming Christmas Eve services. Our church will be giving all seven services that night, three at 5:30 and four at 7:30, so we're enlisting all the help we can get. Want to come? The State locks bad people up; I love to lock good people up! That night is perhaps one of the most vulnerable nights of the year for men's emotions who are in prison. Their thoughts naturally go out to loved ones and family and it is not a night that's easy to be shut away from them with only memories. Therefore channels can be open that may not be open any other night of the year. We are praying that God will use the Christmas message in word and song to reach beyond the emotions and stir the will of many men. Thank you again for your prayers.

William Cawman

9
THE TUG OF WAR CONTINUES

January 1, 2015

> *The year is gone, beyond recall, with all its hopes and*
> *fears,*
> *With all its bright and gladdening smiles, with all its*
> *mourners' tears.*
> *Forgive this nation's many sins; the growth of vice*
> *restrain;*
> *And help us all with sin to strive, and crowns of life*
> *to gain.*
> *From evil deeds that stain the past we now desire to*
> *flee;*
> *And pray that future years may all be spent, good*
> *Lord, for Thee!*

YES, ANOTHER YEAR HAS slipped by so quickly— we are one year closer to a never-ending eternity! How few indeed have spent even ten minutes of the year just passed to give solemn thoughts to what matters the very most. How much longer can mercy be just? Or are we already living beyond that boundary line where our only protection from the

Hand of Justice is that "mercy rejoiceth against judgment"?

It would be almost if not altogether impossible to justify the tarrying of divine wrath had not Peter unveiled the unfathomable mercy of God in these words: "The Lord is not slack concerning his promise, as some men count slackness; but is longsuffering to us-ward, not willing that any should perish, but that all should come to repentance." And, my dear praying friends, by the help of your prayers and by the mercies of that longsuffering God, several more men in prison have found grace instead of wrath this past year. One might say, "But so few?" We would answer, "What if one of them was you?"

But before we either reflect further on the year passed or on the one to come, if Jesus tarries, let me print something here that we wrote a couple of years ago by request of a certain church group, endeavoring to portray Christmas in prison. We insert it here:

> What a glorious and joyful day it was when Jesus Christ was born! Yet, while there was light and joy and rejoicing around a little manger bed in Bethlehem of Judea, the rest of the world was lying in the darkness of sin, knowing nothing about what had just happened in a little stable far away. The traditional manger scene is highly inaccurate— it would be perhaps a year or so later before the wise men found the newborn baby. And so on that first Christmas night there may have been no one to celebrate the glorious event save Joseph, Mary, a few shepherds, and a multitude of the heavenly host.
>
> Since that first Christmas night over two thousand more have come and gone. The celebration of it has continued until now it has almost become a world-wide event of joy and gladness— that is, except behind the cell doors of our many prisons. How things have changed— on the first Christmas but a few on earth knew about and celebrated it; now multitudes will anticipate and enjoy the season except for a few. The first celebration was in a tiny stable, this one will be everywhere except inside prison walls.

On Christmas Day the custody numbers are greatly reduced to a bare minimum. Officers, like everyone else, want to spend the day with family and friends around the Christmas tree and loaded table. The streets and homes of America will be bustling with the long-awaited day. But inside the prison walls there will be an eerie, almost uncanny silence. Christmas dinner will be served much the same as any other day, but with perhaps a slice of turkey and a bit of cranberry sauce. There will be no grandma's pumpkin pie, no bursting of the front door with family and friends— actually, family and friends are busy and have forgotten their imprisoned ones, and the poor forgotten ones feel it deeply and with pain. Yes, they are left for the entire day to agonizingly remember why they are there, and why they are left out of the most celebrated day of the year.

By evening if one were to walk down the long corridor of a cell block he would hear the most pitiful sobbing and even outright crying coming from grown men as they lie across their bunks with the painful sting of abandonment and loneliness. Memories from boyhood flood in and once again they are back in childhood, unwrapping new toys and watching twinkling lights from the ornamented tree. They hear Christmas carols from the nearby church. They taste again the delicious food from the family table. And then it all crashes in again: a little cell of concrete walls; just enough heat to prevent chilling; no Christmas cheer, no carols sung at the window, no Christmas tree, no gifts, no family and friends. They are alone, and it is Christmas.

Is there a star of hope for these neglected men? Yes, Jesus walks those abandoned halls and cells every moment of Christmas Day. Some of the men are still going over the songs sung to them and the stories told to them the evening before by a caring group of people from the church. Some of the men know Jesus and spend the day in His presence and even try to get others to know Him. How many are there like this? Well, on the first Christmas night only a few had light in a dark world. Perhaps only a few know Jesus in a dark prison, but for those few we rejoice. We will go and minister to them again. We will meet them in heaven where Christmas joy and peace will never die.

Yes, Christmas in prison is much like the first one— a Light is there for all who will receive Him. Pray that many more will do so this Christmas!

Our church again this year— with the help of several visitors (among them our evangelist and his wife who held our last revival and found prison life inviting enough that they returned!)— was scheduled for seven services on Christmas Eve. Three services were scheduled for 5:30 and three more at 7:30 plus one in the minimum camp. In each facility we have two housing units with 500 men each. We tried one year combining the two housing units for one service, but after all the chairs in the chapel were filled the officers stopped any more from coming and we didn't want that to happen again so we don't combine the housing units anymore.

We have been praying and the men in prison have been praying that this Christmas Eve service will be blessed with hearts opening their door to the Christ of Christmas to be born in them. Can you imagine the difference there would be in the above description of Christmas Day in prison if a man could awaken on Christmas morning "a new creature in Christ Jesus"?

And now in retrospect after the services: I have seen times where it seemed Satan put forth a deliberate effort to hinder such a prayer and effort as this, but this year God covered us with the precious Blood. The officers were very cooperative and gave us maximum time for each service. There were no codes, either medical or due to a scuffle, and it was a very quiet evening throughout the prison. During each of the services we gave opportunity for men to ask Jesus to come into their hearts. A number of them came to the front for prayer and God only knows just what all was done.

One man that I noticed came forward with tears, and I'm

not sure but what they were still there as we left. I hope he awoke the next morning to the best Christmas he'd ever known. Do you realize that God does not have to be begged to come into a heart? He designed us for exactly that, and all He is looking for anywhere down the journey of life is a soul who is done with sin and willing to let Him come in. I have seen times before when in just a short time of prayer such as these, a man entered into the heart of Jesus and Jesus entered into him and long after he pointed to that prayer as the turning point in his life.

Now, could we suggest this thought? If Jesus is tarrying His coming because His longsuffering is not willing to leave anyone behind, shouldn't we be expecting more to get in? God knows all that we don't know, and if tempted anywhere in the coming year to become a victim of dim expectations, let's surrender those to the One who knows, and because He knows, is delaying His promised coming.

Permit me to reflect a bit on a lost soul I have encountered in the past month. He is the first one of the two fresh prayer requests I gave you last month. At the time of that letter I had only visited with the second one, and thank God this young man, though having been sifted as wheat by Satan, is now finding real peace in believing. As he speaks of his desires for God one could almost forget the terrible damage to his body that Satan afflicted. But the first man is the one I am speaking of now. He sat down and poured out such a tale of ungodly dysfunctional living (if it can even be called that!) that I was left rather dumbfounded as to how to help him.

Actually I didn't even try much on the first visit as he had used up all his time telling me his history. I cannot and would not want to relate it all here, but it was so devastating that at one point he took enough meds to kill himself, but didn't quite get the job done. Consequently his brain is definitely damaged.

At the end of the first visit his primary concern was to find out if the married woman he had been shacking up with on the front porch of an inner city doctor, and who had set him up to come back to prison, was dead or alive. He had heard she had overdosed. I called him down again and took the offensive. I told him I could only help him as a chaplain and that if he really wanted his life to be different than what it had been he needed to put the past and all of its sin behind him and forget about that woman.

That did not satisfy him. He claims he loves her like he has never loved anyone. He is only in prison for a few more months and then he has no place to go and no one will receive him because of his horrible record. I told him there was only one thing that I could help him with, but that is the thing that matters most— what about where he would spend eternity? That thought seemed to pass through his mind like there was no mind there, and he returned to his dilemma: "But where am I going to stay when I get out?"

That night he came to Bible study and at the close came up and stopped in front of me and said, "Chaplain, I don't know if I told you when we talked, but can you find me a place to stay when I get out? And is there anybody from your church that ever passes through the city ———? Can they stop and inquire if Mrs. ——— is alive or dead?"

Honestly, my heart is distressed over him. Is he one of those whom God is not willing should perish? I am sure he is. Then Lord, how, when, where is the doorway into his heart? Was it so sealed up a long time ago that there is none anymore? I confess, I do not know. All I can say is that it is a fearful thing to turn away the Hand of Mercy when it knocks ever so quietly at the door of the heart. And knock it does, for the inerrant Word of God says that there is a "Light, which lighteth every man that cometh into the world." I cannot help but wonder if somewhere back in his rocky history, before he blew his brain apart by an attempt to leave the world, he didn't shut the door to that Light. That part of his history perhaps no one but God and he know about.

As we enter another year of unmerited mercy, let's agree to

put our all into the hands of a loving God, that we too might be a partaker of that longsuffering that is not willing to see one soul perish!

With gratitude for all you have done for these men in prayer, A Blessed New Year to you, William Cawman

February 1, 2015

Satan certainly does not care how he deceives an individual into missing God's perfect will. A man who has been coming to class now for a couple years or more just visited with me at his request. When he first started coming to the class he obviously had a number of spiritual issues that were anything but Christ-like, but now he very enthusiastically reports that God is just marvelously helping him.

He's just bouncing all over the place telling me how wonderful life is going. His whole family is "on fire for God," and his relationship with his wife is better than ever before. His daughter is "saved," and "on fire." The *officers* all see how "he carries himself," and are entrusting him with special privileges, even to running errands for them to the other two facilities. He is never idle.

Whenever he can he is in the dayroom studying his Bible studies. He has dropped out of all the false religious teachings and is staying only "in the truth." If he is not studying he has a rag and squirt bottle in his hands and is polishing and cleaning everything on the tier and witnessing to the other inmates while doing so.

Is he a born-again child of God? Is he victorious over all sin? Why is there something about all this glowing testimony that just doesn't "ring a bell" and cause my heart to sense the bond that only the Blood-washed know? David said, "I hate every false way!" And the old prophet cried out, "There is a way which seemeth right unto a man, but the end thereof are the ways of death." I would love to be mistaken, but my heart somehow senses red flags, notwithstanding the vibrant zeal and glowing words. Oh, what a tragic shock many will encounter when the Great White Throne pronounces, "I never knew you; depart from Me!"

This past month I have been more conscious than ever of a number of men who one time not long ago were bright and bore the marks of genuine divine life, but who now are laboring under a dark and confused-looking countenance. The cause of such is a very strong false religious teaching, which is being hammered into them, that they cannot lose their salvation. No matter what they do or how they are living, even if they are wretchedly sinful in all their ways, it is simply that they are going to lose their rewards, not their salvation.

The material they are being taught says in plain language that they may be living in a state where they have lost all their personal righteousness, but never can they lose their salvation. Their works did not bring them salvation, so their works can do nothing to cause them to lose it. I am not exaggerating, but instead very much abbreviating, what they are being taught, and that by wresting one Scripture after another to prove it.

If God leads you to pray for this dire situation, please pray that God will silence the mouth of these false prophets, who are anti-Christ to the very depths. They are promoting the very thing Jesus died to save us from— SIN! Their material even states that the method God uses to redeem us is that He caused Jesus to become sinful by taking on Him our sin and then in exchange we are counted righteous because it is borrowed or imputed from Him in exchange. Don't you agree this teaching is absolutely anti-Christ?

Above all this aura of sinful and sinning religion we still have a nucleus of wonderful men who will have nothing to do with it and are just as bright and victorious as these others are dark and dejected and argumentative. Thank God for them. They are growing in grace and it takes no imagination to see it.

Paul wrote thus to the Galatian Christians: "My little children, of whom I travail in birth again until Christ be formed in you." Please help us travail in birth again for these precious souls that nothing will hinder "Christ be[ing] formed in them" as the Galatians were. What pain it brought to Paul to watch the Galatians being hindered; what pain it is to watch a soul in prison that had such a bright start be hindered by these viciously arrogant false teachings.

Again and again my own heart just has to lay it before God and realize the battle is the Lord's, not mine. Won't it be wonderful beyond all imagination when God cleanses this entire universe of every effect of sin— even its memory— and forever and ever there will be not one discordant note in the praise and adoration of Him who loved us and washed us from our sins in His own blood?

One day in class recently we had come to the end of our time and the officer had already let us know it was up. A man said, "Chaplain, can I just ask one question because it is really burning on my heart?" Given permission he continued, "This is really heavy on me. I have never been married and someday I want to be, but before I came to this prison I never heard such truth as this. I'm really burdened about when I get out— how am I going to ever find a woman who believes like this to be my wife?"

I said, "Would you let me tell you a quick story? There was a young girl who got gloriously saved and was really enjoying her new life. Then it seemed she went under a cloud and her pastor became concerned for her. Finally he went to her and asked her what seemed to be bothering her. She said that she was afraid she did not have dying grace. He asked her if she was dying. She said she wasn't. He then told her that God would give her dying grace when she needed it to die." I then dismissed the class.

At the beginning of another class one of our best sanctified men came to me and said, "Chaplain, I want to tell you something. This class is really helping me. I mean, it really is! The truths we have been discussing are not only informative, but they are really helping me and I thank you." What a joy to feed such hungry souls. I must say that I don't believe he was the only one, because I could sense the light dawning on numbers of them and there has been a good atmosphere in the classes. Oh, that many will walk in that Light!

Several years ago a young man who is from Sierra Leone prayed through in a Bible study that our pastor was holding and he has never looked back or gone back. Whether or not he fully comprehends with his mind all the theology of holiness, I would not be at all surprised that he has walked into it. I have asked him several times in recent months if he is living victoriously above sin and his answer is as clear as a bell that he is. He is a very quiet humble man and it is a joy to be around him.

He was released the other day and we still do not know where they have sent him. He wasn't sure just what they would do with him, deport him to his own country or send him to his mother who lives in the northern part of the state. He definitely wanted to keep in touch and if not deported right away, come to church. Please help us pray that he will not miss any part of God's will or grace but will go right on. Sierra Leone is one of the major hot spots for Ebola and it would seem they would refrain from deporting him there just now, but who knows? I trust wherever God allows him to go he will continue to walk in the light and be a light to others.

I think I have mentioned it to you before, but for the nearly seventeen years I have ministered at this same prison I have witnessed the tone of the services and Bible studies move from one facility to another. For a few months it seems God is moving especially in one or two places more than in others, and then it will change back. I am very sure it is totally a matter of hearts responding or not.

Seventeen years ago there was a very vibrant and encouraging group out in the minimum camp, which is a small facility of about 350 beds outside of the main security boundary.

Once or twice since it has seemed to revive for a short period, but for the most part it has been one of the more discouraging groups. Part of the reason is that the men there are about to leave and are focused on that instead of being ready to leave. Recently a couple of our good men were moved out there and now there is again a very vibrant atmosphere in the services and studies there.

The other Sunday night I received a call that the volunteer group scheduled for there had called out, so I went in to fill in for them but also found that another group had cancelled for a service inside the prison. I took the inside service first and then went to the minimum camp. I preached the same message, but certainly felt a difference in the atmosphere between the two places. It really shows the fact that God comes where He is wanted and welcomed, doesn't it?

And so today when I went out to the minimum camp for Bible study I asked one of the men to pray and this was his opening statement: "Father, our hearts are panting for Thy truth that is going to be given to us." I don't think that God finds it hard to come among a group like that. It takes me back to a few years ago in the same facility when I was speaking to a group of men and on the front row was a sandy-haired man with a very red face. He was listening intently as I was telling them that the nature of sin is two-fold. There is the problem of our committed acts of sin, but then there is that sin nature that we came into the world with and wants to rise up and give us trouble even after our committed acts are forgiven.

Our brother on the front row put up his hand and with a very earnest look in his face asked, "Can we get rid of that?" If my heart enjoys an open door like that, I wonder what the heart of Jesus feels with a question like that, when the answer to it is the very purpose of His giving His life and blood for us.

Oh, that men would cease arguing over theological viewpoints and plunge into the open Fountain for sin and uncleanness. I have at times told the men that it would serve them well and save them from error if they would quit arguing about who is teaching the truth and what the truth is and simply pray this prayer: "Jesus, I know that You died for me. Whatever it was that You saw I could become that made You willing to die for me, please make me that! Amen!"

Do you remember the man who had the hurting face due to his inability to stop smiling? I wish you could meet him someday, but without him knowing you were there to meet him. I have heard him more than once walking down the hallway saying quietly yet plainly, "Praise God! Oh, hallelujah! Thank You, Jesus!" Now I have met people in my life before that might be very vocal about their religion, but somehow it just didn't ring a bell with me. Not this man! It does ring my bell! And that very loudly! I love to hear and see him for he literally shines with the joy of his salvation. He is not struggling over any of the false doctrines and teachings, for he is too occupied enjoying the real thing.

Now please excuse me for a minute as I just have to insert something here and I do it with a heart full of love. If everyone who professes the name of holiness and is endeavoring to defend and preserve it was enjoying it as intensely as this man is, sufficient indeed, yea more than sufficient, would be their defense of the doctrine and the experience. An old song says it well.

> *When I saw their faces shining,*
> *and the fruit on which they're dining,*
> *I believed the good report and came in.*

And now I want to praise the Lord for an answer to prayer, which I had shared with our local church but not in these letters as far as I remember. The politics and the bizarre religious groups that have to be dealt with have changed completely the workload of my supervisor over the past fifteen years. Fifteen years ago he was having classes and preaching himself, but now there are so many issues that arise from the many "faith groups" (so-called) that his time is swallowed up in that rather than any active ministry or inmate interviews. He has become weary of it all and has been threatening for over a year to either retire early or take a pastorate somewhere in one of his denominational churches.

I asked our church to pray about this as there is possibly no one more conscious of what all he does to keep the door open for us than myself. He has told me numbers of times that if I were not there he would quit without a doubt, but he is conscious of what God is doing and has a heart for it. In fact, whenever there are cancellations from any other Protestant group, we are called upon to fill in.

Well, just today he told me that he informed his conference that he will not take a church and that he is thinking now of even staying until full retirement age. I gave him a pat on the back. Even though he would differ theologically, he would not put a straw in my way or change my course. Thank God for him and please keep him in your prayers.

Laborers together with Him, William Cawman

March 1, 2015

"I DON'T WANT to be this way!" These were the heart-wrenching words of a twenty-five- year-old who has found the pathway Satan mapped out for him totally disappointing. (Anyone else will too.) In his wee quarter of a century on earth he has already had a few prison sentences; he has tasted the bitterness of the opposite of God's plan for him; he has come to a screeching halt down the swift road to hell— thank God he has! Now he is sitting before me by his own request and does not know where to begin to unload his misery and heartache, except that he doesn't want to be this way.

It is Satan's passionate plan for any young life to get them to take his crash course in sin's pleasure and push them fast enough that all of the sudden it seems too hopeless to turn around and go back. Then he needs put forth but little effort to get them to carry on just a little farther, and a little farther, until he has them where he can just stand back and laugh at them while they plummet into hell.

One of these, plucked as a brand from the burning, will be worth all it costs, for it cost the Son of God everything. O Jesus, please help us to rescue a few more while the day lasts! Will you pray for this young man? I tried to tell him that Jesus doesn't want him to be the way he has been either and that he died to change him. I prayed with him and then urged him to pray with expectancy and to forsake every known sin. He said he would. I will see him again soon, Lord willing.

Just after him came two of our good men from the same unit who are walking in all the light and have found God's Word absolutely true that "if we walk in the light, as he is in the light, we have fellowship one with another, and the blood of Jesus Christ his Son cleanseth us from all sin." The first one was so delighted with the opportunity to visit as he was wishing for it but knew we were scheduled to be leaving for a meeting.

As we simply spoke to him as God laid words upon us, he kept saying, "Oh, I can't believe we're having this conversation! This is just what I have needed to talk about. Chaplain, I've listened to all you have said about the false teachings all through the churches of today and I know for a fact that it is the truth. My own father was a minister and advanced to a position of leadership but while he was attending a big convention in another state the bishop found him sleeping with another woman. My mother found out about it before he ever reached home and things really fell apart, but he goes on making excuse for sin in his life. I don't want any part of that. I love the truth you are bringing to us."

The next one is a man with such a hunger for more of God that if there is any temptation to turn him aside it certainly is not the temptation to spiritual indolence or sluggishness. He is taking the college courses from one of our Bible colleges and this is what he told me about it: "I will get to the study books, but right now I'm just absorbed in the Bible itself, so I'm doing all the Bible studies. I can't get enough of God's Word. I have set up a study method of my own besides the studies for that course with the college. Every morning along with chapters from the Old and New Testaments I read a Psalm. Then I meditate on that Psalm all day and then I pray it when I go to bed at night. Oh my, no matter what you're going through, there's a Psalm for it. I find it wonderful to pray them after I've meditated on them."

This man is coming close to the finish line of a very heavy sentence for murder. He is the one we have told you about in previous letters that bludgeoned a woman to death with a hammer and felt no remorse over it. I only tell that (and do so with pain) to point out the redemptive contrast wrought by the Blood of Jesus. He is now absolutely loveable and gentle and teachable and everything else that God's Word says a Christian should be. He had the opportunity of a change of custody, such as a halfway house or such, but he prayed and committed himself to God and felt such a relief when they agreed to just let him finish his time right where he is.

Just the other day he told me this: "When I first heard you teaching I said to myself, 'Wow, there's no such a thing as that! That's impossible. This man is off the wall.' But as I listened and read the Word I began to see how true it was and then I fell in love with it! Now there's other men right where I was and I want to see them get the light, too."

Can I tell you that here is a man who once was a slave of Satan to the core, who is now a saint on his way to bridehood with Christ for all eternity. Hallelujah for the Blood of Jesus! I say, Hallelujah for the Blood of Jesus! You can say it, too, if you want to. If that is not the language of your heart, you need to flee to that Blood until it is.

I want to share a prayer request with you. About three years ago, more or less, a decision was made up in Trenton to delete the post of having an officer in our chapel areas except for Friday Jumah and Sunday night services. Ever since we have been much hindered in finding space for our religious classes and Bible studies during the week and most of the time in the rooms they have provided we are exceeding the fire code allowance for occupancy.

Besides that we never know what office will be available to hold interviews in and many times the men come down and, not knowing where to go, just return back to their cells rather than risk being charged for being where they are not scheduled to be. In one of the facilities we only have a room available for one afternoon a week for any service we want to hold.

It seems ridiculous that the name of the institution is "New Jersey Department of Corrections" and we have neither space nor time to correct. My supervisor has pressed the issue over and over to try to get them to put the officers back in the chapel areas during the daytime hours, and they adamantly refuse to do it. We are praying and we want help to pray that somehow the minds or hearts of those making this decision will change and see the need to put the officer back. This would open up so much more time and space for us to hold these functions.

My supervisor says if God will undertake to work a miracle and get them back open he will schedule a solid week of revival in each of the three chapels. If that should happen I believe I would cancel whatever I needed to in order to be here for such. So as you help us pray for these spaces to be opened up, please pray for the upcoming revival! I love to read where Paul wrote to Philemon, "But withal prepare me also a lodging: for I trust that through your prayers I shall be given unto you." If God sees fit to work this miracle the revival might start before I would have opportunity to write and ask you to pray for it, so I'm asking now.

If you are saying, "Well, if we should pray for it and God does not open the areas, what then?" I will tell you a story I heard from a precious saint years ago. She said that she was attending a camp meeting in Canada and such a swarm of mosquitoes came in that they felt they could not continue. They held an all-night prayer meeting to beseech God to take away the mosquitoes. She said the mosquitoes never left, but God gave them a camp meeting anyway. We really feel the need of these chapel areas being opened back up, but if God does not see fit to do that, your prayers for the revival can be answered anyway, and we need them to be.

Oh, how we thank God for every victory so far. How we love the men who have walked in the light and are shining for Jesus in the midst of this evil prison. How thankful we are for every time God anoints and helps us in our Bible study and class times. But we need a revival. We need an awakening. So many are still groping in the quagmire of human religion and self effort. And then so many are not even doing that. They are just rotting in their sin and growing worse by being here among other sinners.

This past month we were asked to hold revival services in one of our Bible colleges. The students readily responded when we asked if they would agree to pray for the men in prison and be prayed for by them in return. How it touched the hearts of the men when we told them about it— the more so because of it being young people. The world is such a stranger to young people who want the way of God and holiness. Satan has certainly proved successful in pawning his wares to the younger generation, but thank God, he does not have them all! I love our young people who love Jesus and have it settled to walk the way to heaven and leave the world behind. May the Lord add to their number.

I would ask you to pray for a sixty-two-year-old man who is being released very shortly and during the relatively short time he has spent in prison has lost all of his belongings as well as experienced the death of his common law wife. He is naturally feeling some anxieties, not knowing where he will be sent by the Department of Corrections, who it seems do less and less for the justification of their name. I am not sure that he has yet found a solid relationship with the Lord as in

His abiding presence with him, but he is very aware that he needs to follow the path of the just.

The last visit that I had with him I tried to impress upon him the absolute seriousness of opening the door ever so slightly to anything that he knows would not please God. He nodded his assent and said, "Yes, I know that." Pray that he will yet come into the full light of God and His favor and then go right on with Him. I can never get used to watching a soul stand at a fork of life's road and then take the wrong turn. Everything inside of me screams at such, but it is repeated over and over. It reminds me of two drops of rain which fall side by side on the continental divide. No drop of rain ever stays there. It responds to one of two pulls and the two drops begin to drift apart until they are lost in one of two vastly separated oceans. To stand and watch that first "little" step toward the side of Satan's tug is nothing short of horrible, for the track record of somewhere later crossing that divide again is grim.

It would seem that in that first step the soul partakes of a numbing substance that makes the next step almost a natural consequence— on and on until suddenly at some screeching turn in the slippery road, he is jolted by the reality that he never intended to be where he is. And then instead of that jolt of reality giving him the power to turn around, Satan laughs in his face— "No hope now! Look where you are. Look what you've done. You may as well just make the best of the remainder of the wreck!" By the way, I am not fantasizing; this drama is enacted over and over and then over again, and I hate it more every time it is.

While reflecting thus would you permit me to express a predicament that is signally distressing in reference to men being released from a prison in New Jersey? When my mother was a teenager, she with her sisters and other young people their age would spend considerable time in their summer months going to holiness camp meetings around south Jersey. She heard truths preached by many of the last generation evangelists and knew well the atmosphere of genuine conviction for sin as well as the shouts of victory when it was taken care of. Numbers of little holiness churches were scattered nearly all over the district. Today they are all but gone.

The church I attend and love with all my heart, and a very small remnant in two other holiness churches, are all that I know of in the entire state. Now here is a man, and then another, who has responded and heard and accepted the message of the way of holiness as opposed to either the sin-endorsing churches or the charismatic emotional, feel-good ones, and he wants to know where he can find a good church to continue what he has found in the prison. He hasn't only heard from one, but from multiple witnesses, as our good volunteers and various evangelists have come in and given out the clear message that there is a Savior from all sin.

The majority of these men are being sent back to the huge metropolis areas of the northern part of the state and I know of not one church that I can conscientiously recommend to them. A rare case may be going to a city near the PA border and if he is allowed to cross the state line I can tell him of some churches over there, but New Jersey is a barren wilderness to the message of heart holiness. What can I do? What good would it to do recommend a church that will contradict all that they have learned to love and tell them they cannot live without sin?

Does anyone out there hear this plea? Does anyone hear the Lord of Harvest calling to New Jersey? We are waiting!

Thank you, everyone who is praying, William Cawman.

10
It's Called, "Redemption"

April 1, 2015

Whereas I see how intensely the Holy Spirit is working on the hearts of men in prison as a vital part of preparing a Bride for Christ, I am extremely aware of how much your prayers for us are being answered. I want to thank you, each and every one, for every prayer you have prayed for us here in this prison. I wish I could share the reality of what I have just written more effectively than writing about it, but until you come visit us, that will have to suffice. I say again though, and that from my heart, and from the hearts of the men, "Thank you!"

Let me try to give you a few updates in specific. First let me tell you something thrilling about the man I have written of befor,e who in his wild former life bludgeoned a woman to death with a hammer. Yesterday in class he said to me, "Chaplain, I need to talk to you. Something is very heavy on my heart and it has to do with my getting out. I need to write a letter and I want you to read it and tell me what you think." I told him I already had him scheduled for a visit the next day and he seemed so glad.

And so today he came, and that a few minutes early, which was just fine. First he hugged me and told me how much he loved me and then asked if he could pray first.

"Absolutely!"

"Dear Lord, I love You and I want to make it to heaven. You know this is heavy, Lord. You know it might keep me from getting released from here. You know it might even cause the death of my father. But Lord, I've already cried and shed tears over this and now it's time to stand up and do something about it, so please help us just now and let us know just what You want in it. Amen."

Next he asked me to turn to Leviticus 6:1-7 and he read it through. Then he said, "Chaplain, many people have told me that what I'm about to do is not necessary and that it would be foolish, but God keeps bringing me up to it, and then yesterday in class God led you to tell three stories, one right after the other, and they were all for me. I almost thought you were telling them to me. Then one of the good brothers said he knew why you told those stories and it startled me because I thought maybe he knew of this, but he couldn't have.

Now let me get to the point. That Scripture in Leviticus says that when we have stolen something not belonging to us it must be made right. I am in prison on a sentence for manslaughter, but I stole that sentence. I lied to the judge and so did all my co-defendants. I am guilty of murder, and if I hadn't been sent to prison there would have been several other people dead because I fully intended to get them. I stole this sentence by lying and I can't live with it any longer. Now I want to read you the letter I wrote."

He began by addressing the judge very respectfully, and then testified to him and then quoted John 3:20,21, "For every one that doeth evil hateth the light, neither cometh to the light, lest his deeds should be reproved. But he that doeth truth cometh to the light, that his deeds may be made manifest, that they are wrought in God." But when he got to the words, "But he that doeth truth cometh to the light…" he just broke down and sobbed, and right there and then light broke all over us both.

He made it as clear as could be that he was guilty and was submitting himself to whatever needed to happen. He said that many lies were told in the courtroom that day, but he was only concerned about the ones he was responsible for. When he finished reading the letter to me he laid it down and looked at me. I looked at him and then pointed to the letter and said, "That is absolutely the right thing to do. That rang a bell clear and loud."

He grabbed the letter and stuffed it into the envelope and said, "That settles it!" Then he said that ever since he wrote the letter he felt a weight lift off of him.

Now— will you pray that God will get an arrow through to that judge as he reads such a clear Gospel message and such a clear manifestation of genuine repentance? Pray also that the Blood will cover our brother and God's full will be done with him. The marvelous grace of God that is working in this dear man is something far beyond jailhouse religion!

Some time back I had told you about a pastor who had been set up and is in prison as a result of his church taking such a clear stand against un-biblical marriages. I had another visit with him today and saw that once again grace is working in a marvelous way. He could be wrangling with bitterness over the injustice done to him and to the blow to his reputation, but instead he is sweetly rejoicing in perfect submission to all that has happened.

He is a clear thinker in Biblical truth and often contributes in class, but never in a contentious spirit, even when he encounters a truth that is new to him. Just how deep his relationship is and how far he has gone in the purging of his heart I wouldn't know for sure, but he leaves no room to doubt that grace is working.

Several months ago an elderly man appeared in the Bible studies and classes and seemed very alive to all that was being given and then something happened recently to prove him.

He was accosted a number of times by a very small, very young, very belligerent cellmate. The cellmate would curse and holler at him and finally the older man went to the officer in charge and asked to be moved, because he was afraid it could get serious. The officer said he would move him when he came in on Monday.

On Friday he was washing a bowl in the sink when his cellmate came in and began screaming and cursing at him. He said the Lord spoke to him and said, "Brace yourself." Just then the young man socked him violently in the right eye. He said the old him would have wanted to hit back, but God said, "Don't hit him." The older man could easily have handled the young one, being much larger than he and having had military training that rendered him capable of taking a life with his bare hands.

Instead of striking him back he just put his arms around him and pushed him into the corridor so that it would get the officer's attention.

They both went to lockup. While in lockup he was put in with another young man who was just as full of rage. He began cursing him and acting out in various ways but our older man with his eye all swollen out like an apple just prayed and thanked the Lord for His goodness. Finally the younger man calmed down and began to get tears in his eyes. The older man asked him what was the matter and he said, "I've never met a man like you. You have a glow in your face even with that eye all swollen up like that. What makes you that way?" Before long they were in prayer and the young man got saved.

He was with that man for six days and then he was put with a third man who was acting the same way. His first thought was, "Oh no, Lord, not another one!" He was with him only from Friday to Monday, but he also was convicted when he saw how the older man took everything, and he, too, got saved.

Then it was time for both men who had the altercation to go to court line. The younger man went in first and when the older man was nearing the desk, the woman officer handed him a blue sheet, which constitutes a guilty charge, without even hearing him. He asked her if he could talk about it first, but just then he recognized that the inmate paralegal who was acting for him came from the same tier he did. The paralegal said to the officer, "Ma'am, you need to watch the video of what happened before you give him a charge. I was there and I saw what happened. He did nothing wrong." The blue sheet was retracted and he was pronounced not guilty and returned to population.

This man has since told me some of his life story. After some tumultuous early years he married and settled down and became a Christian. He drove a truck for nearly thirty years and then retired. His wife and he moved into a home in a neighborhood that was not really all that great, but they would just mind their own affairs and then drive to another neighborhood to do their business. There was a pretty violent gang in their neighborhood who made a practice of mugging seniors and robbing them, so they tried to stay to themselves and not spend much time on the street.

One day he needed a few things from the store and having some trouble with the car he decided to just walk a short distance to get the things. It was getting towards evening and as he neared his street there was a section that was overshadowed by trees and was rather dark. He suddenly became aware that he was being followed. He looked back and three men were walking toward him. As they neared him he put his back against a wall and they surrounded him and told him to give them all his money. He told them he would not.

Just then one of them pulled a knife and he thought, "Oh Lord, I am about to be cut to pieces, help me." As the man lunged at him he caught the man's arm and grabbed the knife and swung back at him, slicing his throat open which immediately began to spurt blood. He thought, "Oh Lord, I have killed a man!"

While this was happening a woman from her window saw

it all and called the police. The police in that section are not the swiftest to respond and by the time they arrived the man was dead. Now he is spending a few years in prison, but God is using him to help others and no one can deny it, not even the officers around him.

For just a month or so I have noticed a new man in Bible study who seems to really light up with the teaching, and after a few studies wanted to talk to me. He is sixty-six years of age and came from Dominican Republic at the age of thirty-nine. He went to medical college and then postgraduate and is a Doctor of Internal Medicine. His wife gave him four lovely daughters but after they were grown she began to step out on him. He did his best to try to reason with her and get her to stop, but she kept on being unfaithful, so he left her and went to another woman.

That woman became too much for him to live with and he told her he could not continue the relationship. He packed up to leave and she threw his things all around the house and said he couldn't leave. He got them together again and told her he was leaving no matter what and she tried to stand in his way. Then she came at him and he picked up a knife and gave her a stab which was just enough to bring some blood, but nothing life-threatening. Just then her daughter came on the scene and it culminated with his being charged for attempted murder.

As he told me the story he was deeply remorseful and then said, "Chaplain, the thing that troubles me most is whether the sin that I committed will cause me to lose my salvation." Then besides that, he said that his youngest daughter, at the age of nineteen, was driving her car when a man bumped her from the rear. She got out to see what damage was done and he said not to worry about it, he would pay all the damage, just get her paper work out.

When she got into her car to get the papers he jumped in and raped her and as a result she became pregnant. When she found that she was expecting she went and told her mother and together they began to plan an abortion. Her father begged her not to do that, promising that he would take care of her and the baby. Now he is all broken up because he cannot fulfill that promise.

I first of all began to instruct him in the nature of salvation and the fact that any sin causes us to lose it, but that if we come to God in true repentance there is forgiveness. He looked at me as if a light had just come on inside of him and said, "Really? Oh, that is the best thing I have ever heard. I have been so troubled that I could not be ever saved again. I know God brought me to the right man. I have just been in a few of your teachings, but when I heard it I just loved what you were saying and then I went to the Bible and found it was exactly what the Bible teaches. Oh, I am so glad that God brought me to you."

I then tried to give him simple directions as to how to come to God and really confess and repent and believe God to forgive him and come into his heart. He was overwhelmed with gratitude as he left and I promised I would see him again very soon.

Perhaps I have given enough for one month to help renew your prayers and praises!

William Cawman

May 2015

Believe it or not, there are men here in prison who are extremely thankful that God allowed them to come here. Among those who are outspokenly grateful for this is the Doctor of Internal Medicine, a native of Dominican Republic, who I have mentioned in a previous letter. Yesterday I had another visit with him and he was so gracious and full of heartfelt gratitude for what he is finding in God here in prison. He says he is having seasons of wonderful communion with God and knows that he is forgiven.

If you remember, he is the one who was really struggling over whether God could forgive such a sin as he had committed. He told me yesterday that when my daughter had come in and spoken to the men around Christmastime, she had told them of some of the demonic activity that she battles with in Africa. He said that really opened his eyes as to what those same spirits were doing in his life and helped him to get free from them. God really used what she had said to bring light to his confusion and help him to get out. He is now radiating with joy and peace.

This month I have had more new inmates to work with than repeat ones, I believe. A twenty-eight-year-old man wanted to talk to me and his story would seem very likely that he is not even guilty of what he was charged with. He was not even allowed to appear on the witness stand at his own trial. Anyway, he has been sentenced to twenty-eight years for a charge that I have never before seen to carry that heavy a sentence. His attorney says that it is almost a given that he will not have to serve all of that because the State is even admitting that the trial was at fault.

Notwithstanding all of that, he seems to have no bitterness about it and acknowledges that it has definitely brought him to seek after and find God, and that had it not all happened he would no doubt have gone to hell. He comes across as a perfect gentleman rather than the typical prison person.

He told me that some of the men around him warned him not to listen to or get near Chaplain Cawman because he teaches that you can lose your salvation. He said that made him really want to talk with me because he knows one can. I urged him to just hug up to God and ask Him to completely fill him with His Holy Spirit. He seemed very eager and open to that and so we will be visiting again, as dangerous and erroneous as I seem to be.

When a man comes to me I almost always begin by asking very pointedly if he has ever had a really life-changing experience with Jesus. I ask him if he ever repented of all his sins and then was made clearly conscious that God had forgiven them and given him the power to live above it all. It is amazing how many of them can immediately relate to such a time in their life.

I asked one man this yesterday and he, too, immediately knew that he had. He said he remembers how his whole horizon was full of God and what a zeal he had for Him and what love he felt in his heart. But he went on to say that for several years he has not had that inward fire, but has been endeavoring to study the Scripture and live as he should. He then said that he really wished he did have the old him again. He often prays and asks God that he could bring that man back again.

I urged him to begin earnestly seeking God for a renewal of the divine nature within him. He didn't need very much explanation as to how unsatisfying it is to try to live the life without the Life. Please pray for him that he will not be satisfied until he really is born again.

As I listened to him speak in honesty about his lack, I couldn't help but wonder how many there are outside of prison and sitting in the best of churches in our country who also could remember, if they would only be honest, days when they had more of God's power and presence within than they are now in possession of. I don't mean to sound judgmental, but their number, I fear, is legion.

But one, recently, couldn't really say that he had ever had such an experience. He has been trying to live the Christian life, but it has been a struggle without very satisfactory results. He says he has never had any kind of power over sin or any joy in knowing the Lord. He is tired of this way of life and wants something real. I asked him if he knew of any sin that he is presently committing. He said that he is definitely putting his family before God and he knows that is a sin.

He then went on to explain that his wife had gotten into drugs. It had brought a strain on their marriage and in part was what led him into the crime he is here for. But then he said in the last little while she is trying to come out of the drugs and wants to renew their commitment.

Now, whenever a man asks me for advice concerning a marriage or a proposed marriage (which is a subject that comes up very often) I always ask some questions before proceeding to give any advice, for I do not want to be guilty of advising a man to continue in a relationship that is contrary to the clearly written Word of God. So I asked him if this was a first marriage for both of them and he said it was for her, but not for him. I then asked if his first wife was still living and he said she was. I then told him that if he really wants to find a living relationship with God he cannot be married to a second wife while the first one was living.

He said, "Chaplain, I know that and it has been troubling me. In fact I had started divorce papers for her but then I felt like Satan attacked me over it."

I assured him that Satan's attack was inevitable if he made any move whatsoever to really find God's favor, but that was no reason to back away from obedience to God, for God is stronger than all the attacks of Satan. I asked him how long he was sentenced for and he said he will be in prison for fifteen more years. I then told him we needed to look this thing squarely in the face. Without God, what woman with a history of drugs would be likely to wait for him and be true to him for fifteen years?

I then said, "Now if you want to try to twist God's arm and keep a relationship with a woman that is not lawfully yours, and live in a condition that God calls adultery, you will without doubt lose God's favor and lose the woman, too. If instead, you come clean according to God's Word, you can then be free to ask God to fill your heart with His Holy Spirit and live in the clear and go to heaven in the end."

He said, "I know that is the truth and I am going to do the right thing."

He then wanted to join my Christian Living class and wants to visit some more. Please pray for this man, too.

Do you remember the gentleman we told of in the last letter who was attacked by his cellmate and how God intervened for him in court line? Well, he was in a waiting room for various areas and another inmate was there who was very troubled because he, too, had been falsely accused of some infraction here in the prison. There was a third man who was telling him that there was no chance whatsoever that he would not receive a charge because whenever someone is accused of that there is no one that doesn't get charged.

Our brother asked the one who was nervously awaiting his hearing, "Are you guilty of this?" The man said he absolutely was not. "Then," said our brother, "we will pray." Right there he bowed his head and asked God to watch over this man and allow justice to be administered. The man went in and came out without a charge.

In a recent class time we took a marker and listed on the white board the specific categories of sins and many of the sins that then stem from them. We were trying to show them that sin is simply what God is not, just as darkness is what light is not. It really seemed to be effective for many of them really caught the lesson and said how clearly they now understood the nature of sin.

I then told them that many times arguments come up over whether or not a person can lose their salvation, but that there is no use arguing that point until we have clearly the same definition of salvation. Just so, if we are going to find the cure for sin that the Bible teaches, we must first of all have the same definition of sin that the Bible teaches.

We pointed out that a person can take all manner of desperate means to try to remove darkness from a room, but all would be futile as long as the light remained off. Just so, the many books, sermons, support groups, seminars, mentorships, and you name it, that are today offered to make a person a Christian instead of a sinner, are of no avail whatsoever unless Jesus is allowed into the heart. When He comes in the darkness leaves and the soul has instant power to say No to any further sin. Maybe with your prayers we are now ready to proceed to the cure.

Recently a man began attending the classes and listening with evident interest. He walks with a cane and is dangerously overweight. After a few classes he wanted to visit with me and told me quite a bizarre story as to why he is here. He had been very happily married for twenty some years when one night someone broke into their home and shot his wife and then shot him in the back of the head. He remembers being shot and dropping to the floor and then passing out. Whoever did it then put him into the bed and pulled the covers up around his neck. When their son found them a while later, he could tell that his mother was dead and called for help for him.

When they took him to the hospital the doctors gave him up and said he would never pull through it, or if he did he would be nothing but a vegetable. The police just marked the crime up as a murder followed by suicide and never made any further investigation because they figured it was not worth their time since he was going to die anyway.

Well, he didn't die nor is he a vegetable, but due to the fact that there was neither trial nor investigation, he is now in prison over it. Now the reason he wanted to talk to me was to ask if he could share with the class what he is calling an after death experience that he had while unconscious. He said that he saw lights and very beautiful things and that as he approached heaven his wife was at the gate and told him she was happy and free but that he had to go back for God had something for him to do.

All the while he was telling me this so that I would let him tell it in class he was using curse words without any apology. I stopped him and told him that I would absolutely not be allowing him to tell these things to the class and that he needed to really seek God himself to be delivered from such deception. He looked at me dubiously and asked why. I told him that his encounter had not even cleaned up his own language and that he had been using very un-Christian words in talking to me.

I then told him that I have no confidence in these experiences of going to heaven or hell and then coming back to tell people what God Himself has not told us in His Word. I told him that Jesus clearly closed the door on all such experiences in telling us of Dives and Lazarus, and that He said there was a great gulf fixed so that they could not pass back and forth. I felt such a creepy spirit coming from him that I dismissed him without even praying with him, which I never do unless a man is clearly out of line with prayer, as in a Satan worshiper.

There has been a man in my Bible studies for several years now and he always appears to be very upbeat and cheerful, but I just visited with him about an hour ago and when in private he just poured out his empty broken heart with tears and sobs that nearly had me crying with him, my heart was so aching for him. In times like that I am reminded of the words of the song that say,

Lonely without He's standing;
Lonely within am I…

How many there are just like him. Isn't it sad?

Our dear brother that we have written about often, who is just growing in the grace of holiness like summer corn, was also visiting with me today. He said, "Chaplain, the Spirit is just showing me things that He wants me to draw closer to Him in, and He showed me that my dreadlocks (they were short ones) were not the way He wanted me to look. He told me that when I get out of here I might make the saints that I want to fellowship with uncomfortable, and I don't want to do that.

"And then, Chaplain, I need to ask you about something else. I have been paying my tithe for some time, but I went to write out the check to where I had been sending it and I felt uncomfortable. I drew back and asked God why I felt that way. Then I decided to just set that money aside until I knew where God wanted me to send it.

"Well, I have also been trying to take care of my health and by eating right I have lost about eighty pounds and I feel so much better. I thought I would continue to eat right and so wanted to order some fish from the commissary order, and so I took twenty dollars of that money and wrote an IOU slip to God and put it in there. As soon as I did it I felt terrible. As soon as I can I will replace that and never do that again."

Can you believe, friends that this tender conscience is what God has given in exchange for that hardened one that felt no remorse when he killed a woman with a hammer? Thank God that there is not one wreck of Satan's work that the Blood of Jesus cannot undo and restore again into the image He created us in. Where could you find a fuller definition of the word, "Redemption?"

By the way, so far this man has heard nothing regarding his full and honest confession that he sent to the judge regarding his crime. Also, by the way— He is my Brother!

Thank you once again, each one, for all of your prayers for us,

William Cawman

June 2015

Wouldn't it be wonderful if every Christian was growing in grace so rapidly that there would be a continuing chapter to their story every month? Well, thank God for those who are, and the Bible admonishes us, "…whose faith follow, considering the end of their conversation."

In the April letter we told you about our dear brother who obeyed God and wrote to the judge, fully confessing a crime he had lied about in the courtroom. Last month we told you how the Holy Spirit had talked to him about his personal appearance and how readily he is obeying all that God shows him. Well, several weeks after he had taken that weighty step of writing to the judge to come fully clear with his past, he came to Bible study and asked if he could testify. Of course, there was no hesitation on our part of his doing so.

He came up to the front and said that God had spoken to him about one more step He wanted him to take, and then he told all the men in the room about God dealing with him and how he had come fully clear before the judge. Now he said God was asking him to come clear before all of them too. He pulled the cover off of his past and told them all what he had done and when he had finished an obvious wave of blessing came over him and he stepped back and looked up and said with a glow in his voice, "Men, I have no doubt about it that God has saved me and sanctified me, and now with all that in the clear Satan doesn't have one more handle to get a hold on me with."

His face was beaming and the atmosphere was as clear as after a summer thunderstorm. It seemed everyone in the room felt it and began to clap and applaud him. I am quite sure God did not need him to do that for his sake, but for theirs. I wondered how many just then were stabbed with conviction over whatever they have not yet come clear on.

Now, I must confess to you that sometimes I long to see in meetings in outside churches such as we used to see of the work of the Holy Spirit in reproving the world of sin. It seems so rare in our day. The standard procedure seems to be a few minutes of prayer around an altar, followed by a dubious clearing and a return to the seat followed by an unenthusiastic and hazy testimony of some generic hope that an adjustment has come. There is no real clearing of the atmosphere and no vibrant new birth that is hungry and full, all simultaneously and gloriously.

I've never grown accustomed to this, for I was born under the fires of something better than Laodicean lukewarmness. If I could not see this promised work of the Holy Spirit still taking place inside the prison I don't know how I could withstand the temptation to wonder if He is still doing such. But thank God, He is! And old-time conviction still leads to old-time salvation that radically changes in a moment of Blood-cleansing time a vile, wretched sinner into a liberated child of God.

Would you permit me to be forthright and utterly honest in what I am now going to tell you, without accusing me of wrongful criticism or being unjustly judgmental? Most of you know that almost two decades ago God led unmistakably and clearly into a dual ministry, that of prison ministry and also evangelism. That was not my idea— not for anything— but God simply opened those channels and then blessed me for obeying. He continues to do so, and I gladly lay my all at His blessed feet with a love that is growing more intense every passing day. Perhaps it is not good to draw comparisons and the Scripture plainly says that "they measuring themselves by themselves, and comparing themselves among themselves, are not wise." I will not knowingly violate any portion of God's Word, but I don't believe that the following observation would do so.

As I have for several years moved among many of our precious people of the holiness movement in its various sectors, my heart has cried out with pain over the multitudes who are feeding on husks and finding absolutely little or no victory over personal sin. I have encountered this to such a degree in places that it would almost seem to be the acceptable norm— the status quo— of professed "holiness." Paul wept over the Galatian church: "Where is then the blessedness ye spake of?" The angel of the churches wept out these words: "Nevertheless I have somewhat against thee, because thou hast left thy first love. Remember therefore from whence thou art fallen, and repent, and do the first works; or else I will come unto thee quickly, and will remove thy candlestick out of his place, except thou repent." And to another: "These things saith he that hath the seven Spirits of God, and the seven stars; I know thy works, that thou hast a name that thou livest, and art dead. Be watchful, and strengthen the things which remain, that are ready to die: for I have not found thy works perfect before God."

I say again, and say it with painful love for multitudes of souls— they are feeding on husks, "Having a form of godliness, but denying the power thereof..." Multitudes finding no inward power over personal sin, and that while sitting on the padded pews of well-maintained holiness churches.

Then I go back to a setting where even a God-forsaken and utterly sinful society puts men who are no longer counted worthy to move among them. I go to a little office therein and through the door comes a shining face and arms outstretched in anticipation of a brotherly hug. "Chaplain, I want to tell you something." I look into a countenance that defies all ability to have a doubt about the truthfulness of what he wants to tell me. "For two years now, I have had total victory over sin! I haven't touched it one time!" This is not said with one ounce of boastfulness, but rather an overwhelming sense of gratitude and joy. Another comes in and with the same radiance of expression which is obviously stemming from a wellspring of hidden power over sin, he reports with excitement the new territory he is finding in the Beulah Land of Perfect Love.

And do you fault me for wondering why so many, with all the blessings of a holiness church, are so pathetically diminutive in spiritual victory and holy joy, while men surrounded by a hellhole of crime and utter wrongdoing are finding the grace to be "more than conquerors"?

A man who just recently arrived in prison for the first time wanted to talk with me. He has suffered an awful lot because of his carelessness with sin. He has lost his family that he loves and is suffering over it. He is broken and knows that he needs God and he says he really wants to let God have him. I presume from his name he may be Russian or Polish and is barely beyond young adulthood, but he is well aware that he cannot go on like he is.

Please pray that he will go through with God while conviction is trailing him, for I have seen so many who fail to go through and finally, like Felix, tremble no more. Oh, how I want to see him become fully God's man and I know Jesus feels that far more than I am able to. It is so sad that so many have to hit a brick wall before they see the need of a Savior, but such is the delusion of sin's pleasures.

Let me tell you about a couple of staff members. One day we were singing our choruses before starting our class when I saw one of the dieticians who works with the special food trays for diabetics, etc., walking up outside in the hallway. She is an older woman and believe it or not comes faithfully to work in this prison with all of its inconveniences with a walker. I noticed that she cocked her head as she heard singing and then slowed up and stood there listening. She had not yet reached the portion of the room where the men could see her but I could, as there are windows all along that side of the room.

Before long I saw her smiling and obviously enjoying what she was hearing, and then she opened the rear door and slipped into the room. Her walker is one of the kind that can also be used for a seat, so she sat down on it and proceeded to enjoy some more. When we finished I called back to her as the men had not yet seen her and welcomed her to our class and asked if she would like to come to the front and share a prayer with the men. She readily assented and came up and prayed for them, sang them a little chorus, and started to leave. I invited her back as often as she wanted to come and she said, "I just might do this again." Of course, it thrilled the men to see a staff member supporting them in their desire for God.

The other staff member is one of the officers. I believe he is about six foot six or seven, and he is always so vibrant about spiritual issues. For several years I have known and watched him and I have no question that he is walking in the light he has had. He is full of zeal and yet is always ready to learn and even ask questions. I have never told him anything that inclined him to argue with me. I truly believe him to be a babe in Christ. He takes custody of the administration area in one of the facilities where I hold interviews and so I meet him often and he always wants to talk a bit about the Lord. One of his favorite comments when I tell him something is, "I love it! I love it!"

The other day I went to his area to hold some interviews and he walked down the hall with me and as he was unlocking the office door he said, "Can I ask you something? When a person has a real relationship with God, doesn't He witness to that? How does He do that?" Now at this point you need to know that I will not be interviewing one of the inmates until he goes back to the waiting room and releases him, so now it's his turn for an interview. I did not want to rush him away, either, and for a while we talked about his question as he ever so eagerly took it all in. My heart goes out to this man, for I believe since he has walked in the light so far. God is fervently drawing him on into greater light. For a number of years he worked in areas where we did not have this golden opportunity, but undoubtedly God has arranged his present post so that we can often have time together. Will you pray for this officer?

My supervisor who has been used of God to keep the doors open for our church to minister here has been experiencing some multiple health issues. Please pray for Him as God would lay it on your heart, for I don't know what would happen if he were not here. I know he would appreciate your prayers.

Several years back now, one of our former State governors abolished the death penalty in New Jersey. At the time there were, if I remember correctly, fourteen inmates on death row. As far as I know these men were never placed back into the prison population, but were sent wherever they could exist without being in contact with other inmates. At least one of them was sent to the hospital in this prison, but it was not because he needed medical attention, but because he could not mingle with other inmates. He was a very tall, very dignified looking man with medium colored skin, but probably mostly from the black race. He had been in prison, if I remember right, from his thirties, and by the time I found him he was seventy-nine.

I sat down in his cell and visited with him for some time. He was very polite and very congenial, but when I spoke to him about his soul, he responded kindly, "Well, I'm not irreligious, but I'm not religious either." Several times I visited him, once for about an hour. I tried to get through to him how serious it is to be without God in this life, but especially in the next. He listened politely, but seemed unmoved. It rather haunted me to think of over half of his life spent in solitary confinement and no interest in having a Friend in Jesus. So little to lose— so much to gain— but lost, and now lost for all eternity, for he recently died in that cell.

When I heard that he was gone, I wished I had gone more and tried harder, but I can't now, so God, please help me to be more diligent to follow after these lost sheep. Paul said he was free from the blood of all men, but certainly he could only say that under the cloud of unmerited mercy and forgiveness. I humbly claim that freedom, but not to my credit, not from my stumbling efforts, but only because of God's great forgiving heart. Oh, that night that is so fast approaching— may it drive me deeper into the passionate heart of Jesus!

Thank you again for your prayers that God is answering. So many are still in the valley of decision and so much need your continuing prayers.

With love from your brother and fellow laborer,

William Cawman

11
Dear Jesus, You Knew, Didn't You?

July 2015

D O YOU REMEMBER THE words of Jesus in His Parable
about the Sower? One of the reasons that the good
seed failed to bring forth fruit was this: "And when
he sowed, some seeds fell by the way side, and the fowls
came and devoured them up..." Now He also mentioned
several other enemies of the harvest, such as stony ground
and choking thorns, but none of these reasons are quite so
conspicuous in our ministry among men in prison than these
"fowls" which devour the seed that is sown. Let me describe
to you some of these fowls, for they are not all of the same
breed, by any means. Some are vicious and greedy like the
crow; others are subtle and sneaky like the seagull; still others
are persistent and aggressive like the woodpecker.

First there is the greedy crow. No sooner does a man hear
the Word and begin to be awakened by it than a false teacher,
greedy for his soul, takes him aside and counsels him that the
Word he has heard is just simply someone's legalism. God is a
loving God and He would never turn him away from heaven's
gate just because of a few sins in his life. "That Bible teacher,"

says he, "who is telling you that you must live free from sin if you would gain heaven, is just too narrow-minded and legalistic. God knows we all sin. That's why Jesus died and shed His blood, to give us continual forgiveness of sins. In fact, all the sins I am committing right now and all the sins I am going to commit for the rest of my life are already forgiven in the atonement of Calvary. Hallelujah, there is nothing I can now do that will ever take away my eternal salvation, for I am not under the Law but under Grace."

And so the pure seed of the Word, thus snatched away before the simple soil on which it fell has had a chance to develop any discernment, is left just as he was before he heard the Word— fruitless and barren— a sinner.

Then there is the subtle seagull. Well, I remember something that happened to my daughter when she was quite young. We were along the seacoast and she had just purchased a powdered donut. She had taken but one bite out of it when a sea gull swooped down and snatched it right out of her hand and for payment left a white streak all down the front of her. By the way, I am now likening the devil to that seagull. Over and over my heart cries with grief and disappointment over case after case such as I will try to describe to you.

Just a few weeks ago a man appeared in my Bible study and after a session or two asked if he could talk to me. As we sat together he unloaded the grief of his heart; that he had, by a brief excursion into sin, lost everything he had in his life. His wife and children were ripped away from him; his home and job and everything that had comprised his existence was gone in an instant, and he was now left to grapple with the loss. He was so very wide open to my talking to him and praying with him about turning it all over to Jesus and asking to be made a new creature. He readily agreed that it was just what he wanted, and my heart had great hopes that here was one more that was ready for the Blood that was shed for him. But— apparently the devilish seagull came by and snatched away those tender feelings of need and by the next time I met him in

Bible study and asked how he was getting along he said, "I'm all right."

Felix trembled when Paul reasoned with him of "righteousness, temperance, and judgment to come," but he said in response to that trembling, "Go thy way for this time; when I have a convenient season, I will call for thee." The story goes on to say that he indeed did have a more convenient season, for "he sent for him the oftener, and communed with him." But there is no record that he ever trembled again.

Friends, you and I have no comprehension of how often God has encountered a man or woman on their downward course to a lost eternity, but they only trembled for a short season. Why? Because "the fowls came and devoured them up..." Of this breed of fowls there seems to be no shortage, for the above scenario happens over and over and over again. I have no way of reckoning, after all these years of ministering to these men, how many of them came trembling and returned "all right." But they are not "all right." And we see them come and go from the Bible studies and classes and wonder if they will ever tremble again.

Then there is that persistent woodpecker, hammering away relentlessly at the seed sown. Did you ever view the pattern of his work? He pecks a hole through the outer layer and then instantly moves to another spot just beside the first and thus works his way around the whole tree, leaving it full of holes that form a pattern of persistence with no gaps between.

A young Hispanic man a while ago was brightly saved. It was so refreshing to see his shining face and hunger for more of God. But ere long a woodpecker "Bible teacher" enrolled his undiscerning hunger into his class and began to hammer his series of holes in what he first believed, teaching him that he could not lose his salvation. The light went out in his countenance. A hard cynicism took its place. In a short while he wanted to come talk to me and was well armed with Scripture after Scripture that the woodpecker had drilled into him by which he was prepared to prove to me that we cannot lose our salvation.

Detecting his real purpose for wanting to talk to me I told him that I wanted to ask him something that had nothing to do with what was on his paper. I said, "How is your relationship with Jesus? Have you been in His presence lately? Do you have the joy of sins forgiven? Is your heart full of love for Jesus?"

"Chaplain, I want to show you these Scriptures."

"No, I don't want to look at them yet. I want to know if you are finding fresh victory through the Blood of Jesus."

"Yes, I am, but I want to go over these Scriptures with you." But the "Yes, I am" was badly overshadowed by the dark countenance and the obvious loss of first love. This too, continues to plague the growth of the good seed and the woodpecker is still hammering away.

All that I have said to you above is, if anything, an understatement. We are in a battle for the souls of men. The foes are relentless. Ever so many times in God's anointed sacred Word a world of truth is portrayed in but a few choice words. There is no other piece of literature that can match the dynamite of just a few words from that precious Book. The Parable of the Sower is no exception. We witness it in living drama, day after day, among the many men who cross our pathway in New Jersey's largest prison. It is not at all easy to witness it, either.

In other letters we have reported with joy the many victories among those whose trembling hearts turned into good soil and are still bearing fruit abundantly. But sometimes the many that seem to slip through our fingers becomes a heart cry of pain while we watch yet another who for a moment raised our hopes, instead slip into one or the other of those causes of fruitlessness that Jesus told us of.

Now lest that picture be too bleak, will you let me thank you for all that you, our dear fellow laborers in the place of prayer, have done to rescue a few for the glory of God. Please do not let up, but pray on for a real revival of trembling among the men in prison; a trembling that no bird can snatch away; a trembling that will not allow thorns to choke it out. There is but one trembling that finds its way through all these enemies of fruit-bearing and that is the trembling that a soul yields to until the soil of his heart is made to bring forth fruit. Because you have prayed, there is a band of precious men who have escaped these birds of prey and are bringing forth precious fruit. Thank you, and please continue.

How beautiful is God's family and the love that they have for one another. We spent the first few days of June in Malawi, Africa, with our daughter, ministering to hungry souls who sat for three hours at a time on grass mats with their legs straight out in front of them. When we asked them if they would like to send their love to the men in prison in New Jersey, every hand went up very eagerly and every face beamed with delight. We took a picture of them and when we showed it to the men in prison, their hearts were melted and they heartily vowed to pray for the ones in Africa.

So if you can, look beyond that which your eyes can see and picture a band of men in prison in New Jersey and a band of Africans sitting on their grass mats praying for each other. That is exactly what the Church of Jesus Christ ought to be doing, not criticizing and dividing and biting and devouring. How dear is the bond between those to whom He is precious! Satan hates it; Jesus loves it; the angels rejoice over it. Let's join them, shall we?

Speaking of Africa, let me give you a prayer request. For several years there has been a young man who came from Sierra Leone in the prison. Several years ago he prayed through and was saved in a Bible study that our pastor was conducting in that facility. He has never lost that, but has simply walked in the light until I would have reason to believe his heart is cleansed from all sin. Isn't that what God promised as the result of walking in the Light?

I sat down with him and asked him some specific questions regarding his state before God. I asked him if he understood what we were referring to when we speak of the old nature of sin which we are born with. "Oh yes," he fully understood. We asked him if he remembered experiencing an awareness of it in his own heart. "Oh yes," he certainly did. We asked him if he was still having any degree of trouble with it. "Oh no, Chaplain, it is gone!" Where did it go? It was cleansed away as he walked in the Light.

Now he has been released from prison and is in customs awaiting deportation to Sierra Leone. That is one of the countries in which the Ebola virus has been the worst. Please pray that God's perfect will be done in God's perfect timing and that we will have a missionary from Southwoods State Prison in Sierra Leone! He is not resisting deportation for he wants to see his family come to know God as he has found Him.

After returning to the prison from the trip to Africa and then a camp in South Dakota I found that two of our precious brothers who have walked in so much light and were living such exemplary lives here in the prison had been sent out to halfway houses preparatory to their release. I want to leave a very special prayer request concerning that. It is one of the many pitiful efforts of sinners trying to reconstruct sinners that halfway houses have been established around the state. No one wants them in their neighborhood, so where do they get located? Right back in the drug infested alleyways of sin that caused the problem to start with.

I have watched the result of these establishments long enough to know them to be more conducive to relapse than to rehabilitation. It would by far be better to just leave the men in prison until they finish their sentence than to send them where the entire atmosphere is discouraging and demoralizing in no small degree. The idea is halfway back to a new life, but the reality is halfway back into the old life. Most of them I have ever witnessed are not operated with any degree of helpfulness in reintegration into society, and that is why I never encourage men to apply to them. Many times, however, they are sent without their having anything to do with it.

These two men need prayer, now more than ever, that they will be true at any cost to all that God has done for them. Both of them were enrolled in the four-year theology course being offered by one of our Bible colleges. One of them had just finished the first year and the other had just finished the entire four-year course.

Whether it is in Africa, or South America, or with American Indians, or holiness camp meetings, the battle for souls is a battle royal. Would I be right to believe that in these last flickering moments of time, Satan is rising to the forefront as never before to detour souls from heaven? I believe I am. But let me also say that I am witnessing the Holy Spirit at work as never before in His faithfulness to bring a pure Bride home to Christ.

On the way to Africa I was seated beside a young Ethiopian girl. We hadn't talked long before our conversation turned to Jesus. With tears in her eyes she said to me, "I wish I had a relationship with Jesus that I really was sure about." I told her Jesus wanted her to have that, too, and before we parted she took my contact information. Pray for her, too, if God lays her on your heart.

William Cawman

August 2015

"Is anything too hard for the Lord?" By the way, God Himself asked this question. It is so rewarding to watch God move the impossible mountains when a man sets his will to obey Him.

For some time we have watched a man give himself more and more in full obedience to God, and in turn watched God draw closer and closer to him. The man of whom we are speaking is vibrant with energy by nature, but thankfully that energy is being channeled into obedience to God. He has been taking some Bible studies in the form of little booklets that he has to write the answers to, and he has been thoroughly enjoying it, even though there is much of it that is somewhat beyond his capabilities. He is thrilled with the opportunity and when he realizes that he is in over his head he just lays it aside and goes to prayer and asks God to help him and then goes back at it again.

In all of his drawing closer to the man he should be, he realized that God was not pleased with his second marriage. He talked it over with the second wife and she, too, agreed that they were living in conflict with God's Word, and so they agreed to break up that marriage. Now he is finding a real bond with his first wife. I just love to watch God melt down mountains of impossibility that no one else can move, don't you?

If only hearts would give Him a chance to solve their problems and untie their sinful knots, He would so readily do it. That is why He asked the question to His servant Abraham, "Is anything too hard for the Lord?" I am reminded of the old song which says,

> For the love of God is broader than the measure of
>   man's mind;
> And the heart of the Eternal is most wonderfully
>   kind.
> If our love were but more simple we should take Him
>   at His Word,
> And our lives would be all sunshine in the sweetness
>   of our Lord.

And so, in our latest visit he told me that his first wife and all of their now grown children are overjoyed at their getting back together and they both wanted to know, "Chaplain, will you help us take our vows again as soon as I get out?" With utmost delight I will do so! They both say they not only want each other but they want God to now be the Head of their home. Oh, if more people would just let God put their broken pieces back together! What a mighty God we serve! But to experience that might, it's all or nothing— God's way, one hundred percent!

And then if you would like to know how our dear brother is coming along that we have written much about lately, here is what I found from the latest visit with him. He has taken on, not from a sense of duty but out of a heart of love, a twenty-four hour fast each week during which he just prays for whatever God lays on his heart. While I was gone in Africa last month with my daughter, he fasted and prayed for us. What a precious brother in the Lord is that!

And when he prays he then writes out a prayer to each of the Members of the Trinity. Such worship and time spent alone with Jesus serves to create within him an ever-deepening hunger for more and more of God. He will bring back the latest three holiness books I have loaned him with a big grin of satisfaction and say, "Chaplain, I need three more." Thank God that I have built up a good library over the years, and he is welcome to them all.

For a short time now there has been a young man coming to the Bible studies and Christian Living classes. At first I could tell he was rather staggered and almost ready to quit, but he began to listen closely and is really seeking to know more. Just in passing recently I was saying that we ought to desire to be identified with Jesus and the holy way. I pointed out that a biker is easily identified by his long hair and tattoos, etc., so what is wrong with wanting to be identifiably a Christian?

At first he resented my saying that, as his father (who is anything but a good father) was a biker and wore all the appropriate symbolic garb. But then he read the same teaching in his Bible and also heard other men around him standing up for the way of truth, and he came and apologized, and did so with a real gentleman's haircut, too. He said that when he cut his hair he felt like he had had a bath all over, he felt so clean.

He sat down and told me some of his life story (all of which has happened in about twenty-one years) and I asked him if he would write it down for me. He explains in the account why his writing is poor, but let me give you what he wrote just as he wrote it, poor spelling and all.

When I was two years old I fell out of a second story apartment window. The fall left me with a brain injury and a speech problem. When I started school, I was placed in special Ed because of my learning abilitys. I was a little slower then all the other kids my age. So I felt alone and out of place. So I started to get into trouble in class for attention. So getting into trouble became my escape from everything. I was around five or six when I drank a cup of gasoline. I was rushed to a hospital where the doctors saved me. I was kicked back and forth from home to home from my Dad to my Mom. At age seven I was drinken beer and huffing gas. At the age of nine I was placed in a adoption place because everyone gave up on me. I was put in a foster home but I got kick out because I was getting into a lot of trouble. My foster parents put me in a group home where I ran away from them and broke into a church and caused a $150,000 doller werth of damage because I was mad that no one loved me. I was 14 or 15 when that happen. I was sentenced to 4 year in juvenile for that. I got out when I was 18 years old and I started drinking beer and hard liquer and doing blugs. Then I found my-self in trouble once more with the law. I did eight year in prison in Texas for robbery. Got out got a job did good got ingage had a little girl get back into trouble. I over-doed cops saved my life and sent to jail. Judge gave me five years for bulglaly. He told me when I got sentenced if I could find a long term rehab that would take me then he would have me brought back to court and sentence me to probation and let me go to the rehab no I see no one wants to help me get in to one but I know that God will help me.

He is very intense in class as he listens to things he has never heard before. Oh, how my heart longs to see this victim of an abusive, broken-home society find a haven of rest in the arms of Jesus. I know Jesus wants him there, too. When I hear such a story and then think back on the beautiful and peaceful Christian home I grew up in, my heart cries, "Why me, Lord?" Why have You been so good to me? What would my life be right now had I been raised like he was?

And then how many more are out there just like him? Jesus, please help us to reach them. You died for them!

All of the sudden, after a long absence, a man who had been somewhat in the background of my classes, made a reappearance and requested a visit. When I called him in he began to tell me what the past few years have held and then I understood why the absence and the reappearance. He said that he has been in prison for several years now and he had listened to all the preachers that came in and was not finding what he was looking for so he had tried the Muslim religion for a while. After some time he realized he wasn't finding anything real in that and so he began coming back. He again listened to a number of volunteers who come in for Sunday night services and then he enrolled back into our Bible study.

He said that immediately he knew he had found what he was missing. "I said to myself, 'This chaplain has what I want!'" Now after a few Bible studies he wants to enroll in Christian Living classes and he told me that he has never loved Jesus like he does now. He said he is determined to go all the way with God and let Him have his life. Oh, how we wish everyone in the world would find that Jesus alone can satisfy the void within.

We have all no doubt read accounts of a soldier (some mother's boy) dying all alone on a far-off battlefield with no one there to comfort him. It is most heart wrenching to read those many stories. But I believe there is even a sadder way to die, and that is alone in a prison cell and a family close enough that they could come, but they no longer care. It is not a rare case that this very thing happens in a prison hospital.

Without a doubt, Satan promised at the outset of the road they took that they would have fun and friends and everything to make them happy. But so often the Scripture is proved out, in living drama, "...bloody and deceitful men shall not live out half their days..." And since they have lived so as to please self— let suffer who will that they may do that— now they are at the end of the sinner's road, and all have forsaken them while even Satan stands back and laughs.

For some time now there has been a man in the Bible studies and classes, and over the past few years he has been moved all around in the prison. For a while he was in the minimum security division and then back inside again, and finally with a bad case of sugar diabetes and who knows what else was admitted to the hospital. I did not hear that he was there until my supervisor asked if I could go see him, as they didn't know how much longer he would last.

When I got there he was in the dialysis room undergoing his cleansing and I would have hardly recognized him. His face was swollen and he had large ulcers on the top of his head and he was barely conscious. The nurse shook him and told him I was there and I am sure he recognized me and nodded when I asked him if he wanted me to pray for him. There was hardly any response besides that. I trust I did what I could, but I have never really heard a clear testimony from him.

I remember that one time he was worked up over bursting ulcers on his legs that they were not doing much about. I talked to him at that time about getting serious with God and we had a good time of prayer, but I wish I could have a clearer assurance that he is ready to do what he may well be doing while I am typing this to you about him— dying.

One bright spot in this hospital is that another of our precious sanctified brothers has just finished his training to serve as a hospice caregiver to the dying men. From among the men who apply for this offering of love, which by the way is nearly always murderers, they generally choose some from each religious background in order to minister to their own in their own way.

It is a very grim thought as to what a false religion can offer one of its own at death's door, isn't it? But thank God that every once in a while one of our best men gets accepted to sit with these dying men. I have no way of knowing how many souls have been snatched from a burning hell in their dying moments by these precious missionaries who not only attend to their physical comforts but also eagerly seek entrance to their attention to point them to the Savior of sinners. I know for sure that this prison hospital has been the scene of a number of precious souls being borne away by the angels to a heavenly home. Think of it! To die in a prison hospital and wake up in heaven! It's too late for anyone to claim that it cannot happen! All glory to the Lamb for sinners slain!

'Tis mercy all, let earth adore:
Let angel minds inquire no more!

I wish you could hear the response among these men when I tell them that "I was approached by some of God's children around the country (that's you!) and that they told me they are praying for you men in prison." There ripples across the room, not a loud artificial response, but a heartfelt, almost awesome undertone that carries in its embrace a marvel that says without words, "Can it be? Does someone who doesn't even know us, care about us? And they are actually praying for us?"

Unless you are there to experience it you cannot know how strongly this comes across and perhaps words would only weaken it. I know these men; I have felt their heart throb for years now. I am telling you the truth. They appreciate you and your prayers. Isn't the family of God wonderful? And it's all because of Jesus and His unselfish desire to share the love of His Father with you and I.

And to what extent does He desire that? "And the glory which thou gavest me I have given them; that they may be one, even as we are one... Father, I will that they also, whom thou hast given me, be with me where I am; that they may behold my glory, which thou hast given me: for thou lovedst

me before the foundation of the world."
Thank you, from them and from me!

Your brother, William Cawman

September 2105

THANK YOU SO VERY MUCH FOR praying. Never doubt for a moment that God is answering your prayers. Several people in my travels have asked how the two men are doing who had left for the halfway house. Both of the men have been in the classes held by one of our Bible Colleges and were sent away just a short time before the classes were held this summer. They were disappointed that they could not attend, especially since one of them finished the whole four-year syllabus just before leaving.

Just yesterday I was very surprised to see one of them walking across the compound toward me. We are not really supposed to stop and visit on the compound, but he just told me in passing that they found a lump on his lungs and so he was sent back for medical evaluation. He asked for prayer. So today I placed him on my appointments and had a very profitable visit with him. He is still vibrantly in love with Jesus and even though the news of this physical problem hit him hard, he very quickly looked up and committed it all to God. It hit his family really hard and his mother cried and said, "I don't want you to die in prison." He cried as he told me about it. He said it is not that hard for him, as he is ready to go to heaven, but it hurts him to see his family taking it so hard. He is only thirty-four years old. Please remember him if you think of him. By the way of remembrance, he is the man who a few years ago declared with glowing face that God had sanctified his soul at a specifically mentioned moment in shower number five. Thank you for praying!

One of our dear men who has walked in the light and made some real spiritual progress in the last two years came to class this week looking somewhat "under." I called on him to pray and he asked to be excused. The next day I sat down with him and he began to tell me what it was that was bothering him. His mother worked when he was young and he pretty much raised his baby sister, and there was a real bond between them. He received word that her boyfriend in a fit of carnal rage had slammed her face into a stove top, mangling her terribly. She would not go to the hospital because she did not want him to be turned in, so now she will be marred permanently.

Our brother was struggling with overwhelming feelings of sorrow, sadness, temptations to anger and bitterness, and every other evil passion that Satan could hurl at him over it. I did my best to try to sort out where it was originating from and then told him that feelings of hurt and disgust over such an awful display of sinful passion were not a wrong feeling, as long as he did not choose to allow any bitterness toward anyone or any questioning of God.

Then I told him that the reason he was feeling such hurt over it was that he was only feeling the same hurt that Jesus was feeling over it. When I said that to him, his face brightened and tears filled his eyes and he said, "Oh, Chaplain, I never thought of that. That really helps me. Oh, thank you, that really helps me." Won't it be wonderful when we reach that perfect land where sin will never hurt again?

For probably at least fifteen years now I have written numbers of times about a precious inmate who was a double murderer but is now a shining saint. He is the one who entered into the blessing of a sanctified heart and never knew what to call it until he was sent to this prison and heard us teaching about it. Well, he wrote out his whole story and gave me a copy. It is a very touching tale of God's great mercy and redeeming grace. I set up a visit with him this past week for a specific purpose. For all the years I have known him he has unmistakably lived a perfectly sanctified life. He is obviously growing in grace and Christ-likeness, and if I would take the space to tell you the positive evidences of that, it would bless your heart as well as mine. He literally shines with the presence of the indwelling Comforter.

And so I asked him if he could relate to a specific moment when he was consciously filled with the Spirit and emptied of all sin. He smiled and thought a minute and then said, "I'm not sure that I can, but it surely wasn't long after I knew I was forgiven. Such powerful things were going on in my heart that I knew I was completely done with any and all sin. I would say that it was only a short while after I was saved. I do remember that after you and I talked about it and you presented it to me as a second work of grace, I told you what all God was doing in me and you said, 'Well?' Right there I knew the work was done, but I think it was just that there is where I recognized it."

Doesn't this magnify the wonderful promise, But if we walk in the light, as he is in the light, we have fellowship one with another, and the blood of Jesus Christ his Son cleanseth us from all sin"? All the while we were visiting it felt like we were in a precious church service with God's family all around. Our hearts were burning together with His presence and at times we just looked at each other and were speechless before the wonder of His redeeming grace. Don't you want to come visit with him?

And then the same day I visited again with our hungry little bird who is filled and yet hungry with holiness in his heart and holiness in his head. By the way— another murderer. He very often describes some new area of inward growth in the blessed Land of Canaan where he is living and knows it, and then he asks, "Am I feeling right about that?" Is he ever! Wondrous grace of heart holiness that keeps the head straight! I love it!

There is no Bible teacher better than the one named in Titus 2:11-13. "For the *grace of God* that bringeth salvation hath appeared to all men, Teaching us that, denying ungodliness and worldly lusts, we should live soberly, righteously, and godly, in this present world; Looking for that blessed hope, and the glorious appearing of the great God and our Saviour Jesus Christ." This man does more with the holiness books that I loan him than read them, he eats them! And his inward Teacher gives him so effectively an inward discernment regarding all the false spirits and teachings sweeping all around him while keeping him sweetly on the straight and narrow path of holiness. Well now, should this surprise us? Didn't Jesus specifically promise that He would send the Holy Spirit who would guide us into all truth and be our teacher in the things of God?

The men so profited once again this summer from the teaching of one of our Bible School presidents and his wife. This week each summer is set apart and is very akin to the Mount of Transfiguration for the men enrolled in the college. I am quite sure the teacher himself does not fully know how much this week means to the men. I get to hear the reverberations of what they were taught and what they felt during that time of blessing. Thank God and thank the administration for being so open to this ministry and opportunity.

Not all stories are very bright. There are many that are otherwise. For a couple of years there has been a man in the classes and Bible studies who has been somewhat of a trial if one would let him be. He has a large Bible that is marked from cover to cover and filled with notes, etc. He knows it almost by heart, and any subject that is being discussed he can immediately find reference to in his Bible. He is very vocal and his raised hand has to be ignored many times or he would occupy the entire time.

When we sing, he belts the song out with ear-splitting volume, drowning out however many others while brandishing his hands and closing his eyes as if feeling it deeply. When unison reading of Scripture is called for his voice overpowers all others. He is very self-confident, ready to teach others, ready for anything. But for all that, I have never sensed the slightest degree of harmony as to his spirit.

Well, yesterday the Catholic chaplain was over in the detention center and told me that this inmate was asking about me. I opened up the custody tour report to see what had sent him to detention and was disgusted to the core. He was caught committing a very gross and open sin and so was locked up. So much for religion of the head! Believe me, I will not allow him back into any class that I teach without first talking to him plainly about this sin and instructing him that he can keep quiet about teaching others until his own walk is above reproach. Sadly enough, he is undoubtedly a representative of many who Paul would have to address, "Thou therefore which teachest another, teachest thou not thyself?"

Do you remember the young man I told you about a few months ago who appeared on the back row of a Bible study with glaring marks of Satan's bondage all over him? He has the satanic triangle with the eyeball at the top tattooed in his forehead, teardrops tattooed from his eye, a permanently embedded object beneath his nose, ears pierced but now robbed of their disks so that the lobes hang drooping with huge holes in them, many other heavy tattoos and marks all over his body— in other words, Satan used him well. This appearance in itself causes many conflicts, because so many people avoid him as an obvious Satan worshipper.

Notwithstanding all of this, he is growing in his love for Jesus and says that even though he regrets everything that he has done, he is not one bit reluctant to profess now that he is a born-again Christian. Grace is teaching this man also, even though he has a long way to go. He asked me where he could get a necklace with a cross on it to hang around his neck as he thought it would help counteract all the negative symbols. He said he had tried to get one and hadn't been able to. I told him maybe God didn't want him to have one as He wanted His grace within to speak for him, not an outward symbol. He said, "Oh, maybe so." Thank God for teachable spirits.

He is not at all reluctant to talk freely about the marks on his body and how he wishes they were not there. I told him that there was something I have never experienced yet but would love to see, and that is to see the grace of God remove a tattoo. I have seen grace shine out through them, but I have not yet seen that grace remove one. Someone told me that they heard of a man who came up from the baptismal waters without his tattoos. I told him that and he said, "Oh, how I wish that would happen to me when I get baptized!" Would you venture out a little bit, or maybe a big bit, in your requests to God and ask Him if it would please Him to cleanse this man of all marks of Satan? Would it be wrong to ask that? If you could see him you would understand why I am asking. He is a shocking sight to behold.

Then he went on to tell me that when he gets out of prison he wants so much to spend his life telling young people to not take the path that he took. He says that when in prayer he literally cries to think of all the young people that will go down that pathway until he can get out and warn them. Surely that desire is not amiss, for often Jesus sent those He had healed back to their homes to tell what great things He had done for them.

Now if Jesus tarries until he gets out and if that is God's will for his life, then God alone knows whether his outward appearance would help or hinder the message God would give him. After all, God has given us the amazing fact that "Surely the wrath of man shall praise thee: the remainder of wrath shalt thou restrain." I would confess that one of the most humbling things I continually encounter is God's insistence on using the part of my own life that I wish had never been. But then, He promised to give "beauty for ashes," didn't He?

Now I want to give you one more prayer request. Just yesterday a man had requested to see me and so we had a visit together. He went right to the point. "Chaplain, I am not at all happy with my life. I want to be a Christian, but I find myself neglecting to pray like I should and to read the Word. I am disgusted with myself. I feel discouraged and I know I need to try harder, but it seems I keep falling back into my old self."

I said to him, "The first thing you need to do is to get alone with God and thank Him that you are not happy. If you were, you would do nothing about it. The very fact that you are not satisfied with yourself is the Holy Spirit knocking at your heart's door. Now let's get right to the core of this problem. So many people think they are Christians because of what they do. They are powerless to live above sin. You need Jesus to come into your heart and become your Power to live right. He never asked you to be a Christian. He asked you to open the door and let Him come in."

He said, "I am going to do that!" Pray for him.

William Cawman

12
God Never Gives Up!

October 2015

I WOULDN'T DOUBT BUT that serving as a pastor to men in prison bears, for all its differences, many similarities to being the pastor of a church outside of prison. Probably many a pastor looks at members of his congregation very often and wonders just how they really are doing in their relationship to the Lord. Well, I probably also do what many other pastors do after a season of wondering— ask them. Many times the response is somewhat disappointing, sometimes it is very disappointing, but once in a while my ears perk up and I begin to marvel at what measures of God's grace are working in a man that I didn't recognize to be so. Such was a case lately.

I had noticed a man being very attentive and pleasant looking in all the classes, and finally I asked him in for a visit. With joy and positive assurance he began to tell me of how satisfying his walk with Jesus is. He loves all that he is finding and he told me that the choruses we sing at the opening of each class are so precious to him. He says that every day he sings them over to himself and always finds them to lift up his head and encourage his heart. His testimony is positive with assurance.

Before each class we sing four choruses: "To Be Like Jesus," "Let the Beauty of Jesus be Seen in Me," "Into My Heart," and "Make Me a Sanctuary." As many times as we have sung them, I always notice a few of the men doing so very intently and intensely. Why should we change when those four choruses verbalize the very central quest God desires of us? Sometimes I stop and ask them if they do not want to be like Jesus, just who do they want to be like?

Another encouraging note this month was that one morning, while waiting for the gate to open into one of the facilities, one of the officers who was also waiting said to me, "Chap, please don't be tempted to think that your efforts here are not having an effect. Every time I see you I am reminded of the only thing that really matters."

And then you might enjoy this humorous story. A man up in years, who not only attends the classes but adds a lot to them in a very positive way, does so through very flexible lips since most of his teeth are missing. Lately he has had to leave for a while from class to go to the in-house dentist, and just the other day he left the class and in a little while came back in with a full set of teeth. What a change in his appearance! And it was not for the worse, let me tell you! I think all the men were amused enough that I just had him come up front for "show and tell." He happily gave them all a big new smile!

This same man doesn't just make a profession, but he consistently manifests fruits of righteousness. He is living in a four-man cell of which there are very few. His cellmates are either Muslim or nothing at all as to religious belief, and so he is very tactfully working on them and he ardently hopes to have them all saved before they are separated. So far he has one of them studying the Bible and has convinced another that what he has is more beautiful than what Allah has done (?) for anyone. If you think of him, please pray that God will pour His anointing upon him and grant him the desires of his heart.

On the morning of September 11, orders had come from the State government that we were to have something of a memorial for the tragedy fourteen years before. Our supervisor could not be there that day and so he asked the Catholic chaplain to give some reflections and then asked me to offer prayer over the prison-wide intercom. We gathered under the flagpoles in front of the prison. Our Catholic chaplain stepped up to the podium and with no hesitation began to elaborate on some of the teachings of Jesus Christ as to how we are to view and treat our enemies.

My heart was rejoicing, not only in what he was saying, but that he would stand up and say it when he knows as well as anyone else that such references are not considered politically correct anymore. He made no apology for what he said— none whatsoever. Then I closed the session in prayer and then I went as I was instructed to the central command post and at exactly 8:46 am and 9:03 am, which were the exact two moments that the twin towers were attacked, they issued orders for radios to be turned off and I offered a prayer to the whole prison. I did not hear one negative remark about any part of what we did, thank God!

There is no language to describe the joy and spiritual uplift that I find in a half-hour visit with a couple of the dear sanctified men here in prison. One sat before me today and with glowing face as usual said, "I have no problems. I just have no problems, because I don't have any. And it's because of Jesus. I am just living for Him." Now it would be one thing for a man to say that with his lips, but this testimony is coming right out of his heart and absolutely staging the atmosphere all around him.

After a few minutes with him I feel as spiritually refreshed as having just been through a powerful move of God in a camp meeting service. The Spirit of God literally shines forth from him as much as Moses' face shone upon descending from the mount with God. I asked this dear man today, "You may or may not be able to answer this question, but can you point to a moment when you know that all sin vanished from your heart and you were filled with the Holy Spirit?"

Without a moment of perplexity he said, "No, I can't tell you an exact moment when it happened but I know it's done! I know I am fully sanctified!" Do you see, as we have tried to say before, what happens when one walks in the light as He is in the light?

I then asked, "Do you ever sense down in your heart anything that would come up in disagreement with God in any way?"

"Oh no. Never do I find that!" And no face could look like his while telling a lie.

Now this is the man who just recently took the training for hospice care in the prison hospital and is already caring for dying men over there. What a blessing! Pray that God will give him many souls, snatched from the burning.

Oh yes, now a day later as follow up, in class today he prayed, "Thank you, Lord, for that deep cleansing where sin has no more dominion over us!" Do you read your Bible carefully enough to know where he got that from?

That visit was late in the morning, and then in the afternoon I had a second blessing by another one. This man also knows without a doubt that he is sanctified wholly, but that is no stopping place for him. He is earnestly striving to allow God to mold and refine him in his human vessel, and so he often has questions to be sure he is staying in the right perceptions of what God is doing in him. The beauty of it is that never do I have to disagree with him, for the Holy Spirit is teaching him so effectively.

There are peculiar battles associated with living a sanctified life in such a hellish place as a state prison. He feels it keenly and is endeavoring to sort out the feelings of revulsion toward sin all around him and yet love the sinners who are committing it. His sense of discernment is very alive and false professors just do not "ring his bell." Again with this man, the half-hour visit goes by so quickly and we always wish for longer.

Neither of these two men I just told you about are the same as the one of equal grace I told about in last month's letter. I love these brethren, and you would, too, if you love Jesus. I lovingly and patiently confess that I often find disappointment in many people who profess a lot but just don't seem to have the goods that these men have. If that troubles you, maybe it should, for I personally settled it a long time ago that if my heart tells me there's something better, then it's time to go after it. Why not?

There is another of the men that I would not as yet feel as confident about as two or three others, but I am definitely watching him grow in comprehension and sincere hunger. He just started taking the classes from one of our Bible colleges that are being so graciously offered here and has also just finished a shorter study that I gave him. He hardly misses a thing and I have watched him grow, not only in comprehension, but in spiritual grace.

There is a genuine humility that marks these men that is so refreshing. It is a sharp contrast to some others, such as the one mentioned in last month's letter who was so ready to teach others and then committed such a gross and low-down sin. As I had a suspicion, as soon as he was released from detention for what he had done and returned, not to his facility, but to another one, he showed up at the door for class. I had removed his name from all lists and told the officer in charge that I was not allowing him back until I had talked to him. The officer readily agreed as a sin such as he committed becomes known to the whole battery of officers.

When the time came I sat down with him and he immediately began to explain his side of the story without one glimmer of shame for what he had done. I stopped him dead stream and told him that I wanted him to look at this the way he needed to. He was known by all around him as a vibrant enthusiastic attendant upon all religious exercises. Now he was known all over for his sin. What kind of image of a Christian would I be manifesting if I simply swept his actions under the carpet and allowed him to continue to "shine" and come right back to class? I told him that I would not allow him back until the end of the next month when I would talk to him again, but in the meantime he needed to humble himself and ask God to show him his hypocritical heart.

He left the interview with self-image still in full bloom, making one think of Robert Burns apt, yet deeply Scottish poem: "O wad some power the giftie gie us to see oursel's as ithers see us!"

It might interest you that in 1950 the state prison population, USA-wide, was somewhere around 65,000. In 2010 it was 420,000. Could I suggest one huge factor in that explosion? Now, I realize that we are not the "nation under God" that we were in 1950, and so there are many facets of that fact, but here is just one of them. I was a boy living in a small town in New Jersey only one mile square in 1950. The little town had no police force at all. Now that same town with the same boundary lines has eight policemen and four cruisers.

You see, in 1950, nearly every man in that town was a policeman. If one of us boys made any trouble, any man in town could haul us in and work us over and it would only be the forerunner of a second application by our own father when he found out. One Halloween (cursed be that demonic day!) a group of boys (minus the one writing this) went about the town and threw raw eggs at the houses. Now raw eggs upon drying on the side of a house do not wash off easily at all. By the time this happened we had hired a policeman, and so he rounded up the guilty boys and took them house by house and stood by while they washed them all off with soap and water and elbow grease. Eggs, thereafter, at least in that town, remained dedicated to their intended destinations.

After over seventeen years of listening to men's stories of why they are in prison, I could usually finish the story for them after the preface. Boys need fathers! Since we seem to have forgotten and forsaken this imperative, prison has been substituted for fatherhood. Poor substitute indeed!

Many times over the past years I have heard from some of you that you are still praying for one or another of the men who were in the prison system and are now out in society somewhere. That really touches my heart that you would take these men so deeply on your hearts. It is not very often that I have contact with the men after they are released. The Department of Corrections would be very quick and decisive in "correcting" a chaplain, or any other state employee or even a volunteer, for following an inmate after they leave, as they would view that as the employee having developed a personal relationship with the inmate.

Now let me explain something rather incongruous about this viewpoint when it comes to chaplains. I have been employed by the State for the express purpose of helping them recover from a life of sin. The only way to do that is to lead them to Jesus who can make them "sons of God" with power to stop sinning. I am also, thank God, a "son of God." That makes us blood brothers, doesn't it? How close is that relationship? Thank God for every one of them that I do hear from who is still loving our mutual Heavenly Father!

Thank you,

William Cawman

November 2015

On October 27 our supervisor was to have an operation on his lower back and was planning to take two weeks off to recover. On the twenty-first he had all three of his chaplains come to his office to outline procedures and responsibilities for his absence. After he had gone over everything he then told us what they were planning to do to his back. I then said, "All right, now let me tell you about my back surgery." They readied themselves for my hospital experience and this is what I told them.

Late in the year of 2000 I was holding a revival meeting in the panhandle of Idaho and while there, maybe because of the bed we were given, I discovered that at some time previous I had ruptured a couple of disks in my neck. They flared up and gave me a very stabbing pain in the middle of my back, a pain across my left shoulder and numbness and pins and needles in my left hand and little finger. I went from there to a church in Ohio, and whenever sitting on the platform in the straight-backed chairs I was in misery. When I stood up to preach it would let up some.

One night the pastor announced a healing service and immediately I thought I would go to the altar and ask for a healing, but I felt the very clear hand of God holding me back. I didn't understand at the time and so continued on for about four months. I was getting ready to go to Guatemala for a youth conference and felt I just couldn't go that way so visited a doctor up at Jefferson Hospital in Philadelphia. He took an MRI and told me he needed to operate on it and so set me up for surgery the following Tuesday.

On Friday night before it was scheduled I was having a Bible study in the prison and at the close of it I announced to the men that I was headed for surgery on my neck the following Tuesday so would really appreciate their prayers. No sooner had I said that than I was pinned to the block wall as they all were trying to get their hands on me saying, "Chaplain, we're going to pray for you right now." I woke up the following morning without a trace of the pain and never had the surgery and the pain has never returned.

The Catholic chaplain immediately began to bounce all over and wave his hands in the air and thank God. My supervisor said it was wonderful and just like God and would welcome such for himself. But the Islamic chaplain looked stunned. He sat there looking at me for a moment and then said, "Is that really true?"

I said, "Absolutely it is."

He said, "Really?" and the look on his face was complete astonishment. For some time he sat there with his eyes on me, just thinking about what I had told them. Allah has yet to do such for the first time, I am sure. I'd like to know just what all went on in his mind and heart for a while thereafter.

Our supervisor had been talking for months that he might just retire and get relieved from the battle of the many forces coming against us. I was concerned over that for he has certainly kept the door open for the full Gospel to be preached here like no other supervisory chaplain would have. I had requested prayer at our local church about the issue and then this prospective surgery came up. That seemed to sway him even more to just retire early. He knew I was praying and resisting his retiring and the Catholic chaplain was as well, but the Islamic chaplain was all too ready for him to get out of there by any means at all, confident that he would then be chosen to take over.

Well, God answered prayer. He went home over the weekend and prayed over it and came back and told me that God had made it clear to him that he is to take as little time off for his recovery as possible and then come back stronger than ever before. What a burden rolled off of me to hear it. For over sixteen years we have worked together and there has never been the slightest conflict between us and he has not let anyone or anything hinder our efforts and has rejoiced with us in the victories. God still answers prayer!

Speaking of which— about two weeks ago a man had put in a slip to see the chaplain and when I went to him I found a man that Jesus was certainly speaking to. He was then forty-four (now forty-five, but more of that in a minute). He is a native of Colombia and came to this country at the age of twenty-eight. He was raised a Roman Catholic but being a very intelligent man he could not reconcile all the errors therein and gave up on it. He expressed the fact that all his life he had a great big void inside that made him unhappy. He became a very violent person and remained that way until recently. Being disenchanted with the Catholic faith he tried Islam for a while, but again he couldn't reconcile the errors and inconsistencies. In this condition he finally appealed for help.

As I listened to him I could literally hear the aching cry

of a soul that nothing had ever satisfied. He had gone quite far in schooling, even obtaining some doctrinal degrees in Catholicism. I began by pointing out to him that surely he believed there was a God somewhere who had created him. He did. Then I said, "You have a right to know Him." I happened to have a devotional book with me and I gave it to him and told him to read his Bible and seek to know the true God and I would call him back after a couple weeks and see how he was doing.

When he came in again, his face was filled with peace. He began this story: "Chaplain, I was born on October 16, 1970. I really didn't plan it this way, but on my forty-fifth birthday as I sat in my cell I said to myself, 'I want to give myself a wonderful birthday present,' and I opened my heart and gave it to Jesus and He came into my heart. Oh, what a change there has been ever since! I love Him. I am ready to say that I am a Christian. He is changing so many things in my life and it is so good."

I turned to John chapter one and to 1 John 1 and began to talk to him about what had just happened in his life. I talked to him about the Power that comes to the soul into which Jesus comes, the Power to be a child of God. I talked to him about the Light that comes in with Jesus. Then I turned to 1 John and read to him about what happens when we walk in that Light. Then in verse three I showed him that we now have fellowship with the Father and with His Son, but where is the Holy Spirit in that? He immediately said with a huge smile, "Inside of us." Then I told him about the time as a fourteen-year-old boy walking home from school when Jesus came into my heart.

He looked at me and said, "You were fourteen?"

"Yes."

Then he put his face in his hands and burst into tears. Soon he said, "I feel so bad that I wasted forty-five years."

I said, "Yes, but thank God you're home now!"

"I am," he said.

I tell you there was such clearness in his testimony that it left no question marks as to his new birth. He then asked to enroll in my Bible study. We will be sharing some more times like this I am sure. He still has quite a few years to serve, and I am excited to have another missionary among us. After his first Bible study he met me in the hallway and said with an amazement in his face, "I am so honored. I am so honored." I had always thought only of honoring God, but he gave me a new bright horizon. I, too, am so honored that God would visit me!

Just before visiting with him I had another man for the third visit. This man is in a fierce struggle to find the God he seems to really want, but cannot find. I have to confess that I have been there at one time in my life, and oh, how my heart aches for him. Of course, I cannot know his heart and what might be hindering him, but he is certainly sick and tired of the way he is. How I long to see him really pray through and find the Power he so much needs.

His bewilderment and unhappy state led me to preach to them the following Sunday night on the thought, "How sure is your hope of heaven?" I told them that if you would ask around the world, no matter the religious format or lack thereof in the life, everyone would say they wanted to go to heaven, but how sure is their hope of that? They were not shouting back at me, but I believe the thought was penetrating.

In the first paragraph of the September letter I mentioned that the man who said he was sanctified in shower stall number five had returned to the prison here, after having been released to a halfway house, because they had discovered a lump on his lung. The next report we got was that it was not malignant and we were rejoicing with him, but just yesterday he came in and told me that he had just received his full medical report and that it is malignant. The doctor feels it is lymphoma, and is hoping it is the lesser of two kinds of that, but to know for sure they are sending him for another opinion.

He will undoubtedly have to undergo chemo and radiation. He then told me that He has no argument with God, for he knows that He does all things well. He feels ready for life or death, whatever comes. He just asks prayer for his unsaved family members who are taking it so much harder than he is. He is only thirty-four years of age and is a picture of health otherwise. I know he would be so glad of your prayers.

For a few weeks now a new man has appeared in my classes and Bible studies in Facility 1. He is an intense listener and after a few sessions began to ask further regarding some of what we were teaching. He did so, however, without the least air of contention or disagreement, but rather with an obvious hunger for truth. It was very evident that he had been immersed in the sinning religious philosophies of today's "Christianity," but he was not coming across in an argumentative way like so many others who have been thus poisoned. He would ask a question and then say, "I'm going to pray about that."

He asked to visit with me. When he came into the office his face betrayed him as a humble, sweet, loving man. He began to tell me his story. He was raised in a church, but had drifted out into the street life and for thirty years he had, by his own words, (1) disappointed his family and distanced himself from them; (2) broken and ruined every single relationship he ever entered into; (3) only worked enough to get a bit of money to support his drug usage and drinking; and (4) wasted everything he ever obtained until he was poverty-stricken— no place to call home, no money for food, no friends to lean on. Isn't Satan a magnificent director and manager of a human existence?

Then he began to tell me how through all of those dreary wasted years there was never a time when he wasn't conscious that God was continuing to pull on his heart and to disallow him to be happy in that state. He went over times when he knew God was standing there, and finally allowed him to go to another prison where he somewhat began to awaken spiritually. But he said that there was nothing offered in that prison that answered the deep need within him and so God allowed him to come here to this prison to hear what he was hearing.

As he talked to me I was drawn to open my Bible to Jeremiah 31:3, "Yea, I have loved thee with an everlasting love: therefore with lovingkindness have I drawn thee." I read it to him but as I was doing so, I very vividly realized that we had something very much in common. I, too, spent way too long in a spiritual wilderness, albeit ever so differently formatted from his. No matter the dereliction that separates us from the love of God, it is sad, ever so sad. And so realizing this and having read this Scripture to him we looked into each other's eyes and both were failing to hold back the tears.

Then, all of the sudden, a whole new thought entered into my heart. I turned to Revelation 20:12, "And I saw the dead, small and great, stand before God; and the books were opened..." I had always only thought of those books as containing our deeds, by which it goes on to say we will be judged. But suddenly I saw those deeds interspersed with ever so many faithful mercies of God by which in various ways He had done His best to get through to us and turn us from those deeds. It did two things to me: (1) made me realize afresh that by those very memories of God's mercies "every mouth will be stopped," but also, (2) how if we have heard His voice and opened the door, we should fall before Him with gratitude unbounded. He and I are now delivered! Are you?

With love for you and Jesus,

William Cawman

December 2015

ANOTHER YEAR IS ALMOST history, and with that thought comes the ever-increasing uncertainty of the future. Oh, how imperative that we be ready for whatever that may hold.

Last month I told you about a man from Colombia that was

gloriously and powerfully saved on October 16, alone in his cell. He was instantly transformed and he knows it. He is a very well-spoken and well-learned man and holds degrees in Catholic theology, but that leaving him empty he tried turning to the Muslims. That also proved empty and he put a request in to talk to me, telling me of his background of violence and disappointment and how unhappy he felt on the inside.

I directed him to turn to the Bible and prayer, gave him a good book, and told him I would see him again shortly. He came back two weeks later a changed man! Normally I would not have waited that long to see him again, but I was gone in a revival meeting and the blessed Holy Spirit is so much more able to help a soul like that than myself, anyway.

Now for an update: his face is literally glowing with his new life in Christ Jesus and he is one hungry little bird. I gave him a few more books, and among them was the life of Ralph G. Finch. He brought it back and as he laid it on the table he said, "That book— that man— was powerful! I read it through and took notes and it blessed my heart. When I read the account of his receiving the Holy Spirit, just as I read of him putting his hands in the air and the Holy Spirit coming upon him and him falling back into the arms of that black man, the same fire fell all over me! I love that man!"

I then told him that he had been my pastor for six months when I was a small boy. He looked stunned. "You knew him?"

"Yes, I did."

His face went into his hands and he just sat there for a moment like that. Then he said, "Chaplain, I'm hungry. I need more food. Can I have some more books?" So that evening I gave him *Heart Searching Truths* by R.G. Finch and *The Way of Holiness* by Samuel Logan Brengle.

He then asked to join in my class as well as the Bible study on Friday night. That Friday night the evangelist holding our church revival went in and preached to them on "The True Light." He listened intently, evidently understanding every single word, and then told the evangelist, "I have that Light in my heart, but it brings a burden to me." The evangelist wondered at first what he meant. Then he explained, "I have a burden for all those around me that don't have that Light." He told me he went to the Spanish service as he thought hearing it in the Spanish tongue would be good, but he said he felt there was no life there like is in the Bible study.

He told me that a great cleansing had taken place inside of him and he loved it. All of his wrongs he has made right. There were two or three people that he hated bitterly and wanted to get revenge on when he would have a chance, but in one moment all of that was gone and gone forever. He declared that he feels absolutely no stirring of sin within or without at all. He said, "I am so excited because the second half of my life is going to be completely different from the first half."

And so now, several days later than what I had written above, he comes to class after five weeks of being a "new creature in Christ Jesus." I noticed him as we sang our choruses. His face was almost mesmerized as he looked from one man to another and drank in the words they were singing. It is very obvious that he is still standing amazed at this newly-found grace. At the close of Bible study he came to me and said, "Chaplain, every day it is better than the day before." I guess I will have to believe him, that he lived his life up until now a very violent man, for one would never guess it from his radiant and innocent looking face. The old song says, "Who can cheer the heart like Jesus, by His presence all divine."

He brought back the book *The Way of Holiness* by Brengle and had read it with delight, but he is not finished with *Heart Searching Truths* by R.G. Finch, as he said he is taking every chapter and studying it and applying it to himself. Did you ever see someone sitting in their driveway having just returned from the car dealer with their brand new car? They cannot leave it alone. They are devouring the manual to see all the possible potentialities its manufacturer provided for them. They even like the smell of it, notwithstanding there could be nothing in such a smell compatible with one's bodily well-being. Somehow our dear newly-born brother reminds me of such a demonstration of infatuation, but the difference is that what he is entranced with will be eternal and healthy at the same time, and provided he never looks back it will never grow old either.

This past week the state chaplains were all expected to attend a training session in one of the northern prisons about two hours away. My supervisor asked if I would mind to drive him and the Catholic chaplain up and I agreed. We had a nice time visiting, both coming and going, but as to the meeting? About half way through my supervisor looked at me and said, "They all need to get saved!" Out of about thirty chaplains, ten were Muslim, and two more were so ecumenical that when we had to break for the Muslims to pray, they prayed with them. However, when they wanted to take a group picture, not one of the Muslims joined for it.

At the close of the session, two retiring chaplains were honored. One of them was a Muslim and had long served in chaplaincy, and just before the closing prayer, he stood to his feet and said he would like to give a word of parting advice. He then said, "When you pray in public, pray specifically in the name of the one you are praying to. We are all civil enough that you don't have to hide it and think you have to be politically correct."

Now let me tell you about a rather interesting class discussion this past week. Somehow, I don't remember just how at this point, we came to the question of whether Jesus Christ was always from all eternity the Son of God or whether He became the Son of God when conceived by Mary. For some time we examined various Scriptures concerning this. 1 Pet 1:20: "Who verily was foreordained before the foundation of the world, but was manifest in these last times for you." Rev 13:8: "And all that dwell upon the earth shall worship him, whose names are not written in the book of life of the Lamb slain from the foundation of the world." John 1:1,14: "In the beginning was the Word, and the Word was with God, and the Word was God... And the Word was made flesh, and dwelt among us..." Psalm 2:7, Acts 13:33, Heb 1:5: "Thou art my Son; this day have I begotten thee."

There was absolutely no disagreement among us as to the eternal existence of the Second Person of the Trinity, but there were some very interesting thoughts given as to what office He held in the two eternities, the one before the existence of mankind and the one that is yet to come. Finally, I brought the discussion to a close with the comment that we were all like the three blind men who came across an elephant and did not know what it was. One of them was running his hands over its legs and declared it to be like a tree. Another got a hold of its trunk and said it was like a fire hose. The third was hanging onto its tail and saying it was like a rope. I said, "Men, we are all of us just that handicapped in our ability to comprehend a God who fills earth and heaven and cannot be measured. But isn't He wonderful?" No disagreement.

There is a man who has attended the classes for about a year, I suppose, but has been rather hit and miss for a while. I called him down for a visit and he said that he has not been coming to class much because there are several things he cannot agree with that we are teaching and he doesn't want to start an argument.

He said that he doesn't believe there is such a thing as a radical change that instantly puts an end to the sinning business. He feels that it is a matter of time. It is a gradual process by which we become finally better. How long it will take him is a very dubious perspective due to the fact that time is a very inadequate savior, and that fact, coupled with such a dismal lack of desire, no doubt has him already in reverse.

It is so sad to see how Satan wins the love and obedience of souls and then takes them as rapidly downhill as he can until they simply give up ever trying again. What a contrast between this eternity-bound soul and the other one told about in the beginning of this letter. I remember years ago hearing an old preacher say that the most painful thing about having a spiritual vision is those who don't.

Sometimes I look over a Bible study group of somewhere around fifty men and wonder just how many of them really are walking with God and living covered by the Blood. Once in a while I discover that someone really is when I would not have particularly guessed it, but I fear there are so many who are still living under the spell of some imagination that all is well, rather than the true witness of the Spirit. Oh, how my heart longs to see that change, but all I can do is be faithful in obedience to God and leave all the rest to the Holy Spirit.

And then, if you would permit me to be frankly honest, I also wonder about the same scenario in congregations outside of the prison. According to the very plain words of Jesus, "Many will say to me in that day, Lord, Lord, have we not prophesied in thy name? and in thy name have cast out devils? and in thy name done many wonderful works? And then will I profess unto them, I never knew you: depart from me, ye that work iniquity." Such a warning keeps my own soul ever reaching for more of God in my own heart and for others.

On Sunday night, November 22, in the church service someone called for the song "Amazing Grace." On the second verse a young man on the front row just turned around and knelt at his chair and began to pray. We finished the song and he was still praying so I asked a few of the men to gather around him and we went to prayer with him. We prayed for a while and then he arose and said he had found victory. I spoke a few words to him at the close of the service and encouraged him to continue seeking after the Lord and he said he would.

After the men had left the service the officer came in and asked me if the man was all right. I told him he was, that he just wanted to pray and find the Lord so we prayed with him. He was a tall blonde officer, rather young himself, and he just looked at me very inquisitively as though he had never seen such a thing and didn't understand at all. Perhaps our president* was sadly correct— we are no longer a Christian nation, so much so that many have not the slightest notion of what it takes to come into the presence of God.

That Sunday night I had two blind men come to the services, one in each session. I wondered if perhaps being blind might not be such a bad misfortune if one has to spend time in prison.

I have for some time now felt an increased sense of urgency in preaching to the men in prison. Time is certainly running out and so many are still not ready if the Lord should come back. While, thank God, there are a few men who are hungering and thirsting for the deeper truths and higher ground, the multitude are still in need of a genuine awakening. And unless they find it soon, it may be eternally too late. That thought keeps a keen edge of seriousness about standing before them even one time.

Several new awakenings have taken place and I am trying to follow up on that while the waters are troubled for them. Please help us pray that these will go all the way through with God while He is calling them. Very often, the troubled waters do not seem to last very long. In fact, I have often experienced visiting with a very awakened man and then by the time I visit with him again he has consoled himself and the disquietude has largely dissipated. That is so sad to witness, but it happens again and again.

God is still answering your prayers, so please don't give up!

With gratitude,

William Cawman

---

*Barack Obama was President of the United States at the time of this writing. —*Ed.*

13
HIS MERCIES CONTINUE STILL

ANOTHER YEAR IS gone! What we were looking forward to so shortly ago is now history, and still the Heavenly Bridegroom tarries. Let us not forget that Peter told us clearly that the only reason He delays His coming is His "longsuffering to us-ward, not willing that any should perish, but that all should come to repentance." Oh, how urgent that we work with Him while the flickering shadows of earthly day linger.

Over and over I sit and marvel at what I hear as men tell their life story in a few minutes. One such is a man who was born in New York to Puerto Rican parents. His dad was a policeman, but also a heavy drinker, and his son remembers vividly being made to play Russian Roulette with him. Then at a very young age his father died, then one sister overdosed, and the other sister ran away. Devastated, he took to the street gangs as his family and refuge. At the age of sixteen the gangs told him that in order to become one of them he must kill his best friend, and so he stabbed him seventeen times, which accomplished the required goal. From then on he led a life of unbelievable violence and crime, spending much of his time in prisons.

At one time someone took a butcher knife and stabbed him just in front of his left ear, sending the knife all the way through his head and out of his neck on the other side. He survived it. He has been stabbed and shot over and over. One time, three shots were fired at him at close range but not one of them hit him. After Jesus found him just a couple of years ago, he prayed that, if it be the Lord's will, he be able to get out of prison to show his children what their father should have been.

One day the Department of Corrections came to him and told him "to roll it up." He asked what they meant and they said he was going home, that his case had been overturned and all charges dropped and he was being released to go home. Rejoicing, he went to his home and began to testify to his wife and children of the great change God had wrought in him. Six days later several squad cars pulled up to his home and he was told that he was going back to prison, that his release was totally a mistake. Back to prison he came, but rejoicing that God had answered his prayer and given him that opportunity to witness to his children and family.

One would think that all of this horrible history would be visible in his countenance, but until he told me all this I would never have dreamed of all he had been through. He has been very responsive in class, has a very bright countenance, and seems to be genuinely in love with Jesus. Such is the grace of our Savior! If you think His creation of man was miraculous, what about His recreation! What a Savior!

If you could visit with our new brother from Colombia you would readily forgive me for writing continuing updates from him. This is not one of those sadly oft seen whatever experiences that leaves a person either in the incubator or the morgue. He is alive! In the last issue we told you he was still exploring the book *Heart Searching Truths*. He brought it back and said, "Chaplain, I don't know how you thought to bring that man into my life, but it is powerful! I am receiving so much good from it."

Then he sat back and put both hands together under his chin and said, "Reverend, I know that the Holy Spirit is in my heart. I feel Him there. He is working in me. But I know there's more. I know there's more. I know God has changed me completely in things I could never change myself. I had hatred in my heart and it is completely gone. I have power over sin. But I know there's more. I can't say that I've had that Baptism of the Spirit that Finch had, and I want it." I believe there will be more good news very soon, don't you?

These letters are often written in parts through the month as things happen in answer to your prayers, so two weeks after the paragraph above, here is more: Today, Dec. 10, I visited with him again. He entered the room with a face literally aglow with joy and grace. We visited a bit and I asked him if it was still good. He beamed the answer immediately, "Better."

He has been attending the Spanish services and they, too, must have realized the Spirit in him and so the teacher asked him to teach one night. He prepared a message over two weeks and then as he gave the simple message of salvation to the men, those who come just to visit stopped their visiting and began to listen. When he finished he asked them to bow their heads and pray for salvation to enter. Every head bowed and two men came to him afterward and said they had let Jesus come into their hearts.

He then said to me, "Reverend, when I heard you speak it was different than anything I had ever heard. You gave the message so clear and simple that there was no argument. Of course, with Christ within we can live free from sin! I am not struggling with a single sin in my life."

I then told him I had something to present to him. I had already asked the Bible school president, who comes here each summer to teach the men and gives them a four-year study course, if I could enroll him. I have never in my life seen a babe in Christ advance so rapidly. He is possibly the brightest conversion I have ever witnessed, and that right out of a black confusion of Catholicism and Islam and a violent lifestyle. I explained the course of study to him and then asked if he would be interested in enrolling. Instantly his head went into his hands and for a bit I didn't know if he was crying or praying.

When he came up from that I saw that he was completely overwhelmed. He leaned forward and said emphatically (he is very well spoken with just a hint of accent), "You won't believe this: I had just finished writing letters to sixteen Bible colleges across the country because I wanted this so much. I know this is the right one. I will go back to my cell and take all sixteen of them and tear them to shreds, for God has led me to the right one!" Isn't God... isn't God... isn't God...? Yes, but read Isa. 40 and then you will know how lost I am to tell it!

In just one or two days he had already studied the Book of Genesis and was starting Exodus, completely over-whelmed with joy and satisfaction. When I gave him the list of study books besides the Bible studies, he looked them over with anticipation and then noticed one of the books by the title of *Till Death Do Us Part*. "That will be very good for me," he said, "because I have been divorced for a num-ber of years and I will tell you about it. We got a divorce years ago when I went into prison and now my wife is mar-ried to another man and lives way down in Texas. I cannot help that now, but there is another young lady in Colombia that has been willing to start over with me. But let me tell you, when Jesus came into my heart, the Holy Spirit said to me, 'Close that door! She is not for you nor is any other woman while the one is still living that you were married to.' So I have closed that door and now I will give my whole heart and time to Jesus alone."

It is thrilling to watch a born-again soul find his heart all in agreement with the written Word of God! Do you remember that John, under the Divine Anointing, said this very thing: "We are of God: he that knoweth God heareth us; he that is not of God heareth not us. Hereby know we the spirit of truth, and the spirit of error."

Let me take that a little farther. Before he left the visit he said, "You know, I have heard all my life the name, 'Jesus.' I have heard all my life the name, 'Christ.' But now whenever I hear that precious name, 'Jesus Christ,' it makes hair grow up on my bald head!"

I then pointed him to the Scripture in 1 John 1:3, "That which we have seen and heard declare we unto you, that ye also may have fellowship with us: and truly our fellowship is with the Father, and with his Son Jesus Christ." I asked him if he was a believer in the Trinity. "Oh yes, I am."

"Well," I asked him, "where is the Holy Spirit in that fellowship circle, for it says that 'truly our fellowship is with the Father, and with his Son Jesus Christ.'" He pondered that for a moment and then brightening up clasped his hand over his heart. "Exactly," I told him. Until He dwells within us we may have lovely emotions about Him, we might even say we love Him, but there is never fellowship until the Spirit within us makes contact with the other two Persons of the Trinity. Says Paul, "Now this I say, brethren, that flesh and blood cannot inherit the kingdom of God…" But the moment He enters, oh, what a fellowship! And of course it is unthinkable that there would be any disagreement or discord in that fellowship!

Oh my, I am getting blessed just writing this about it. Do you have this fellowship? Our dear brother from Colombia surely does, and his chaplain does, and we are finding that gives fellowship between us also just as John said it would.

Oh, that everyone who names that Precious Name had the Holy Spirit truly dwelling within. There would be no strife and division among those who claim Him as their Savior. There would be one great truly united Church just as Jesus bled and died for. Well, someday soon this is going to be, for He is coming for those in whom He truly abides, and there will never be heard again the voice of disharmony throughout the entire universe! Oh, what God has in store for those who truly belong to Him. Let's be sure we do!

Well, now for the Christmas Eve services. We invited a number of people from as far away as Indiana and had them all cleared for security and then gave in a proposal for the evening for seven services. It just so happened that having gotten all of that arranged well ahead of time, God saw fit to allow my heart to act up abnormally just a few days before, and so while the services were going on I was endeavoring to unwrap my Christmas present— guess what I got? Two stents in my heart! That is not "all I wanted for Christmas!" but I got them anyway.

So much for that bump in the road, except to say that while the doctor was probing around inside my heart, my men in prison were praying for me, as well as a prayer band way over in Malawi and many here at home. I feel so humbled and yet so thankfully privileged to belong to the great family of God. I mean that with all my heart! I love my family! And would you let me take this opportunity to say to my loving family, "I never needed you more, and I never loved you more! Thank you, thank you!"

Now Christmas Eve is a time of deep emotions among men in prison, and we always run the risk that after all our planning and visitors coming, someone will cause a disruption that will hinder or even shut down part or all of the prison activities. We were praying much that such would not happen, and thank God, it did not. However, another thing that can cause dysfunctional episodes at such times is that often the officers in charge of the chapel areas and in charge of entrance procedures are new to the job because they are substitutes for the regulars. This did cause some delays and a bit of time lost, but all in all, God did overrule and I believe much good was accomplished. Please pray now that many new souls will continue to be born into the Kingdom. We surely thank everyone who volunteered to come and help us!

By the way, I just received a letter from a man who was

gloriously sanctified a number of years ago here in prison but had to go serve a number of more years in another state. For several years I lost track of him and often wished I could know how he was doing. Just before Christmas I received a letter from him at last and it contained an up to date victory report. Thank God! Once again, I and the men in prison thank you for everything!

William Cawman

February 2016

OFTEN I SIT DOWN TO write something that has happened right after sending out the last newsletter, but I know that is because you are continuing to pray for us. Thank you. I will do that now, just after the turn of the year.

As I told you in the last letter, I had an unexpected episode with my heart and as a result had two stents put in. At times like this I am reminded and humbled afresh at how much these men in prison as well as my Christian family's prayers mean to me. When I returned into the prison between Christmas and New Year's, the men set up such a rejoicing that it was extremely touching. As I listened to them singing again what we have sung over and over— "To Be Like Jesus"— I was very conscious of something: I really, really love these men! They are my brothers in Jesus.

I noticed that many of them were singing the chorus with understanding and reverence. I stopped them after the first time and said, "Men, we have sung this chorus many, many times. We will continue singing it, but please don't sing it just from memory, for it is our heart cry. We really want to be more like Jesus!" They assented eagerly and we sang it again. I thank God that a number of them are certainly more like Jesus than they were one year ago, some just months ago. The Holy Spirit is certainly preparing a Bride for the Lamb of God.

Then in Facility 2 there is a man who I have grown to

really appreciate in his love for Jesus and it is so good to see him growing in grace and spiritual stature. I was telling them that, on the Sunday afternoon just past, I had said to Jesus in prayer, "Lord, last Monday a defect that I was totally unaware of was located in my physical heart. Do You see any defect in my spiritual heart? If so, Lord, I really want to know it." After a period of waiting on the Lord, I was overwhelmed with the words of Fanny Crosby's song, "Blessed assurance, Jesus is mine!"

When I told them that, our dear brother's face lit up with radiance and he resounded, "Oh, what a foretaste of glory divine!" There was no question but that he felt that in all of its God-given reality. Isn't it wonderful, and isn't it just as essential as it is wonderful, that we can KNOW that Jesus is ours and that we are His? I love this way to heaven!

Due to the fact that I am in the prison for a week or two and then gone in meetings elsewhere, I usually don't observe what the world calls "holidays." In fact, I rather enjoy going into the prison on days when nearly everyone else is gone, because it is quiet and I can have interviews with little competition. And so, on Martin Luther King Day I had scheduled a full day of interviews. There are very few officers posted in most areas so I just go to the medical area and since there are no doctors in, they gladly give me a room to use.

The first man I saw had just come to the prison on New Year's Eve from a county jail. It was his first experience in prison at the age of thirty-four and he began to tell me how he got there. He had been drinking and was driving his car when he had a terrible accident. The floorboard of the car was pushed up to within a few inches of the steering wheel and the driver's seat was only about a foot from it. The engine was thrust clear back into the passenger compartment. No one can figure out how, but with a broken back and shoulder he climbed out and started walking along the car. He says he only remembers saying, "O God, You must not be done with me yet." Then he fainted and woke up in the hospital, unbelievably, still alive.

He had been raised a Catholic but his mother had gradually drifted over into a strongly Pentecostal church with all of its drama and tongues and gifts. He had followed her but somehow wasn't very impressed that all of that was valid Christianity. Then the wakeup call happened that I just told you about. Now he is wide open and wanting to know the true Christianity. I signed him up for Christian Living classes and Bible study and he was ever so glad. Please pray for him that he will not stop short of the real thing and that for which God has spared his life.

The next man was also newly there and he went right to the point. "Chaplain, I have a question. I heard you say in Bible Study that we can lose our salvation. Is that really true?"

I said, "Well, let me ask you a question. Could I lose my deuselflexer?"

He looked puzzled and said, "I don't know. I don't know what that is."

"Well, then, how can we decide if we can lose our salvation if we don't know what salvation is?" I then asked him to define "salvation." He stopped and thought for a bit, obviously having never pondered that before, and said that it was the assurance of heaven. I told him that the assurance of heaven was something that accompanied salvation, but was not salvation itself. I asked him to think again about that word. He then said that it was the state of being saved. I told him that was entirely correct, but saved from what? Again he had to think and then said, "Well, from eternal damnation." I asked him what would cause a person to be eternally damned. He gave some more thought and then said it was sin. I again told him he was correct, and so of necessity salvation must be a state of being saved from sin. He readily agreed.

"Now that we have a definition of what we are talking about," I told him, "we can now discuss whether we can lose it." I then used the simple illustration of saving a man from a burning house and bringing him into a state of being saved from the fire and its consequences. But I asked him whether if that man then ran back into the burning house to rescue his billfold he was still in a state of being saved from the fire and death? He readily agreed that he was not. And then with that the truth suddenly hit him. "Wow, wow! I see it now. What you are saying is the truth and I have always heard that you couldn't lose it. Wow! And here I thought I was saved!" I urged him to not linger in that state but to earnestly pray to God that He would really come into his heart. We had prayer and then I asked him to please let me know when he received the witness that he was really saved. He smiled and said, "I sure will!" Please pray for him, too.

Now our dear brother from Colombia has been living in such clear and unbroken victory that it would almost appear that he received two works of grace at once. And frankly, I love that kind of regeneration! But today he came in to see me and began to speak of the truth I had been preaching to them at the last class regarding the consciousness of indwelling sin as opposed to the consciousness of guilt. In deep and pensive seriousness he said, "Reverend, something happened yesterday that made me remember that truth. I have been telling everyone that yes, it is absolutely possible to live without sin, for when God saved me He broke every sin in my life. The murderous hatred that I had carried for two people who I fully intended to kill was instantly gone. Every other sin I had been involved with was broken and I can honestly say that from the day Jesus saved me I have not committed one sin. But yesterday someone spoke very rudely to me and I felt something come up in my heart that I had not felt before. I spoke to them truthfully, but without the love that Jesus would have had. Immediately I felt horrible. I went to them and apologized and I've been asking God to take that out of my heart—completely out!"

I asked him, "Would you describe the pain that you felt when that happened as a pain of uncleanness, rather than the pain of guilt?"

"Exactly! That is exactly the way it felt." I did not even

find it necessary to urge him to seek for cleansing from it, for he was deeply into it already. That revelation of remaining sin was so painful to him that I am confident he will not be long in finding the Blood that cleanses from all sin and uncleanness.

I had mentioned in a previous letter the man who by heritage is a Puerto Rican, but who was born in New York and whose father was a police officer who was continually getting drunk and making his son play Russian Roulette with him. I think I told you also of the violent life he had lived from an early age when he ran away from his father and found his home with the street gangs and had been shot and stabbed through the head. As he has been sitting very quietly and humbly listening to the teaching of holiness in the classes, his face has evidenced that he is just walking in the light without a single kickback or argument.

The other day as I was teaching the men I could see that his face was indicating that his heart was about full to overflowing. Suddenly he just got up and came up to the front and threw his arms around me and said, "I love you!" On the way out of class he came again and said, "I just love these teachings." He is manifesting just one more witness to the words of John, "We are of God: he that knoweth God heareth us; he that is not of God heareth not us. Hereby know we the spirit of truth, and the spirit of error." When Jesus has truly come to live in the heart He certainly does not argue with His own Spirit within us.

Another dear man who is up in years and has also been walking in the light came to me before the class and said, "Chaplain, I just wanted to tell you something." Then he referred to something we had taught them the previous class time and that had apparently been new light to him. "Do you know what I did about that? I went back to my cell and got on my knees and asked God to forgive me and cleanse me from that!" He evidenced not one iota of reluctance to let it go, either.

Over and over again we are reminded that Jesus' words were so true when He said to His disciples, "Abide in me, and I in you. As the branch cannot bear fruit of itself, except it abide in the vine; no more can ye, except ye abide in me. I am the vine, ye are the branches: He that abideth in me, and I in him, the same bringeth forth much fruit: for without me ye can do nothing." And He meant absolutely nothing! But the reverse is true also that "I can do all things through Christ which strengtheneth me." If Christ is in us there is power to rise above every and all sin and live the life so impossible to live without Him. And that "Power" is not something, but Someone!

A few weeks ago a man was released on parole who had been very faithful in the classes and Bible studies. The following Sunday he came to church for both services and has been coming ever since. Let me give you a little window into what these men face when they get out. The Department of Corrections placed him in a motel and the parole officer warned him to be careful as there were drug dealers and prostitutes all over the place that would try to entice him. He pulled his little Bible out of his pocket and said, "Sir, I'm not interested in any of that stuff; I'm a Christian." The parole officer said, "I don't care about that!" I wonder sometimes why it is even called the "Department of Corrections."

But now that is not all that a man faces. He has no family, no identity, no driver's license, no money, no credit— just his record of where he has been. Until a person has tried to get on their feet from a situation like that they have no idea what all is involved. Where does one go first, and how does he get there? You can only imagine (and that will fall short of the reality) what tidal waves of discouragement and temptation Satan hurls at a man in these circumstances.

It is no wonder that so many fail and fall back into old dependencies of drug dealing or stealing or whatever their former lifestyle was. The bottom line is this: sinners are powerless to help sinners. Even the best of man-made programs fall so pathetically short of meeting the needs that only divine miracles can bring about. That is why these men need prayer even more when they are released than while they are incarcerated. What a cruel, cruel world sin has made this planet!

God is helping our brother, though, and we are doing all we can to help him, too. Please help us pray for him that he might escape every snare Satan has laid for his feet and grow stronger through all the difficulties and trials.

And then, I feel so deeply that I want to express to you once more, our praying friends and the family of God, how much we appreciate and value and thank you for your prayers. How I wish I could share with you more effectively the joy of watching God answer them. Please keep up the good work. Jesus loves you for it too! Matt. 25:40.

Yours for Jesus and the men in prison,

William Cawman

March 2016

God is still answering prayer! Some time back I requested prayer for the political situation in the prison, for at times it seems the evil element would be almost to push us back or out. I also told you about our new Catholic chaplain who is a Nigerian. He has continued to be so helpful and is as well always ready for me to testify to him of God's grace in my life. He has become a huge asset to our whole religious program. In about one year of his coming here, with no previous experience as a prison chaplain, he has enveloped the whole concept of what is going on and is exceptionally efficient and thorough in doing not only his job but in helping wherever else he can.

I was walking out of the facility where our main office is and the assistant superintendent was walking out with me. I stopped him and said, "Mr. ———, I want to tell you something. I have been here in this prison for eighteen years and I have never seen a partner in our department so efficient and helpful as Chaplain ———."

He readily agreed with me and then said, "All of you are exceptional in all you are doing. And then…(he grinned) there is ———." Yes, we all know who doesn't cooperate. But back to the assistant superintendent; I have known him for nearly the whole eighteen years I have been here and from the time he was a junior officer until he worked his way up to where he is now. It is another answer to prayer that he is the man who is now my supervisor's supervisor. We couldn't have a more cooperative man to work with. So thank God and we will continue to pray for His protection.

After that conversation I was with the Catholic chaplain in his office and I began to testify to him about how precious Jesus was to me in my prayer closet that morning. I told him that my prayer was, "Draw me nearer, Jesus." He got so happy he was jumping and saying, "That's it! That's it! I love it! I love to be around people like you who make me see God shining all over them." I said, "Yes, it's not us. It is Jesus in us!"

Then I told him what I sometimes tell the men, that if you reach under a setting hen and take out a few of her eggs and replace them with duck eggs, after a while you will see a bunch of little yellow balls following her all around. They all look much alike from a distance, but let them get near the farm pond and half of them will plunge right in and the other half will go nowhere near it. That's the way it is when Jesus is truly living in our heart. We don't have any more desire to go into sin. Again he just ate it up and said, "That's good. That's really good! I'm going to use that!" I told him to help himself. He addresses me as his "brother in the Lord," and tells me he loves what I'm teaching and wants to come sit in on more of it.

Our Colombian man is desperately seeking to be fully sanctified. He testifies that from the moment Jesus entered his heart he has not committed one single sin. He is devouring all the holiness books I give him as well as the Bible college work. He told me that often in the Spanish church services he is asked to speak to the men, and even though he is very eager to tell the men of the life of holiness, he feels he cannot do it until he has experienced it himself. I told him that was exactly what Jesus did with His disciples, also; He told them to tarry until they had been baptized with the Holy Spirit. I do not believe he will be long in finding the "pearl of great price."

One thing makes this dear man suffer now. There is a book that floats around religious circles by the name of *Christian Muslim Dialogue,* or something very similar to that. I have read the book with wrath! It is written by a Muslim and "proves" by the Bible that the Bible is untrue and contradictory and that Jesus never died or rose again. It goes on and on with blasphemies of the most horrid nature.

When I said something to our brother about it, he hung his head and told me how he suffers over the fact that when he was a Muslim he translated the book into Spanish for its publication in that language. I trust I'm not wrong to say this, but in so many ways this man makes me think of Saul of Tarsus and then Paul the Apostle. Thank God that the same Power that transformed and turned Saul around has also made a complete change in this man.

A few days ago I went over to the hospital to see a man that I've had in classes for several years. He had sort of slipped off the radar and I had even heard that he had died, but then I found he was in the hospital. I went into his cell and he was in the middle of his dinner but had laid it aside and was calling loudly and frantically for the nurse as he had messed himself up in his bed. I tried to say a few words and had a short prayer with him, but I could tell it was a poor time to expect him to focus on anything other than his dilemma.

As I left the room I was struck once again at how ugly the end of sin's road is. The poor man has only about six months left until he could be eligible for release after a number of years, but it doesn't look like he will ever make it. How sad to spend the last days on earth in such a pathetic situation and then leave but a faint hope that it will be well in eternity. I walked down the hallway and saw the nurse who was being summoned so loudly visiting with one of the officers, totally ignoring the call. How long he continued to lie there and scream for her I did not stay to find out. Satan, you are such an atrocious thief and robber and a horrible taskmaster!

I would ask you to pray especially just now for several men who recently came into the prison and are probably being really awakened to their spiritual state for the first time in their lives. One of them briefly told me some of his biography as he now looks back over less than forty years. His father was a regular user of drugs and then disappeared out of his life at an early age. His mother was a drunkard most of the time and ran with bikers and both she and them molested and abused him all during his young and adolescent years. Finally he went to live with his grandmother, but drifted out into the street gangs and took the slippery road that leads ever more rapidly downward.

Now he has been in prison for some time but recently came to this one. He told me that just a few days before he had gotten down and prayed to Jesus and asked Him to forgive him and take all that away. He feels that God heard his prayer and for the first time in a long while he is able to smile. I tried to direct him to really seek God in earnest and become all that Jesus died to make him. He says he wants to do that and I trust he will.

Our lesson for Friday night Bible study recently was about David and Goliath. I asked the men if they had ever heard the children's song about it and not one of the one hundred plus men had ever heard it. I sang it for them complete with the motions and they enjoyed it just as thoroughly or more than any children I've ever heard sing and act it out. Then we went on with the lessons in the story for them. Don't ever any of you ask me to do that, please! That was prison version only!

The real lesson I wanted them to get from it is that unless we have been finding victory over all personal sins (bears and lions) in our secret living, we cannot expect to have victory when the crisis comes. They certainly gave utmost attention to it, as they generally do.

Perhaps just in case you might be tempted to think that every visit between a chaplain and an inmate is highly productive of spiritual good, let me try to describe my first visit on the morning of President's Day. This man has been in the prison for about one week and has submitted a request form on which he has checked the box which says, "By requesting the above programs I am declaring that Faith Group as my Religious Affiliation." He has further checked the box for "Protestant Christian." In addition he has checked the box that reads, "Spiritual Counseling [By Appointment Only]." Upon the lines available to further explain any particulars that he desires he has written: "Spiritual, Holyness [sic], Hebrew, Jewish, Egptian [sic]."

Upon opening our acquaintance he informed me that he didn't know what to put down as he is very "unique." He had been ordained a "prophet." I tried to avoid that detail, but he would rather I not. I tried to evade it by asking what religious programs he would be interested in joining. He said that he didn't want to attend any Bible studies because he didn't want to bump heads with any other Bible teacher because he had already been ordained a "prophet."

Since we were now incapable of avoiding this endowment, I asked him who ordained him a prophet. He replied that a Philadelphia clergy did so, but he didn't remember his name. I asked him if this was his first time in prison and he said it was the first time in a state prison, but he had been several times in a county jail.

He proceeded to enlighten me with the details that while in one of these bids he began to discover the gift that was in him. He put out the shingle that any man who desired his services could come to his cell and he would prophesy his future. Every man that came received from his astounding insight into the future that he would be released the next day, and lo, everyone thus enlightened was released the next day.

One day as he sat upon his bed the "lord" spoke to him and said he could either accept the assignment he had for him or he could lay back down on the bed and stay there. He told the "lord" that he would accept the assignment. I asked him what the assignment was, for you see by now I was desirous to know all I could regarding this illustrious personage into whose presence I had been marshaled and at such a time as this.

He replied that the assignment was to accept his calling as a prophet. Since that time he had not needed to attend other men's Bible teachings for he was himself a "servant of the lord." He then began to inquire about the Jewish services. I asked him if he was Jewish. "Well, that doesn't matter, because I am not Christian or Jewish but simply a 'servant of the lord.'"

He revealed that he had also had quite a wealth of Egptian (his spelling) and other ancient studies incorporated into his resumé. Then he began to rattle on and on with one disclosure after another of his truly marvelous capabilities and potentialities, and so I decided to bring it to a terminus. I suggested that it might be well for him to just lie low with his program until he was released and then find a place for himself.

"Yes," he felt also that such would be appropriate. I prayed in closing without bidding godspeed and we parted. As he left he shook my hand warmly and said, "My name is ———, but I was ordained as Prophet Adonia" (accent on the "i").

I pulled up his face sheet to learn, if I could, what would have possibly induced the State of New Jersey to halt the development of such spectacular and impressive potential as this. I learned that he was there for endangering the welfare of a child through abuse and neglect, coupled with a third degree escape history and terroristic threats.

Such was my honorable interview with the Prophet Adonia. In case you are wondering, it has long been a dominant trait in our family genetics to enjoy various types of people.

I was told by two of the inmates that one of the men who had been in the classes was in the prison hospital and that the doctor had given him only a few weeks to live. I immediately went over to see him and he greeted me and said he had been trying to send for me. He was obviously in very poor condition with stomach cancer and after two surgeries was now left to die. I asked him how it was with his soul and he seemed very confident that his sins were forgiven and that he was meeting with God in prayer.

He is only thirty-two years old and dying in a prison hospital. That would be unspeakably sad except for heaven, wouldn't it? How many others have also died there in the past eighteen years since it was built, and that with no hope of heaven. Satan surely is a rotten paymaster.

Thank you once again for all your prayers this past month. May the Lord reward each of you as only He can.

In His love,

William Cawman

14
THEN JESUS CAME!

April 1, 2016

P LEASE DO NOT RELATE one single thing in this letter to the
date above. The many answers to your prayers, the deal-
ings of the faithful Holy Spirit with the hearts of men,
the seriousness of eternal destinies, are matters too somber to
admit of any of the attachments traditionally connected to this
day of the year. We are in a real battle for real souls. Satan
hates it with an inveterate wrath. Jesus loves every victory won
on this battlefront. As long as God keeps the doors of the prison
open just as He opened them to start with, our loyalty to this
ministry will not waver. God knows how seriously we have
promised that to Him.

We would not deny that there are repeated disappointments. It seems that in by far the largest majority of cases we
see the following pattern. First a man is stopped in his tracks,
whatever those tracks were and wherever they were leading
him. Then he makes a bit of recovery from the initial shock
and begins to reappraise his life and its meaning. And for many,
this is the first time they have ever been stopped long enough
in their mad pursuits to permit such.

It is not only safe to conjecture by observation, but it is also consistent with the written Word of God, that the faithful Holy Spirit does not bypass a single one of these souls at this point. Long and earnestly He has followed them like the "Hound of Heaven," patiently, persistently, with almost unbelievable longsuffering. And now, perhaps in many for the first time, He has their attention, to some degree at least. It is very often right at this fork of the road that we have our first encounter with them. Now what?

Over and over we have been right at this point in a life in the past eighteen years of laboring here in the prison. Never can we take this lightly or without deep concern. We long to see them, while He is knocking at their door, open it and let Him come in and change all that has been as well as all that might yet be. We cannot place a percentage on these cases of those who do respond in full to Him, but the fraction is minimal. This hurts! It hurts the heart of Jesus; it hurts our own heart; it hurts the soul He is knocking at, if they only knew it. But it seems so often that they don't know it. Why?

Permit an effort at the reasons why so many slip through our fingers. I don't mean by saying all this to be discouraging or pessimistic, but it is sadly the truth— so very, very many let the knocking of the Holy Spirit grow faint without responding wholeheartedly, and then they grow accustomed to the awful state of His absence. One reason for this is found in the Biblical statement itself that the Holy Spirit "shall not always strive with man." While God is longsuffering, patient, faithful, and persistent as well, He will not insist on knocking if from within there is a desire for Him not to. He is a tender and loving Dove, and He can be grieved not only by man's resistance, but by his procrastination as well.

We cannot but observe over these many years that a person does not stay long under the convicting finger of God's Spirit. Many a time we have sat and listened to a man pour out his brokenness, and then stop just short of opening his door to the further work of God. Oh, how often we have longed to urge him to go on in, and we have, but there is a part that no one can do except himself. By the next time we visit with him we can sense that much of the urgency, much of the broken-ness, has already begun to wane and dissipate.

Another reason why so many slip through this crossroads without taking the right turn, is that we have such an abun-dance of the multiple false prophets that abound every-where. Having never taken the way of truth themselves, or else having turned aside after having done so, they now are aggressively opening the doors of false security and ground-less hope to men that they can slip under the wire, so to speak, of God's written requirements. On their rapid way to a lost eternity themselves, they are maliciously and vi-ciously turning others aside from the way of that truth which pricked their heart and conscience when first awak-ened. I hate their works— I really do! And in case you think me wrong for saying so, could I quote a few lines from the Word of God?

Psalm 101:3: "I will set no wicked thing before mine eyes: *I hate the work of them that turn aside;* it shall not cleave to me." Psalm 119:104: "Through thy precepts I get understanding: therefore *I hate every false way."* Psalm 119:113: *"I hate vain thoughts:* but thy law do I love." Psalm 119:128: "Therefore I esteem all thy precepts concerning all things to be right; and *I hate every false way."* Psalm 119:163: *"I hate and abhor lying:* but thy law do I love." Psalm 139:21,22: *"Do not I hate them,* O LORD, that hate thee? and am not I grieved with those that rise up against thee? *I hate them with perfect hatred:* I count them mine enemies." Zech. 8:17: "And let none of you imag-ine evil in your hearts against his neighbour; and love no false oath: for all these are *things that I hate,* saith the LORD." Rev. 2:15: "So hast thou also them that hold the doctrine of the Nicolaitans, *which thing I hate."*

I do not hate these people who turn these awakened souls aside. I love them and want to see them change, but I hate what they are doing to precious souls that God and the prayers of His children have brought to a critical fork in the pathway of their lives.

And then without a doubt, another reason why so many slip by us is that "when he sowed, some seeds fell by the way side, and the fowls came and devoured them up." Satan actually considers this prison to be "his" territory. He has let me know such in no uncertain terms many times over.

But now I am happy to tell you that not all are thus bereft of that which the death of Jesus provided for them. By the blood that He shed, by the faithful wooing of the Holy Spirit, and by your prayers, God has found in a number of hearts a welcome, and He has come in. While sometimes we are pained by the many who turn aside, we are also enriched by the few who really let Him come in and thus come forth new creatures in Christ Jesus.

You might ask how many of these there are? I cannot answer that. Every so often I discover with joy that a man I didn't realize was gaining such ground, comes open with a story of God's amazing grace to him. The Blessed Holy Spirit is doing His work, and He will until the Rapture removes Him, along with those that are His.

This past month I was made to rejoice in that a man who had told us he wasn't coming anymore to the Bible studies and classes because he didn't agree with what we were teaching, changed, and is coming back again. I trust it will be with him as one Paul spoke of: "For perhaps he therefore departed for a season, that thou shouldest receive him for ever."

What he specifically did not agree with is that there is a provision in the Blood of Jesus whereby the sinning business can be terminated, and that immediately. He felt that such would take much time and perhaps never reach perfection. What a shabby Christ that would be! Indeed, it places Him profoundly inferior to Satan, who did not need time to make us sinners, nor did he fail to make us perfect ones, either! Please remember this man in your prayers. I long to see him come altogether into a Biblical Christian.

Another man who is now unquestionably a true Christian, saved and sanctified and happy to be so, testifies that when he first heard the teaching that we could be made free from all sin, he simply said to himself, "Oh no, that just could not be true!" But he said that he went to his Bible and began to read, and lo and behold, he found it there. No marvel— that's where the rest of us found it too, wasn't it? What a blessing this man is now! He is radiantly happy in his walk with God. He is passionate that others find it, too. O God, give us many more just like him!

Once again this past month we had the privilege of taking the evangelist scheduled for our church revival into the prison classes for a week. After speaking in several of the classes through the week, he and his wife and son came for the 5:30 p.m. Bible study on Friday night. When he had to leave after that one to go back to the church for the service, his son wanted to stay behind for the next Bible study.

How my heart was thrilled to sense the response of the men when they heard an eighteen-year-old young man pray and testify to them. They indeed had appreciated his father's sermon to them, but what an impact it obviously had on them to see a young man so deeply in love with Jesus and so in love with them as well. It really spoke to their hearts. Oh, would God such young hearts were not so rare a testimony to this sin-sick world.

At the close of last month's letter I told you of a young man who was dying of stomach cancer in the prison hospital. I had gone to visit with him and thank God, he did feel that his sins were forgiven and that he was in communion with God in prayer. The following week I was scheduled to be away and so I asked my pastor if he would go over and visit him when he went in for the Wednesday classes. Of course he was very eager to do so, and so I called on Tuesday to try to get a clearance for him to visit in the hospital.

While the social worker was taking down the information I was giving her and had mentioned the name of the inmate to be visited, she suddenly called me back and said, "Guess what? I just now got a notice that the inmate you wanted your pastor to visit died last night." I never expected him to go that quickly as he didn't seem that far gone at all when I had visited with him.

You have probably heard that our national government is taking a very scrutinizing look at our prison system and proposing some soon-coming changes. It is an embarrassment, whether they want to state it that way or not, that now with the legalization of some drugs, it is rather ridiculous to have men imprisoned for what is now legal. Just what all the implications of this is going to be, one can only guess, but we will leave all of that in the hands of Him who called us to these men and continue to work while the day is.

Thank you again for your prayers for us.

In His love,

William Cawman

May 2016

ARE YOU STILL praying for our Catholic chaplain? He really appreciates it. He has begun sending men to me that he finds are really in need of help. He told me that he feels more of the Spirit of God in me than he knows he has and so he wants them to get help from me. Then he said very enthusiastically, "I want what you have!" I told him it was certainly not me, but Christ in me and he knew that. I will take every opportunity that I have to continue to invite him into the better way, and I will count on your prayers.

He told me when I had returned from a meeting that a dying man in the hospital really needed me to talk to him. I have known this man for a number of years and watched him as he went pathetically downhill physically. I went over to his cell and entered his room. As soon as he saw me his eyes lit up and then filled with tears, "Oh pastor, did you come to see me? Oh, thank you." He took my hand in his and what a grip he got on it. He was not going to let go. He looked up to the ceiling and started to thank the Lord, "Oh Jesus, thank You for letting the pastor come to see me. Oh Jesus, thank You!"

I asked him if he felt God's presence with him.

"Oh yes, I do," and he held his hand over his heart.

I asked him if he knew that Jesus' Blood had forgiven all of his sins. He shook his head Yes with positive assurance.

I asked him if he had any family members that were contacting him. He shook his head sadly No.

I said, "Well, you have a Christian family who loves you, don't you?" His face brightened up with that. I visited with him a bit and read Scripture to him and had prayer and then told him that I was going to have a service downstairs. "Can I come?" he asked, very eagerly. I said I would ask the officer if he could come downstairs for the service.

I stepped out into the hallway and went to the officer's desk and asked if he could come down. He said as long as the nurse thought he was stable enough to make it. Then I turned around and there stood one of our good sanctified brothers who sits with dying men as hospice help. He said he would make sure he got there. I went on down to the service and the officers announced a church service. Soon a Puerto Rican man came in and I will tell you about him when I finish the story of the first man.

After a bit, here came our good brother, bringing the sick man in a rolling chair. The movement obviously had upset him and the poor fellow was emptying his stomach into a basin on his way down. The brother taking care of him handled him so gently and took care of the basin for him so that he could be in church. We had a precious time together that night, just the four of us and Jesus. I felt so rewarded for being there with them.

The following week I was away again in a revival and when I returned, the volunteer from our church, a man who once was in that prison himself and who had taken the service in my absence, told me that he had also had a precious time. So on Tuesday morning I went directly to the hospital to see the two men.

The man who had been so sick had not been able to come the Sunday that the volunteer was there, and I found him in bed with the blankets wrapped tightly about him, very obviously worse than before. When I approached him his eyes again got wet with tears at my coming, but I could tell he was very sick. I laid my hand on his arm and he said, "Don't move me."

I said, "You're in a lot of pain aren't you?" He shook his head. I said, "Brother, soon God is going to give you a new body and you will have no pain anymore."

"No pain," he said with relish. Then I renewed the question as to his sins being forgiven and he again answered with great assurance.

Just then a female officer walked into the room whom I have known for a number of years. Her husband was also an officer, but due to physical difficulties he has retired. Both of them are very sincere Christians and so she readily joined with us in the rejoicing that his heart was at peace with God. Then a couple of doctors came in and I excused myself. Whether I will ever see him again on earth I would have but little confidence. The presence of Jesus in the room was reassuring that I will see him again someday, but maybe not on this earth.

But now let me tell you about the other man in that Sunday night service. I had not seen him before to remember him, but it didn't take long to begin to recognize a clear ring in his testimony. Part of this he told me that night while we were waiting for the other man to come down and part of it that Tuesday morning as I took time to sit down beside his bed and just listen.

He was born in Puerto Rico, but came to this country at about five years of age. He is now forty-eight. He has often gone back and forth, but has now been in prison for twenty-five years with about five left to go. A while back he just about bottomed out physically from AIDS and kidney failure and other complications. They sent him to Trenton to the hospital and a doctor told him that he was in bad shape and that he would not live much longer unless they did some things for him. He said that he had bleeding on his brain and needed brain surgery. He needed a blood transfusion. He also needed dialysis. The inmate told the doctor he didn't want any of that; he just wanted to die. His mother came in to visit him and begged him to surrender to Jesus and then take the treatments, but he said he had accepted Jesus and just wanted to die.

A couple of days later he was thinking about Jesus hanging on the cross. He thought about the soldiers coming to break the legs of the two with him, but that they did not break His legs because the Scripture had prophesied that not a bone of Him would be broken. Then he thought about the soldier thrusting the spear into His side and suddenly his heart was broken to pieces. He sat there and cried as he realized that Jesus suffered all that for him.

Right there he opened up his heart and surrendered to Jesus, and as he was telling me about it I was left with not a shadow of question but that he was genuinely born again. He said from that time he became so happy and still is. He is happier right there in prison than he has ever been in his life before. He said, "I am locked up on the outside, but I'm not locked up on the inside. I am free!"

He immediately began to make all his past wrongs right as best he could. There were men in prison that he hated and had fought with and had to be kept separate from. When he met one of them he would say, "I need to talk to you." The other man would look at him with doubts as to what was coming next and then he would say, "I'm not the same man you used to know. I have Jesus in my heart and if I have ever done anything to hurt you, I'm sorry. Please forgive me." Immediately they were friends.

Well, a day or two after Jesus came into his heart the doctor came to see him. He said, "I don't know what has happened but the blood in your brain is all dried up. You won't have to have brain surgery!" Then he sat there on the edge of his bed and showed me the port in his chest and said, "I read about the three Hebrew boys who told God that He could save them from the fire but if not, they still would not bow. I have told Jesus that He could heal me if He wanted to and make my kidneys all well again, but if not, I will not go back. This is too good!" About that time the officer came and told him that they were waiting for him in dialysis.

I had a request from another inmate that I have also known for years and have watched him come and go from church and Bible study attendance. I've often wished to see him become more serious about his soul. He came in and sat in front of me and said, "Chaplain, I am just lukewarm and I hate it. I've known something better than this. I know what it is to really have the joy and fire in my soul, but it seems now I'm just powerless to rise above this lukewarm condition."

I told him that I knew that territory to my shame; that I also found myself addicted to lukewarm living and spiritual laziness, but that one day God helped me to set my will and get up out of that lazy state and head for Father's house. I urged him to do the same and I trust he will. Time is running out for the business of spiritual insincerity, isn't it?

Another man has come to my attention after a few times in class. One of the volunteers filling in for me in my absence noticed his distraught condition and urged me to visit with him. His story? He comes from Texas and however it came about, he had a girlfriend of some foreign descent in New Jersey. He had a couple of days off from work and so decided to come see her. He drove up from Texas and went to her house and knocked on the door. There was no response and presently two police officers pulled up and informed him that the girl did not want to see him. They handcuffed him and threw him in the back of the cruiser and began to search his car without any warrant. They found a firearm that was legal in Texas but not in New Jersey. From there they took him into custody under multiple charges: (1) an illegal firearm, (2) stalking, and (3) intended murder. Why? He found out that one of the police officers was now the girl's boyfriend.

I listened to his story and then understood why he was so obviously disturbed. I tried to reason with him that it would do no good to be angry at God or anyone else for that matter, but to begin to seek God's help to find His way through it. He said that at first he tried that, but then it seemed all of the sudden his case turned around for the worse and now he is just battling to have confidence in God. I felt for him, but it seemed that he was so wrought up that I could not get through to him. He just kept going back over the same territory again and again and I could not bring it to a close.

I finally told him that we could talk again sometime but that others had appointments also. He stood to leave but just could not for regurgitating all of his frustration all over again. I tried honestly to do my best to point him to the arms of God, but I fear it was a failure as he could hear nothing but his awful predicament. Someone has said, and perhaps truly, that more people will be in hell over the sin of despair than any other sin. That may not have been the original sin, but Satan is so adept at getting them to see no way out, and finally despair takes completely over the reason, the will power and the desires. God Himself cannot help a person who is so deep in despair that they will not come to Him.

Please keep praying for our Colombian seeker after holiness. He is still after it with all there is of him, but told me that he feels his hang-up is pride. After telling me that we went into the class session and I was trying to explain as simply as I could what it really means to be sanctified wholly; not really specifically for his sake alone. Every little bit I would notice his face break into an extremely understanding smile, and after the class period he came to me and said, "That lesson really helped me a lot!"

This dear brother is not going to settle for an emotional uplift or a quieting of his conscience. He has seen the disease and he must have the cure. Pray that he will very soon enter in. Satan hates this genuine work purchased by the Blood of Jesus and he will spare no means to either obscure its simplicity or to detour a soul around it. Thankfully, the old song says, "But the Spirit led unerring to the land I hold today." There is no question about that side of this covenant relationship. Just pray that he will not miss the way and err on his part.

In case you think our supervisor does nothing but be supervisor, he has been out since February with a surgery to his back. I am absent about half of the time and the Catholic chaplain has done an excellent job of filling in what has to be done, but the recording of attendances at all of the religious programs has stacked up on his desk until the pile was every bit of eight inches high. I had a day or two with some time in them and told him I would try to take that part of the burden from him for which he was most grateful. I spent several hours at two or three times and managed to reduce the stack to about five inches high. That is just one of the many functions that have added to our workload. Please pray for the speedy return of our supervisor. I do not covet his task even in the slightest, but thank God we have him to do it, or I don't know what we would do.

Thank you once again from my heart for your prayers for us,

William Cawman

June 2016

Many of us who went through lengthy and fruitless struggles in seeking the blessing of entire sanctification can now look back and say with such gratitude and love that in spite of all those struggles, "But the Spirit led unerring to the land I hold today!" The songwriter expressed it that way, and perhaps no better way could be found.

Well, I am so happy to tell you that after a season of struggles, our Colombian brother has entered the "Land," and is expressly happy about it. One day a few weeks ago I was dwelling in the class on the subject of what holiness of heart really is and how it sanctifies and yet leaves us still human beings, and every little bit I couldn't help but notice that his intensity of concentration would suddenly give way to a burst of radiance all over his face. I knew that God was endeavoring to show him that the work was done, but it never works for us to get in the way of or take the place of the Holy Spirit. He can do His work so wondrously without our aid.

And so after I had returned from a meeting I sat down with him and he began. "Reverend, I must tell you how it is. About a month or two ago I took the entire day to earnestly pray and seek for the work to be completed in my heart. I did not that day experience any great emotion, but from that day until now I have not had one single struggle with any sin arising from within my heart. I know that the Holy Spirit has complete control of me."

I said, "I would really doubt that it would grieve God for you to put your foot over into the Promised Land and claim it. Do you remember that God said to Joshua, 'Every place that the sole of your foot shall tread upon, that have I given unto you'?" With that his eyes filled with tears, his hands covered his face, and then he began wiping away the tears of joy that were flowing. I wondered if he still thought he had not experienced an emotional blessing!

Thank God for another sanctified witness in the prison. I had to leave the next day for a meeting, but the volunteer from our church who took the Bible studies that night said that he testified clearly to being saved and sanctified, and urged the other men to find it, too. He is the first one for a while in Facility 3, while the other two facilities have more than one. So do you see that your prayers for a revival in this prison are being answered? Let's ask largely, shall we?

For several years I have written different incidents regarding a man who was working hospice in the prison hospital and had seen a number of men go from there to heaven without a doubt. Now he is working in a program on the special needs unit called the "Shadow Program." He is assigned to several needy men and he helps to take care of them and guide them, and this is also a very worthy calling. Now another wonderfully sanctified man has taken his place in the hospice capacity and so the other day I called both of them in together for a visit so that they could talk about it and share ideas. It was a blessed time together with these two brothers, one about as black as they come and the other about as white as they come— blood brothers because of Jesus!

After they had talked a while about the hospice work, they began to testify to their personal victories. The one who has been there the longest— about fifteen years— was telling the other man that when he goes to a service where they are not teaching the Biblical theology that he now knows to be right, he feels the need to be patient towards them in his feelings, because he had a pure heart even before he heard us teaching the way of holiness and freedom from sin. He said when he heard the proper teaching his theology changed but the work in his heart went right on. This man leaves not the thinnest gauze of question over where he is living. He has never taken a backward step in his love for Jesus and his life of personal victory over all sin. Visits like that, I confess, do my heart good!

I wish you could hear a certain man pray. I'm not sure, but he is probably from Haiti as he has a French name. Whenever I call on him to pray he beams with joy and then says over and over in his prayer, "Oh Jesus, thank You, thank You, thank You!" Then he'll say a few words and again, "Jesus, we thank You, oh thank You, thank You, thank You!" It is a prayer no one can argue with, for David said, "Thy praise shall continually be in my mouth." It is refreshing to listen to him pray.

Last month I told you of a man from Puerto Rico who is in the prison hospital and was near death's door, until he gave his heart to Jesus and now is even some better physically. He has been growing in grace and enjoying his walk with the Lord.

Our pastor's son was in the hospital for a Sunday night service and the man was telling him that it is now bothering him to see some of what is on the television. The pastor's son told him that he didn't have one to be bothered by and the man could hardly imagine that. The next week as I was visiting him in his cell he told me about what the pastor's son had told him and I said, "No, I do not have one in my house either."

"Really? That's something!"

I said, "No, I have never had one in my house and I can hardly bear to be around one. My house is very peaceful and I can just talk to Jesus anytime."

Then he began to tell me about his mother. She was a very wicked person, too, until God began to get her attention. Then he said she really gave herself entirely to God. He said she told him, "J———, I'm so glad for what God has done and is doing for you, but you must not stop until you have given Him everything. You see, you might walk into a house and look around and everything looks neat and clean, but then you begin to smell a bad odor. You go searching for it and finally find way down in the basement somewhere something rotten that is giving off that odor. Now J———, you must not stop until there is nothing like that down inside of you or it will give you trouble again. You need to surrender all there is of you to God."

I say, "Good preaching, Mom! Keep it up!" Do pray for him that while his love for Jesus is hot he will go all the way and get rid of that rotten thing way down deep inside.

A man who had been doing so well in Christian Living Class was suddenly sent away to a northern prison. He has been gone now for perhaps over a year, when suddenly he walked back into the Bible Study. My first thought was, "Oh no, I hope he hasn't backed up and done something to be sent back over." It was a couple of weeks before I could get a chance to talk with him. He came in and with a huge smile said, "Whew! Chaplain, am I glad to be back!" Then he went on to tell me that the prison up north was so dark and godless that even though it was easier for his family to visit him up there, he just felt he had to get back here. He requested the move and finally it was granted.

He said, "I didn't know how good it was here until I got up there. The whole atmosphere was dark and oppressive with evil. Chaplain, I'm telling you, you and your church are bringing something into this prison that isn't up there. I thank God for you and for the presence of God that is here in this prison. I guess if the time away did anything for me, it made me really appreciate what we have here, and I'm going to tell others that, too."

And here's another update: do you remember some time back the story about the big Italian man who said that the Lord sanctified him in shower stall number five at 10:35 in the morning, if I remember the time correctly? Well, he had been released finally to the assessment center for shipment out to a halfway house when they discovered a lump on his lung. They sent him back and after many tests he has been undergoing chemo and has one more treatment left. The lump is very small now, and if any of it is left after the final treatment, they plan to use radiation on it.

He formerly had a huge bushy beard and very black hair, but now he is totally bald and clean shaven and has put on about twenty pounds. For several months he has been so sick that he was hardly ever attending any services or classes, but he is beginning to feel better now and came to see me.

"Chaplain, I have the victory! Through all of this, God has kept me strong in Him and even when I was sick I had victory in my heart. I've had to keep calling and cheering my family up and tell them whatever happened it didn't matter; it was all in God's hands and I belong to Him." Then he told me that through it all his mother (the whole family was strong Roman Catholic) broke down and got saved. "And she really got it!" he said.

The same day I was visiting again with the man who I've told you was so brutally hard in his sinful life but is now as sweet as Canaan honey. He was telling me that God has been really working on his approach to other men. All of his life he has used his large-bodied frame to throw his weight around and command respect with it, but God is mellowing him and making a gentleman out of him. It would be difficult for most of us to imagine what a change must be effected in a man past mid-life, who has lived in violence and fearlessness and aggressive behavior, to bring him back into the image of Christ. But thank God for the Blood, and thank God for the teachableness of a sanctified heart.

After telling me about that, his face suddenly lighted up and he said, "But I have victory, too. Listen to this: I went through the line to get my food tray and the day before I had given my chicken to someone who didn't get any. When I got up to the window they said the chicken was all gone. Chaplain, I really wanted some chicken, but you know what? Nothing evil or ugly came up inside of me! It made my heart rejoice, because I know what used to be there."

In case you think that is not such a significant victory since it was simply over a piece of chicken, little do those of us who get all the chicken we want know how much the food means to men in prison. For this very reason, several years ago now, New Jersey quit serving meals in the mess halls because so many riots broke out over the only bright spot they had— their dinner. Now they just haul in containers of food onto the tiers and the men eat either in their rooms or a few at a time in the dayrooms.

I will share a bit of humor over this food situation with you. Some time ago, out in the minimum unit, there was a man who obviously enjoyed his food. He was round everywhere— literally everywhere! One day I ventured to call on him to pray before the class. "Dear Lord, thank You for all the food we've had to eat!" I can't remember what followed, for I was too occupied assimilating his introductory gratitude and the obvious basis thereof.

Eternity alone will have the accurate record of how many souls from this prison have truly found and kept the "Pearl of

Great Price" in their hearts. One inmate came into the prison but a few months ago, attended a few classes and I had two visits with him. He freely admitted that his life was a hollow wreck without God. I urged him to really seek after God and expect to find Him. He asked how he would know when He found Him and I assured him that he would know. A short while afterward I had but a brief moment to ask him after a service how it was going, and with a very genuine smile he said, "I know I have found Him. It worked!" I never got to see him again and he was released. I hope to meet him in heaven.

In class one morning something was said right at the beginning that caused me to begin speaking to the men along the line of being effective in their private devotions. I told them that prayer was spiritual warfare and that the devil would do all he could to keep them from spending time and really praying into God's presence. I spoke of the time that Daniel prayed and fasted for twenty-one days without any breakthrough, but then when the Angel Gabriel touched him he said, "Fear not, Daniel: for from the first day that thou didst set thine heart to understand, and to chasten thyself before thy God, thy words were heard, and I am come for thy words."

I spoke then of Job and how he could not sense God, and all the while God was watching on. Then a very good praying brother put up his hand and shook his head. "Chaplain, I was just yesterday praying up against a brick wall until finally God broke in. I was going to ask you today why that was and here you already answered it."

Thank God for praying men! Thank you for praying, too!

W Cawman

15
EVEN THESE HE DIED FOR

July 2016

Another month has slipped by so rapidly and the first half of it I spent with Debbie in Malawi, Africa. To be very candid, I really would love to have just stayed there, but the Scripture says that "the spirits of the prophets are subject to the prophets," and so I returned and went back to prison. The fifteen pastors that we ministered to in Malawi sent enthusiastic greetings to their brothers in prison, and the brothers in prison received it with just the same. I will be passing out a sheet with all the pastors' pictures and names on it so that the men in prison can pray for them. Isn't God's family wonderful? And it's all because of Jesus and His selfless love.

Every Sunday night at 5:30 one of us tries to go to the prison hospital for a service, but if only one or two come, sometimes we just visit and pray with them. I have told you about the Puerto Rican man who, after twenty-five years in prison, and so physically wrecked that he was about to die, gave his heart to Jesus and has been so changed. The past Sunday night I went in and he was the only one that came and he had so much on his heart that he wanted to tell me.

First of all he said that he didn't start in this way to stop or back up, but that he settled it to go all the way with God. Then he told me that he had a confession to make to me and hoped I would not get angry at him. I assured him that I would not and then he really opened his heart.

He had been doing so well in loving and obeying the Lord, but two Muslim men that receive dialysis with him began to accost him rudely and roughly as they were getting their treatments. Finally one of them brought up a false accusation against him to one of the sergeants. He felt anger arise in his heart and actually got up with his tubes still attached and started for the man. The nurses immediately called a code and brought in officers to calm him down, and with that he realized what he had done. He felt terrible. He asked all that were there to forgive him, but went back to his cell to suffer intensely. He was so grieved that his testimony of Christianity was so marred and that he had given place to his old temper again. He said he had been asking God to forgive him, but he still felt so terrible about it.

I listened to his honest confession and then I told him that I wanted to talk to him about what was really going on. I explained to him that when Jesus comes into our heart, there are still dark roots of sin that need to be cleansed out and that God was allowing him to see what was in him that he might ask God to remove it. He understood perfectly what I was telling him and said he knew that the root needed to come out. I urged him to earnestly seek and ask and expect God to cleanse him from all sin by filling his heart with the Holy Spirit.

He then wanted to pray and also told me that the time had come and he had to get the television out of his room. I am expecting another victory for the precious Blood of Jesus very soon.

Now let me take you into office 1048 in Facility 2 while you listen to the life story of a barely twenty-five-year-old from Dominican Republic. For the first six years of his life, he tells us, he had food to eat and clothes to wear, but hardly any contact with his parents except for holidays. Then at the age of six his parents divorced and his mother came to the USA and married another man. He stayed for a time yet in Dominican, but his father paid no attention to him and his older sister raised him.

When he finally came to the USA he found his stepfather a bit more comfortable to live with, but by the age of twelve he was taking drugs and going downhill rapidly. At seventeen his parents finally caught on to what he was doing and more or less just wrote him off. From that age until August 12, 2014, he tried six times to commit suicide, for his life was so unbearable he didn't want to live.

In 2011 he overdosed and went into a coma for a number of hours, but God spared his life. He once cut his throat and another time slit his wrist. Twice he tried to hang himself, the second time just before August 12, 2014. His brother found him and took a machete and cut the rope, but had to take him to the hospital.

On the date mentioned above, he was lying in the hospital when someone handed him a Spanish Bible. In desperation he opened it up and his eyes fell on Jeremiah 52, verse six. His attention was immediately arrested, for this is what he read: "And in the fourth month, in the ninth day of the month, the famine was sore in the city, so that there was no bread for the people of the land." One might wonder why that verse, but God knows His business better than we can comprehend. He instantly saw his birth date: April 9. And God spoke to him that it was not His will for him to live in a famine. He began to seek the Lord and to this hour cannot read that verse without goose bumps popping up all over his arms.

Within the next six months he forsook all the drugs and alcohol. He had been having relationships with three girls all at the same time. He went to each of them and told them he was finished. He was not going to sin with them anymore. He went and had his satanic tattoos covered over with solid blue to hide them. He started reading his Bible and going to church.

Then his court date came up and he was sent to prison on multiple charges of illegal arms and drug possession.

After coming to prison and just the weekend before he was telling me all of this, his birth father was planning to come see him, but then at the last moment he told his sister that he wanted to go fishing instead. It was just about a finish blow of rejection to an already fragile relationship. Now the precious young man who has been through all of this in just one-quarter of a century is struggling to really know God and forgive others. Please pray for him. Little do we know how some others live and what a raw existence really comes out of the devil's warehouse.

Now I am going to share some very open honest feelings with you. As I stood for hours before a group of fifteen pastors in Malawi and taught them with a strong emphasis on the necessity and privilege of a holy heart, I did not once sense a single one of them pushing anything taught to the side of his plate. What a blessing! I can't say that I have always sensed that in our own land. Many times one would feel that the fork is being used more often to push things aside than to put them in the mouth. And so, after three days of intense teaching with these men, I will honestly confess that I really, really wanted to stay in Africa. But I came home.

And then I went into the prison. Class time started as usual with prayer. Then no sooner was the "amen" offered than another broke out in prayer. It certainly seemed genuine. Then a dear Haitian brother who has been conspicuously growing in the Lord asked a personal question regarding living victoriously in the Christian life. One after another of the men began to quote Scriptures, all of them positively declaring victory over sin.

The atmosphere grew more and more excited as again we went to prayer. God was being honored, exalted! More promises were quoted, and I felt reluctant to interfere even in the least with God's obvious troubling of the waters. All of the sudden I felt my heart welling up and saying to me, "I really love these men!" And so, whether in Africa or New Jersey State Prison, I am pledged anew to be His, body, soul, spirit, affections, obedience, and if I have anything else— that, too!

Our dear brother from Colombia is exploring the land beyond Jordan, but has met a few giants also. I love to watch a soul walk in the light and find what a positively magnificent teacher Jesus gave to us in His indwelling Spirit. It is so refreshing to behold the work that He does without any previous head knowledge of His marvelous ways. Nothing is more spiritually crippling than to know all about Him but not *know* Him. Jesus said that to know Him is life eternal!

And then some of you will remember the Italian man who said he got sanctified in shower stall number five at 10:35 in the morning on August 13, 2013. I have mentioned since that he was diagnosed with cancer in his lungs in the form of a tumor. They have done extensive chemotherapy on him and the doctors now say that they cannot find any of the tumor remaining and that his blood work is back to normal. But today he told me that the doctor said just in case there is one little cell of cancer left somewhere they want to do five weeks of radiation.

I said to him, "What an example! You see that doctor cares about you. So does God, and that's why He doesn't want one little cell of the old carnal nature left anywhere in us. And thank God the Blood of Jesus is a sure cure even if chemo and radiation are not!" He beamed with understanding and then went on to tell me how through all of this his heart has just grown stronger in trusting the Lord and loving Him. He will now have to go to Trenton and be housed in the infirmary there until the radiation is finished.

And then another man came in for a visit who has not been here long, but just wanted to thank me for getting him into the classes and for what he was getting out of them. He was all marked up with tattoos and said he had led a very rocky life even though he is not very old, but that in coming to the classes and church he is a totally new man. I asked if he had consciously repented and been forgiven of his sins and he said, "Oh yes, and I know that Jesus is living in my heart!" Testimonies like that just bring such a reward for the hours spent in laboring among them.

But now, thank God for Christian homes! Thank God for young lives who are spared all the scars and tattoos and haunting memories in the night, and regrets and habits and all of the other elements of Satan's dominion. There is forgiveness with our God, thank Him for it; but no one needs all the wreckage and baggage that a term in Satan's bondage gives. Nothing is more beautiful than a life surrendered early.

One time after I had taken a few young people in and asked them to give their testimonies, I then said to the men, "Now you have heard the way it should be, but don't despair. Turn your life over completely to God and pass that on to the next generation."

In Him,

William Cawman

August 2016

Please excuse these letters from being a bit late this month as I was in Haiti in two camp meetings and did not get back home until the second of August.

During the second week of July I had the privilege of having a staff member from the Fort Myers Rescue Mission with me in the prison. It was a mutual blessing, both to the men and to him. It is rewarding to watch the men respond to a new voice preaching to them the same message of full salvation, and it is a blessing to watch that new voice relate to and fall in love with men in prison who have found what is being preached.

That does not mean at all that every man who attends the classes and Bible studies is as yet fully embracing the truth. Some go back to the tiers to criticize and disagree with the

truths taught, and that is undoubtedly not a whole lot different from anywhere the genuine gospel is preached. But it is
unmistakably a great value to hearts that really belong to the
Lord to hear another trumpet sounding the same note.

One special feature of this was that the man I took in is a
black man. When I first began preaching the message of holiness in the prison, it was tittered throughout that it was just
Chaplain Cawman's theology. Over the years as many others
have preached in harmony, that has pretty well died down,
but there has remained some degree of feeling among many
that such is a white man's religion. My heart rejoiced as I listened to that barrier being broken by one of their own race
preaching full deliverance from sin.

One man in particular really pulled on our hearts during
this week of visits and studies. A few weeks before he had
expressed to me his disappointment in his own relationship to the Lord. He had known early on in his life what it
was to be truly forgiven and born again, and now for years
he has not had that same satisfaction. He has drifted in and
out of the classes and lived in a spiritual wilderness of varying states of stagnation.

My heart really goes out to his cry for help, for I remember
when I too was bogged down in that addictive state of sad
spiritual anemia. I told him that I understood his feelings, for
I had been there. I told him of the day when God in His faithfulness dropped a life-size picture of my shabby state down
before me and how it alarmed me and caused me to look up
from my well-worn rut and cry to God that I had to be different. I told him that he would have to take hold of his will and
override his emotions of fear and failure and begin to deliberately walk out into God's deliverance.

He declared that it was exactly what he wanted to do, and I
trust he will. He has had long enough to prove that his own
way isn't getting him there. He has been locked up for twenty-
eight years, ever since he was eighteen years of age. He ac-
knowledged that he had been unwilling to give up all, that he

was just holding onto that ten percent. The visitor from Ft. Myers asked him what holding onto that ten percent had done for him. He said it had given him misery and disappointment. Oh, that hearts— and there are many of them inside and outside of prison walls— would just listen to the ever-pleading Voice, "Oh, why will ye die?"

Our dear brother who is allowing God to take complete control of his life came bouncing in with joy and excitement.

"How are you getting along, Brother?"

"Fantastic! God is just so good to me. I cannot understand why He would love me so much."

"How are your family relationships coming along?"

"Oh! My wife and children are closer to me than ever and it is growing stronger all the time!" This is the man who walked in the Light and divorced his second unlawful wife and is now being reunited to his first wife and their ten children.

Requests to be seen by the chaplain can certainly bring forth a variety of human and spiritual needs. Recently a man who is new to this prison came walking into the office where I was seated and I immediately thought, "What do we have here?" He would have been a very handsome young man and still is, except that as a tattoo artist he has indelibly ruined his looks.

On his right temple was tattooed a vivid lightning strike; on his left temple an assault rifle; words that I did not want to stare enough to read across his throat; intense pictures all the way up his arms; and who knows what else beneath the prison garb. On his face sheet there are listed fourteen separate tattoos.

He began his painful story. He was raised in a home from which his father departed when he was but an infant. His mother in trying to protect him and his sisters from the filth of the world about them, greatly restricted their television viewing and their social circles. At an early age he began to revolt against these restrictions and soon was taken up by the street life and all that it held.

Disappointed with life as he was experiencing it, he found his way to Ft. Myers, Florida, and began to hang out on the beach near there. He there met some Rastafarians who adopted him into their way of life and philosophies. He seemed for a time to find comfort and peace living in their society, but as is often the case, their radical viewpoints led them into conflict with society and the law, and he wound up being arrested for weapons and robbery.

The Brother from Ft. Myers Rescue Mission was with me as we listened to his painful history. We both heard at once that he was telling us two things. First, he had hoped that the group he was with would have provided the answer to life he had been looking for. There was nostalgia in his words and looks that told us he would like to return to the measure of peace he had found there. But secondly, he was saying very loudly— almost screaming, though he was unable to interpret his own heart— that he was still empty on the inside. He could not hide it. He was lonely on the inside of the door, Jesus was lonely on the outside of his door.

When he finished telling us this brief history, I asked him this question: "If you would be honest with me, in spite of the measure of peace you seemed to have for a time in your life, is there still a void inside of you that is not satisfied?"

"Yes, there definitely is." Tears began to form in his eyes. I went on to tell him that first he needed to thank God that there was still an empty hole inside of him. I told him about Nicodemus and Paul and the Rich Young Ruler, who though they tried to walk a perfect and orthodox walk, yet they were conscious of something missing down deep within. I asked him if he believed that there is a God who created him. He did; in fact, he said he is reading his Bible and trying to find help. I told him that Jesus was knocking at his heart's door wanting for him to let Him inside of that empty hole within him. He said, "I want that, I really do."

We prayed with him and talked some more and it felt like the loving arms of Jesus were just wrapping him up in love.

By now he was crying and then he said, "I already feel so much better, I hope I don't look like I've been on drugs." We assured him that if he would just continue to walk in and toward that Light, he would soon be so happy where he had been so distressed. I said to him, "Jesus will not leave you and we will not leave you either. You just keep praying and walking in the Light and I'll soon visit with you again. I won't leave you here." He left with a whole new countenance than he had when he came in.

Cases like this remind us over and over that those faces and bodies we meet out on the streets that would appear the farthest from any part or thought of God, may just be telling us— screaming at us— "I need help! Please help me!" Please help this dear man by your prayers; please do. I told the Brother with me, "It is men like this that often make me feel I just want to move into their cell with them and help them, and then I have to remember that only Jesus can save them, and He can move into their cell with them!"

The next day we were again holding interviews one on one with the men, and a very young looking man from either Peru or Ecuador came to visit. I have been watching this man for some time as he has grown brighter and brighter with the work of God going on within him. He has such a young-looking face that it is hard to imagine but that he would be hardly out of his teens. He has a little over two years yet on his sentence and his father lives way out in California.

His father has been very pleased with how his son is changing and he told him that he is going to quit his job and move back east to be with him while he finishes his five years of parole, during which he cannot leave this state. He told us that he told his father not to do that, that he would be all right and he did not want his father to sacrifice for him. I said to him, "Please listen to me. Don't tell your father not to come live with you. You mean more to him than his job. Let it be that way. You have a treasure that many, many don't have. You have a loving father. He cares about you and he wants to be with you. Don't ever deny him that privilege."

His face lit up as though a burden had just rolled off of him. "I will tell him that," he said.

This young man has been growing in spiritual grace and knowledge so wonderfully that I then asked him about enrolling in the Bible College classes that are offered. He readily jumped at the chance, and I believe he will do very well at it, too.

The man who followed him for a visit was the precious one we have written about numbers of times who is as opposite as night and day to what he used to be. He enjoyed the visit so much with the Brother from Fort Myers and then told us that since this Brother is black and came in preaching holiness to them, it absolutely changed the attitude of some of the other men who had been holding out that this holiness message was more or less a white man's religion. I was nearly shouting on the inside, for that is exactly what I had been praying for.

Oh, the wonderful grace of Jesus that makes us one in Him, no matter our background, our color, our track record, our IQ or lack thereof, or anything else. Jesus loves every soul that He has ever given to live upon earth, and once He dwells within us, we love them all, too!

God surely anointed this Brother and while he felt the reward was all his, I happen to know that God used him mightily in speaking to the men and they loved it. I am very sure it will not be the last time he visits us here in this corner of God's great harvest field.

The events of this letter are all from the first two weeks of July, as the last part I spent in Haiti. The people of Haiti enthusiastically sent their love and promise of prayers to the men in prison, especially the Haitian prisoners, and I know that when I show the men in prison the picture I took of over five hundred Haitians with their hands in the air for them it will melt their hearts.

Thank you to each of you again who are praying for us. God is answering prayer without a doubt, and yet we are hungry to see more of His power manifested and more hearts respond to it. It continues to be nothing short of a miracle and an answer to your prayers that God is keeping the door open here in this prison to preach and teach, without a single hindrance, the message of full salvation. Never once has there been a repercussion that went anywhere, except for a few disgruntled listeners now and then, that has hindered or put a squelch on preaching the whole truth without a bit of political correctness— which, by the way, could not possibly be more incorrect. We certainly will not take this liberty for granted, however, so please help us pray that the door will remain open as long as there are souls there that want God. And there are! Some dear souls here in prison want God more than they want anything else, including their liberty from prison.

Yours once again with gratitude and love,

William Cawman

September 2016

I WANT TO REPORT TO YOU that the Holy Spirit is still preparing a Bride for our soon-coming Christ, and He is not bypassing any candidate here in this prison. It is so precious to see men growing in their walk with God and learning to keep the fire burning in their hearts. I have told the men that it would never be expected of me as a state employee to interfere with the count, but that one glad morning I want to see the count messed up just as dramatically as can be, as numbers rise to meet the Lord in the air. I won't need to be concerned about the repercussions or the consternation or my chance of further employment, for I will gladly go up with them.

I told you in a previous letter about the man who came here from Texas to see what he believed to be his girlfriend and when he knocked at her door he was arrested by two cops who then searched his car and found a handgun which was legal in Texas but not here. He is in prison under charges of stalking, attempted murder, and unlawful possession of a weapon. He found out subsequently that one of the officers who arrested him is now the girl's boyfriend. I have tried several times to help this man, but he is so absolutely distraught by the injustice of it all that he has no open channels through which I can enter.

A week or so ago I noticed that he is showing his despair worse and worse. He looks just like a raw nerve ready to snap. I stopped him on the way out of Bible study and told him I would put him on the appointment for a visit. He dejectedly but emphatically said, "It's no use. I'm hopeless. I'm just going to hell!"

I put him on the appointment sheet and he came, but was determined that he had passed up every chance to ever get right again. I began to reason with him that nowhere in the Word of God is such hopelessness coming from God. In order for me to say anything to him I had to just keep rudely interrupting his endless talk of doom and despair. A couple of times I actually had to raise my voice above his and tell him to stop and listen to me. I hope something registers with him, but I don't know. He spends sleepless nights and frazzled days regretting and fretting, and I don't know how much longer he can go on like this and keep any trace of sanity. Satan is cruel beyond description!

I also mentioned a bit to you about a man in the prison hospital who was brought to death's door and then opened his heart to the Lord and let Him come in. The other day I sat down with him and he filled in some gaps in his story until I pretty well got the picture of his life, although he said there are many things he still didn't tell. Would you let me relate his story so that you might see once again the truth of the words, "Hallelujah! What a Savior!"

When just a small boy, his mother, even though she provided food and lodging, was heavily addicted to drugs and drinking and men. He slept on the couch in the living room but spent many sleepless nights with a knife under his pillow for fear of the men she brought in and how they continually beat her up. Then when he went to school he would just fall asleep at his desk and so he never learned to write well. Just coming into his teens his father was taking him somewhere in the car and stopped and took out a bag of heroin. After he sniffed a bit he handed the bag to his son and told him to sniff it. He said he didn't want to, and his father said, "Ah, come on. Don't be a punk!" So he sniffed the heroin and nearly passed out.

At the age of sixteen a man kept coming around for his mother and treated her so mean that he began to hate him with a passion. One day when he was beating up on his mother he found an axe and clobbered the man so completely that he thought he had killed him. Then he ran away to his grandfather and told him he would never go back home. His grandfather called his mother to come and they tried to get him to go home with her again but he refused. They asked him what he was going to do and he said he would take to the street, that he knew how to handle himself.

While running the streets and sleeping wherever, he became a hit man and stabbed and shot many people and became so enraged with hate toward everyone that he turned into a literal animal. For one of these episodes he was arrested in Pennsylvania and sentenced to eight and one-half years in prison. In prison he was no better for he was by now completely overtaken with rage. It didn't bother him at all to kill and hurt. As he was about to finish this term a chaplain tried to reason with him and get him to seek the Lord. He told him he didn't have any time for Jesus stuff and that when he got out he would again just act like a wild animal.

Upon his release he went to Chicago and in his own words "did a lot of trash there." Then he went to Florida and repeated it all over. He was arrested and handcuffed and sent back to New Jersey. Somehow he got off without going to prison and just continued spiraling out of control.

One night he was driving a car with another man with him and drugs in the car and in themselves. He told the other man he could not drive any longer and the other man said he couldn't drive either, so he set the cruise control on ninety miles per hour and let it go. It crashed through a couple of fences and then smashed into a block wall. He noticed the police behind him, so he jumped out with the drugs and ran for cover. He found a shed and deposited the drugs in there and then started from house to house with his collar bone broken and his arm bone sticking up out of his arm. The other man was pinned by the transmission which had come through the firewall and broken his back. Somehow he was taken to the hospital and put back together.

A while later he was driving again at night, and was going past the shed where he had hid the drugs. He said to the person in the car with him, "I want to stop here and see if those drugs are still in that shed." They weren't, but when he got back to the car a man was standing over it with a gun in his hand. The man said, "I know who you are."

"How do you know me?"

"I'm the policeman that followed you down the road that night when you were swerving all over the place. I thought surely you'd hit a tree, but you plowed into that block wall instead." With that he stomped on the gas pedal and tore out of there. Here he had hid the drugs in a shed that belonged to the police that was following him.

A while later he was in Atlantic City, New Jersey and was messing around with a girl in an apartment building. She left to get something and he stayed there and when she came back she started yelling at him to leave and so he took a knife and stabbed her. He thought he had put the knife through her heart and then wondered how to cover his tracks, so he set the building on fire and left.

This time it caught up with him and he went before the law and ended up in this prison sentence that has now lasted twenty-five years. He is now forty-eight years old, body torn to shreds nearly, with scars all over him and AIDS and kidney failure and bleeding on the brain and who knows what else. While in another prison before coming here he met a paramedic in another cell. He asked him, "What is the worst thing you ever saw as a paramedic?" The man said that the worst thing he had ever witnessed was when someone stabbed a girl in Atlantic City and then set the building on fire. He said that the man thought he had stabbed her in the heart, but he got her lung and so she burned to death while still alive.

During these twenty-five years in prison, not to count the eight and one-half years in PA prison, he continued almost to the present with his hatred and violent behavior. He just simply hated everyone and everything. Finally, broken in body almost to the point of death and needing several surgeries which he refused to have, he heard the gentle voice of Jesus calling to him. He opened his heart and was instantly changed into a new creature with not one drop of hatred remaining in him. He has asked all he can to forgive him and he is now so gentle and loving and loves for our church people to come and see him.

Sometime before all this someone told him that he would not know his mother; that she had become a Christian and had stopped wearing pants and was wearing a dress and letting her hair grow and was completely delivered from drugs and drink. He couldn't believe it but said he really didn't want to, either, as he had no use for that Christian stuff. All that changed in a moment when Jesus came into his heart. Oh, how the grace of God can change the leper's spots! All glory to the power in the Blood!

The administrative department up in Trenton decided that it was no longer politically appropriate to label the eighty-bed facility over in one corner of the prison "The Detention Center," so now we must all try to remember that it is "The Restricted Housing Unit." Nothing else changed, only the politics.

Along with that the same intelligencers decided that we

must have two mandatory interfaith services for anyone in this unit who would desire to come. They even drew up a booklet of subjects that we are to speak on. I looked them over and to my surprise there was not one of them that I could not speak on with profit; however, perhaps not the way they would do it! This was quite surprising knowing the three who drew it up. One of them is a Muslim, one a high-ranking Mason, and I don't remember what the earmarks of the third one are.

At any rate, the first time I went over to hold the service no one was interested. The second time four men showed up and I was there with the Muslim chaplain. All the while I was thinking to myself, "What if I were on the other side of these bars? If I were a Christian would I be comfortable with a Muslim along with a Christian? If I were a Muslim would I want a Christian there?" I shared these thoughts with our Catholic chaplain and he fully agreed, but do it we must. I have no problem at all when it is the Catholic chaplain and myself. He gives them some very good points and then says, "Now Chaplain Cawman will talk to you. You listen to him!" When it is the Muslim chaplain and I— well!

Three of the men seemed to appreciate and profit from it. The fourth one just shook his head and said it didn't help him at all and nothing or nobody could help him. I responded that it was because he had his door completely closed to help. I told him many men in the prison were finding help and were actually glad that God had allowed them to be here. But a closed door he wanted to have and so we had to leave it. Oh, eternity! Oh, worm that will never die! "When the living stream is so near by; why, oh why will ye die?"

With love and appreciation,

William Cawman

16
AND GOD'S WORK WILL GO ON

October 2016

"Surely the wrath of man shall praise thee: the remainder of wrath shalt thou restrain." (Psalm 76:10)

WHATEVER THAT PROMISE MAY refer to in its entirety, I would like to at least give you an example of how truly God means what He says. And thank God that he does! The editorial staff of the TNIV "bible" gives this alleged purpose for its existence: They proclaim it to be the best Bible yet because it gives us what God meant, not what He said. What a shame that "god" (the reason for the un-capitalized words I have just used is that neither is the "god" they are speaking of the true One, nor is the adulterated and manipulated publication any longer God's Word) was apparently so linguistically inept and so unable to express himself that it took a publishing company to interpret Him! And so, here is in all truth what God meant— He meant what He said! So there!

Now to get back to my story. In one corner of our prison there is a separate building with about eighty beds in it,

which has been called, until recently, the "Detention Unit."
Such is commonly referred to in prison language as "the
hole." Now as you are aware, we have reached such a glorious state of civilization in our generation that we must refer to everything and everyone in "politically correct" terminology. And so several months back we all received notice that the unit referred to would no longer be allowed to
be called by its former name, "Detention," but must now
be called the "Restrictive Housing Unit." RHU now it is.
Along with that stroke of brilliant reincarnation it was decided by the powers that be in our state capital that the
chaplains in each prison would be required to hold "interfaith services" in this newly renamed facility. Furthermore
these powers formulated the sermon subjects and material
that we were to preach.

Now let me back up to tell you the previous endeavors in
that same unit. A number of times I visited the unit but
usually only at the request of an inmate housed there. Not
always was a man put over there because of his own wrongdoing, but many times an inmate could be "set up" if another inmate or an officer who did not like him chose to get
him off of one of the other units. Sometimes even, a man
might be sent there until investigation was made if some
contraband was found in his cell and it was not known
whether it was his or his cellmate's.

Usually when I received a request, especially from a man
who had been in one of my classes or Bible studies, I would
first of all open the state computer and read what the tour
report had to say about him from the officers' standpoint. Then
I would go and listen to his story and try to put it all together
to properly help him.

Nearly always as I would walk around and past the cells in
this unit I would be bombarded by voices coming from them:
"Chaplain, can I talk to you?" I would go over to that cell.
"Chaplain, can you do something for me? I didn't do anything to be in here. I haven't had a bath for a week. Can you

talk to somebody?" "Over here, Chaplain. Can you give me something to read?" "Hey, Chaplain, over here! I shouldn't even be here. My celley had some weed in his locker and we both got busted over it. Can you talk to them for me?" And so you can see why after a while I only went upon request or unless it was a man that had been in my classes and I had reason to believe was not guilty.

Another reason I had decided a number of years ago to go over only when called for is that the inmates if sent there were only there for fourteen days, after which they were either turned back to their unit or sent away to a solitary confinement prison. Let me give you another example of how fruitless it seemed, just to lay a background for what I am getting ready to tell you.

Several years ago we had a rabbi as an inmate. The officers made it tough for him as they were not a little disenchanted with a high religious figure having committed a crime. Somehow he was set up over a bottle of prescription medication that he claimed was actually his from the medical department, but which was declared contraband. He was sent to the (at that time) Detention Unit on a Friday morning. I met my supervisor in passing and he told me about it and said that probably one of us would need to come in on Saturday and get his *tephillin* and take it over to him so that he could say his prayers.

I said, "Why don't we just leave him without it and maybe he will discover something better." "Good idea, Chap. Let's do that." Within an hour a call came to the prison administration from the state commissioner, who at the time was on a golf course in Texas, that we were to take the *tephillin* over to him. Accordingly I went all the way in to the prison on Saturday for the express purpose of taking the rabbi his *tephillin* so he could pray.

Now this entailed driving sixteen miles one way, going through entrance security procedures, walking all the way back into one of the facilities to the chapel area, unlocking the cabinet where they were stored and then going back out of that facility over to the Detention Unit! I went to his cell door and tried to hand them to him through the food port. He almost ignored them as he began to vent his frustration over being there. "Chaplain, you've got to do something. I'm going to die in here! I didn't do anything to deserve this. I was set up. They found a pill bottle in my locker and it was mine by prescription but they said it was illegal."

I said, "Here is your *tephillin* so that you can say your prayers." He took it and continued with his complaint. I reminded him that I was there so that he could say his prayers. He reluctantly took the phylacteries out of the case and began to wrap them around his arm and forehead, all the while continuing his gripe. Finally he was quiet for but a few minutes as he went back and forth with them on and then resumed his protestations as he removed them again. From there I had to go all the way back into the remote corner of the facility where I got them and return them to the locked cabinet again— for what?

Now I have belabored the history of the Detention Unit in order to show you that God full well keeps the promise stated at the head of this letter. So here goes:

A few months ago a panel of three within the august halls of our state government came up with the implicit instructions that we no longer have (although nothing physical has changed) a "Detention Unit," and therefore we dare not call it that. We now have a "Restricted Housing Unit." Within a month or so came this firm order from the same department that we as chaplains were to hold "interfaith services" every week therein. Now the three men who came up with this and developed the syllabus might interest you. One is a Muslim, one is a high degree Mason and the other one I do not remember. The one who is a high up Mason was sent to our prison for several months and the longer I was around him the more evil I felt coming from him. Now watch how God makes even the wrath of man to praise Him.

Here is a partial list of the subjects we are to preach in the RHU:

1 The Power of God's Love;
2 Learning How to Forgive;
3 Don't Lose Your Joy;
4 Bad Habits Can Be Broken;
5 Where Is Your Obedience;
6 Faith Is;
7 A Commitment To Change;
8 Patience Is A Virtue;
9 Living A Healthy Life;
#10 Kindness Can Go A Long Ways;
#11 I Am An Overcomer;
#12 Awareness of God's Presence;
#13 Just Let It Go;
#14 Accept What God Allows;
#15 An Excellent Spirit;
#16 Why Are You Angry?;
#17 How To Handle Our Haters;
#18 Don't Count Me Out;
#19 Getting Rid of Your Guilt;
#20 Letting Go of Hatred;
#21 Jealousy Is a Sin;
#22 How to Deal with the Setbacks of Life;
#23 Confidence In God;
#24 It Doesn't Hurt to Say I'm Sorry;
#25 I am A Survivor;
#26 How to Deal With An Inner Conflict.

Now can you see a single one of these that a holiness preacher cannot use to good profit, even if many of the titles smack of New Age mindsets? I was actually very pleasantly surprised when I first read them over, knowing that it was a requirement that we use them and knowing the men who compounded them. But thank God, He is still keeping His promise: "Surely the wrath of man shall praise thee: the remainder of wrath shalt thou restrain."

And so we began, but not without misgivings as to another aspect of it— that of the "interfaith." Let's view this from the Muslim point of view. Is there any tenet of the Quran that encourages fellowship with another "faith?" Absolutely not! If Mohammed's instructions are literally followed out the only obedient thing to do upon a meeting of a Muslim and a Christian would be an unsheathing of the sword.

The first time I was there it was with the Imam. He didn't say much. He mostly left it to me. I went back into the main part of the prison and the Catholic chaplain and I were discussing it. I said, "Chaplain, if you were a Christian inmate sitting in that cell, would you be comfortable for a Muslim to accompany the pastor of your belief?"

"No, absolutely not!"

"And supposing you were a Muslim inmate, would you want a Christian minister to come along with your Imam?"

"No, of course not!" And he just shook his head at the very idea.

Could I tell you something? I have been in several sessions now, sometimes with the Catholic chaplain and sometimes with the Muslim, and I would have to say that God has used it! When the Catholic chaplain is with me he will give some good advice and then tell them, "Now Chaplain Cawman will talk to you. He knows how to help you better than I do." This is always typical of his humility. He then listens and loves to hear what I tell them. I think a lot of this man and sometimes wonder just what and how far his relationship with God has gone.

The Muslim? Well, he realizes the parameters we are working under and complies very well outwardly. Just what he really is feeling inside regarding it all I wouldn't venture to guess. If it is what you might expect, then let's go to the second half of the promise we are writing about: "the remainder of wrath shalt thou restrain."

And so you might wonder how the inmates respond to this?

Well, that is about as different as people are different. Here's from one: "Yeah, I'm workin' on it. I'm doin' better than I used to. I decided that gettin' mad an' bein' angry at everybody wasn't doin' any good anyway."

My response: "Sir, you will never be successful at changing yourself. You need God to come into your heart and really change you into a new man."

"Yeah, I been readin' my Bible." About then I realize just how helpless one man is to help another without the conviction of the Holy Spirit, and yet this is just about universally what is going on in the name of Christianity today. They call it "New Age." it is not new at all; it is exactly without any alteration what caused Lucifer to become Satan: "I can change myself. I don't need God." It is what induced Cain to think he could just offer a sacrifice of his own invention. It is what motivated the building of the Tower of Babel. It is, in short, the very core of the sin problem. "I will be God!"

But here is another response. This man has said nothing; there has been no change of expression on his face. He has just shifted his position every few minutes necessitated by the steel bench he is sitting on. And so as not to neglect any avenue of help we ask, "And how are you getting along? Has this helped you?"

"No."

"Is there anything we can do to help you?"

"No."

"Do you want help?"

"No one can help me. I have tried that before. No one can help me. It's just the way it is." And I wonder, what way is it?

But I then say to him, "Of course, no one can help you if you have your door closed to help. If you want help you will have to open up and ask for it." His head shakes in the negative manner. His door is closed. I now wonder, how will this session look to him from a lost world? So near, and yet so far.

Oh, the sad stories that come from the pathway that Satan painted so beautiful at its outset!

Once again please let me thank you for your many prayers for these men in prison. They appreciate it more than I can express to you; they really do.

With Christian love,

William Cawman

"GREAT IS THE LORD, AND greatly to be praised in the city of our God, in the mountain of his holiness." Such was the bursting forth of the Psalmist's heart, and my own heart says a resounding "Amen!"

Back across the years of these prayer and praise letters I have every so often told the continuing story of a man who, coming out of three generations of Mormonism, found something so much better that he still marvels with amazement, and we do, too. Several years ago I introduced him to a— I almost wrote "retired missionary," but true missionaries do not retire, so missionary indeed she is. They have been in correspondence for some time. Some of that correspondence has been in Spanish as he loves to speak that language since he learned it well while serving a missionary stint in Colombia. Just recently he wrote what follows to that missionary and I asked permission to share it with you, it is so good.

> These past two months have been full of both challenge and blessing for me. I apologize that it's taken so long to write. Soon after receiving your last letter, I received the news no one ever wants to hear, that my routine blood exam showed all the signs of cancer. The doctor was convinced it was a problem somewhere in my esophagus, stomach or intestines. I walked out of the doctor's office stunned. The Lord has always preserved my body so well that I've never had bad medical news before.
>
> I went directly to the Lord with my fellow Christians, and

sought prayer that night at a service we call "Friday Night Fellowship." The prayer I sought was to continue in full surrender to whatever He has for my life. I don't want to be anywhere He is not— geographically, physically, or spiritually. We prayed that whatever challenges, suffering or persecution He wants me to pass through, to keep me there and meet me there because I want to be wherever my beloved Jesus is. I also encouraged them to keep praying for a pastor from Africa who wanted to preach to us to get a visa, and permission from NJ to preach to us, funds for travel, and all he needed to get him here.

A friend from that service called a close friend on the "outside" and asked for my name to be placed in their "Circle of Prayer" newsletter. One night, late at night, I was praying this through by myself, and suddenly I felt the touch of Jesus. It was deeply impressed upon me that He was here, and would remain with me from that moment. I was home. In that moment, He gave me what I've been calling "victory," because I really don't know what else to call it. He gave me, graced me, with the absolute calm that no matter what His will was in this, or anything for me, He had heard me and the prayers of "many," and would keep me close and glorify Himself. After that I actually couldn't wait to see what He was going to do, because I felt Him moving in me— in more than just physical healing.

I testified of that to the church here. But there was something more going on. When I went back and read your last letter about the second work of grace, about an abolishing of the original root of sin, it seemed to give some light on what I'm experiencing. It is the deepest healing and sweetest communion I've ever known. I'm in awe that the world holds no appeal whatsoever. This experience is just as strong now as it was that night.

The immediate result of that touch of Jesus was felt in my body. The doctor was surprised that preliminary tests a few days later were encouraging, but I just smiled, knowing that the prayers of "many" were being heard, that Jesus was close, and that "this sickness is not unto death, but for the glory of God, that the Son of God might be glorified thereby" (John 11:4).

I had to be sent to a hospital for extensive tests which required anesthesia. When I woke up, the doctor came by and told me that he usually doesn't give results immediately; he prefers to send them to the patient's personal physician, but that he just wanted to tell me that he'd never seen anything like it. I'm 54 years old, and I had the insides of a teenager; "pristine" he called them. Later, my personal physician was so impressed she actually printed out color images from her computer to show me.

I just received the results of a follow-up blood test. There is no sign of the original problem; my red blood cell count is nearly back to normal after it had declined for over a two year period as confirmed by several tests during that time. A problem more than two years in the making is suddenly gone. I wish I could tell you more of the details of what the Lord has done in this, but I'm not sure how to describe it, other than a second work of grace, if perhaps that's what it is.

One thing I do need to say is that the Lord has healed some deeper things than just my body. He is so faithful; He over-answers prayer. His healing has included certain emotional scars that have long been part of my life. Best of all, He's graced me with an ongoing experience of His closeness. He's healed some spiritual things, too. We just don't think we're as deaf and blind spiritually as we really are until He shows us just a little more of Himself, heals us a little more, and turns up the Holy Spirit. The humbling thing is that this is His touch, this is nothing of myself. The only thing I've done is continue in prayer and meditation on His person and His Word, and giving Him full surrender. That's all I ever planned to do. But now this wonderful blessing has come along.

Healing and curing are not the same thing. He decided to cure my body in this case as a testimony to His glory. If the Lord had decided not to cure me, that's okay; He had already healed me inwardly. He's still moving in there, in me; moving in a new way. Meanwhile, for those who better understand physical miracles, I'm 54 years old, out on our dirt track running 5 miles in 45 minutes 4 times a week, doing sets of 18 pull-ups at a time, and working out of the weights as "that Christian guy who was told he had cancer a couple of months ago and it's gone now." But others see more deeply what the Lord has done, and for all of it I give Him the glory. There are those who are more perceptive, asking how I maintain such a peace in this place. I smile and look deeply in their eyes and tell them, "I have a very, very powerful Shepherd Who I can trust absolutely; would you like to know Him?"

I want to thank you for the beautiful hymns you sent in your last letter. I particularly like "I Am With You" and "Never Alone."

The Lord blessed me again recently with a wonderful visit from Rev. ———— [the college president who has been giving several men in the prison a four year theological course]. We had a wonderful visit. We shared our lives and had a time of prayer together. It's the highlight of the year for me to get a visit, that's very rare for me. Rev. ———— was on his way to see Rev. William Cawman, and stopped here first. I'm ready to begin the fourth (final) year of the study program now, and expect to get the books anytime.

I enjoyed so much reading about the camp meeting in Kentucky… I would love to be in such a setting in the woods for a wonderful spiritual feast like that. I'm a fairly skinny guy, so I don't eat a whole lot, but the Lord has made my spirit fat, and I love a good spiritual feast. Perhaps someday, according to the will and timing of God, I could go there for a camp meeting. That would truly bless my soul.

Remember the Bible project that was just getting into full swing when I wrote to you last? We were getting Bibles donated for a congregation in Nairobi, Kenya. The Pastor of that congregation had visited us here, and we promised him 30 Bibles for his very poor congregation in that country where it's difficult to get Bibles. Pastor kept thanking us, and told us that for most of the families who would receive Bibles; it would be the only book in their homes because they are very poor. There was a series of wonderful miracles as we fulfilled that promise, miracles that show the power of God.

Getting the Bibles purchased and into a facility like this was a miracle; it took six weeks, due to the odd way security procedures are here. The power of the project was not only the Bibles, although that is powerful enough certainly, it was also that each person took time to write their personal testimony and story in the Bibles. Some even included a photo. In Kenya's culture, this is a very important thing regarding a gift, that it be very personal...

We were under a deadline to get the Bibles back out again, because they were being sent to Oregon so that they could be taken to Nairobi by missionaries who were leaving in mid-July. Due to the delays in getting the Bibles, by the time I had all 30 Bibles ready to go with testimonies, it was only a week before our deadline of mailing the books to Oregon. We'd arranged the donation of postage to Oregon and everything. Then one day at a meeting I was deeply impressed upon to go and get the box of 30 Bibles and we prayed over it. While we were praying God opened the way. A half an hour later, by God's grace, the Bibles were out of the facility. They were sent to Oregon the next day.

The miracles of the Bible project didn't end there. When the Pastor in Nairobi received the Bibles, he sent us an overwhelming letter about his praise to God. Of all the people he met on his trip to America, of all who'd promised involvement and help to him, the only ones to keep their word were the prisoners in this facility. Pastor says he's being very careful about which families to give the Bibles to. He's selecting homes in which there's at least one person who can read, and who is also faithful to God. He wants to choose by the Spirit so that they are ones who will share the Bible reading with those nearby.

Pastor's leaders are reading one testimony from a Bible each week in their Sunday service, and then giving that Bible to a family. We also received photos of some of the people who'd received Bibles, holding up the Bible. A smile is worth a thousand words of what joy the Word of God brings. My fellow inmates and I here are looking at these photos and just praising and singing to God that He used us, "the least of these," to bless His children on the other side of the world.

I thought it worth a whole letter to share this with you. While the Muslims are recruiting followers in prisons, God is using prisoners as missionaries around the world!

Rejoicing with you,

William Cawman

December 2016

I HAVE SOMETHING VERY SPECIAL to tell you. Five years ago from this very letter, the title was not "Prison News Letter," but "My Savior Has My Treasure." At five o'clock on Sunday evening, November 20, 2011, Jesus took my precious wife of forty-one and one-half years home to Him in heaven.

At five o'clock on Sunday evening, November 20, 2016, exactly five years later to the moment, I stood beside her graveside and made a phone call to confirm the answer to a question I had asked four days earlier. With that fresh confirmation, my precious Jesus brought another treasure into my life. Cindy Nale, a precious lady hidden away in the hills of northwestern Pennsylvania, promised to be my treasure. Five years ago I laid to rest with my first treasure a plaque that had hung over our bed ever since our wedding day of May 27, 1970. It read, "God Gives His Best To Those That Leave the Choice With Him." He is still doing that, and I love Him more than ever before.

Cindy's husband was taken in a sudden accident in 2008 and my wife and I were at the funeral. Cindy has two daughters and then a son. I have a son and then two daughters. We are looking forward to loving our increased family.

Never before has a picture been included in these letters,

Chaplain William Cawman and his wife, Cindy

but I am making an exception, for I know you would want to see my treasure.

For five years any thought of another treasure was deliberately laid to rest at the feet of Jesus. My answer to any thought for the future was simply and emphatically this: "I belong to Jesus." I still do. But for a little while now, this treasure by the name of Cindy kept coming up inside of me. As often as I laid my attraction to her at the feet of Jesus, just that often I felt it again. I began to sense that I was perhaps being too difficult, but God was ever so patient with me for He knew how much I loved Him and how I feared ever getting out of His perfect will. I went to my pastor and wife and sought counsel from them and came away quite the opposite of being discouraged. I wrote a letter simply asking if she recognized in our friendship an attraction she was willing to talk of.

She did... More later.

Now I must come back to prison, mustn't I? I have told the men in the prison, not only of my treasure, but that she wants very much to visit them in the prison. How they did rejoice! Our dear brother, who I have told you of who cannot keep the smile off his face, simply beamed and said, "I won't do what I want to do in front of everyone." My supervisor as well as the other chaplains were absolutely thrilled about it.

Let me tell you a touching story about my supervisor. On the morning of November 1, he was reading his Bible in his private devotions. His little grandson, who lives with them, came to him and said, "Poppy, what are you reading?"

"I am reading about Jesus."

Immediately the little boy ran to him and threw his arms around him and said, "Poppy, I love you for reading about Jesus!"

Then his grandpa told him that he reads about Him every morning and then he talks to Him in prayer.

Grandson said, "Poppy, can I be with you when you talk to Jesus?"

Grandpa said, "Well, when I talk with Jesus I like to be all alone with Him."

"Oh, Poppy, I want to be with you when you talk to Him."

"All right, grandson, you can be with me when I talk to Him."

Do you remember our Colombian brother who came out of a life of violence, as well as Catholicism and Islam, on October 16, 2015, in one moment of letting Jesus come into his heart? Well, it wasn't far down the road of his walking in the Light that I felt he was intensely ready for our four-year holiness theological course of study. When I asked him if he would like to enroll, he instantly buried his head in his hands for a while and then came up with tears. He told me he had sixteen letters lying in his room ready to mail to Bible colleges across the country because he wanted it so badly. He knew in a moment that this was the right one, and the others never got mailed.

That was probably around the turn of the year 2015-2016 and he just brought me his finished work for year two. A couple days later I took him the syllabus and books for year three. He looked at me with a glowing yet mischievous grin and said, "I'll bring this back Friday!"

I wish you could see his shining face! He is loving Jesus with all his heart. One of the books required in the third year of study is *Purpose in Prayer* by E. M. Bounds. The way we have it is bound together with other books of E. M. Bounds. I pointed out to him that in the first year he had already covered *Power Through Prayer* but that at that time (knowing him) he may have read the whole book. "Yes, I think so, but that's all right. I will read it all again, because I need help with prayer." I believe Jesus must be looking down upon this dear man and saying to His Father again, "I have given unto [him] the words which thou gavest me; and [he has] received them…"

And do you remember the man who came up from Texas to see what he thought was his girlfriend, only to be arrested at her door and cuffed and hauled off to prison under several false charges, because one of the officers who arrested him was now the girl's boyfriend? I told you of how he is such a picture of despair and stress that it hurts to look at him. I've tried to help him but it seems I cannot get an open window for he is so fraught with anger and frustration over the ills done to him.

The other night in Bible study he came down and as we sang he stood there with his hair all messed up, his eyes all bloodshot from lack of sleep, and he could not sing for yawning violently. I couldn't help but wonder how much longer he can endure without a total snap. I would love to help him, but it seems he is so deeply entrenched in his despair that he cannot hear any voice but his own. Yes, Word of God, "the way of transgressors is hard!"

Now, I do not mean to go overboard in writing of the former Mormon, but after the letters I sent you last month I received another and it is just too good to not share with you. So hear him a little further:

My Dear Brother in Christ,

Greetings to you in the joy and peace of our Savior Jesus Christ, our beloved King. I was very happy to receive your letter. Well, actually I rejoiced, got on my knees, and thanked the Lord! I always hunger for the deeper word of God (beyond the lighter material, and there's always ample fluff, as you noted)... What those wonderful scriptures and hymns you shared in your letter have declared is: He finishes what He starts, and so we need to cooperate. And even when we do, He is beyond finding out. He takes me deeper into the love of Him all the time.

I have a question for you: Do you ever feel like you're only at the beginning of Him? Do you ever long for glorification? I have to admit that sometimes I would really, really like to have a resurrected body and mind that has no pain or infirmities, but even more for that eternal state of being in glorification with Him; like you say, rejoicing around the glorious throne of God and of the Lamb. Of course, then I settle down and enjoy His wisdom and timing. But do you ever feel like you're always just getting started? Do you think He designed us to long for that?

Obviously I can't even conceive of what glorification will be, so I'm longing for something and Someone I've only scratched the surface of experiencing and can't imagine. You once described to me a mutual indwelling, and I knew instantly that it was possible, and more than that, I knew He not only wanted it for me, had not only been preparing me for all my life for it, but fully intended it to be realized. I know what that is now; and for the love of Him I want others to know Him, and to know that reality, before time runs out.

Yes, I have had people attack the second work of grace teachings of the scriptures. However, one thing you taught me, based on my own background and how you helped me navigate it, is that what many people oppose are actually the very things that they should oppose. What I mean is that it's rare that anyone I've heard oppose it actually understands the second work of grace teachings correctly or fully. So I ask them questions. I ask them to explain what they believe "Christian perfection" to be. It is usually always revealed that what they had thought the message of holiness to be is not what it is at all, or that key parts of it are missing. A return to seeking out the scriptures and praying for the Holy Spirit's revelation then begins in their private time with Him.

Let me tell you something; I am so confident in the Holy Spirit. I don't' have to convince anyone of anything. If I can encourage anyone to "play on God's freeway," (to slow down and spend time with Him and in His word and seeking Him and His truth) then He will hit them with His truck.

For sake of space he then explains in detail how in his early married life he and his wife saved up money to drive 60 miles to Chicago and there eat a real pizza. From then on they never bought a frozen one again. Ever! He continues:

You once gave me similar advice regarding Jesus Christ and His double salvation. "Taste and see." You know what; I was so aware of my spiritual poverty, and so unsure if this soul could make the trip, that I almost didn't take your advice. God had broken me. He was calling me, but He'd broken my bones. He'd shown me how frozen the cult gospel was, and even worse He'd shown me the desperate wickedness of my human heart. But I'd not yet truly tasted Him. Since the time of your invitation, I've marveled that I hesitated, but I later learned that when our Lord and Master told His disciples that they must eat His flesh, many of them turned completely away. But you know what, I didn't. Praise His grace and His mercy for that! That was Him!

The Lord got me with the parable about a man who prepared a banquet, but the people he invited didn't come, so he went out and invited the poor. "Come and dine." I'm so poor in every conceivable way, and He's inviting me. He is so faithful, so merciful. Anything I am, except poor, is due to His riches. I'm not above anything, including being tempted. I don't know all the deep workings of God… Sin is still possible, it just seems irrelevant as a choice when He is so clear… How could I not fall down as one dead? He broke me, then He killed me! Praise Him! He's made a new creature.

Thank you, dear friends, for all of your prayers this past year. God is answering!

William Cawman

17
AND THEN I MET SOMEONE ELSE

THERE ARE EVER so many things that happen in a chaplain's daily life that do not qualify as suitable material for a prayer letter, but that does not prevent them happening. After a season of time has passed in which one has interviewed hundreds of needy men, one would be just about to conclude that he had met one of everybody. Then he meets someone else. Perhaps for the sake of balancing the rest of the material in this book, that "someone else" needs to come to light. So be it someone else, these are also real people and these scenes really happened.

Such as the man who was waxing ever so eloquent in his prayer before the service: "O Lord, bless our chaplain tonight. Make him a sounding brass and a tinkling cymbal!" Not a snicker was heard. Albeit the chaplain sent up a quick thanks for the promised One who interprets our prayers when "we know not what we should pray for as we ought." And then at another opening prayer this petition ascended: "O Lord, bless our chaplain. Bless his shortcomings and his longcomings." This time the chaplain simply responded, "Amen!"

My supervisor had just returned to the main office following an interview with an inmate. He was shaking his head as he said to me, "Next time, you're getting him." Supposedly he considered that sufficient preparation for the "next time," which was not long in coming. As we sat down with this distinguished looking individual, we were introduced to him by himself as "Deacon ————," a trace of emphasis on the prefix. After the said introduction he launched into his burden. He had grown up in a certain church but had wandered away and gotten into drinking and drugs. There were some people in the church that owed him some money and weren't paying it, so one night while they were having service he walked by and threw a pipe bomb in the window and burned the church to the ground. (I later checked his record to verify this and it was just that way.)

Now he said he had encountered a problem that he needed advice on. He had written the church a letter asking them to forgive him because he was hoping that after he got out they would take him back into fellowship, but he didn't realize that the church had a restraining order against him and the judge got the letter and gave him another five years in prison. This time it was I who came back shaking my head and telling my supervisor that I was very tempted to say to him, "Oh brother, you must not grow weary in well doing," for perhaps it would be best if he just remains here.

In a few weeks another request came to us from Deacon ————. Again he "needed some advice from a man of God." He then went right to the point. He had been sent a money order for twenty-five dollars from his mother-in-law in Georgia and the prison post office had stolen it. He had a receipt to prove it. He stated that he had decided to sue the State for the damage. He had reviewed his inmate rights and discovered that the ceiling on an inmate liability against the State was $2000 and so he was "giving the State a break" and only suing for $1500.

I said, "And so you are asking me for some advice?"

"Oh yes!"

"Well, when they get your letter, your prosecuting attorney

will get a copy and the parole board will get a copy and you will sit in here until you max out. Do you know how many times you could have made $25 while you're sitting here maxing out?"

"Oh, well, that's what I needed; some advice from a man of God."

A few more weeks passed and what should appear in the in-house mail but a request that a chaplain see Deacon ———. In he came, waltzing in his vibrant gait just as ever he did while usually carrying a portfolio by his side.

"Chaplain, I needed some advice from a man of God again. See (and he held out about a hundred-page document, very carefully and professionally prepared by an outside attorney) I am suing the State again. You see I was out in the courtyard witnessing for Christ and an officer came out and told me to knock it down as I was getting too loud, but see, I have a right to witness for Christ and next thing I knew I was on my knees with my nose bleeding and handcuffs on. So I'm suing the State because I have a right to witness for Christ."

I said, calling him by the name his mother gave in lieu of the ecclesiastical title he so much preferred, "———, do you ever want to get out of prison?"

"Oh yes!"

"Well, you're not going to if you keep acting like this. You are in prison and the Bible tells you that you are to be in subjection to those in authority over you. Do you understand that?"

"Oh yes, thanks, that's what I needed, was some advice from a man of God."

I continued, "———, you come to church and sing like an angel and then go back to the tier and act like the devil. Now quit one of the two."

"Oh yes, that's what I needed, was some advice from a man of God."

A few more weeks and one day I went to see someone on

the special needs tier. Lo and behold, I look up to see "Deacon" ——— waltzing across the floor with his portfolio in hand. He spied me and changed course in my direction.

"Hi, Chaplain, they have me over here on the crazy ward now, but I like it here. They have some real good programs here. You see, I didn't like my cellmate and so I asked my officer to move me and he told me to get back in my cell. So I went into the laundry room and got a pop bottle and put some cleaning fluid and bleach in it and then got all my things together and then went and dropped the bottle on the floor in front of the officer and told him he had five minutes to get me out of there, so now I'm here on the crazy ward."

Sometime later he was moved to another prison farther north. After a while we were at a chaplains' meeting and I met the chaplain from the prison where he went. I asked him, "Did you receive an inmate from our prison by the name of 'Deacon' ———?" An understanding smile accompanied a positive answer. I said, "Please don't consider him one of our finished products!"

Off and on for a long time a man would come to my classes and just sit there, contributing not a thing, behaving very well. It didn't seem he ever had any special needs or asked for any help. After several years of this I decided to get acquainted with more than just his face and so put him on the list for an interview. He came into the room and sat down on the other side of the table from me and just looked at me with the same expression— or lack thereof— that he wore in class.

I said, "How are you getting along, brother?"

"Oh, OK, I guess. I mean, I'm not in any hurry. God wasn't in any hurry for me, so I'm not in any hurry for Him. You know, it's like when you're baking a cake, you know. You put the milk and flour and shortening in a bowl and mix it up, you know, and then you put it in the oven and bake it. See I had a couple two-year hits, but God saw I wasn't finished so He gave me another ten. So it's like now He has me in the oven and He turned the volume up. You know, God knew all this would happen. It was all in His plan for me."

The facial expression continued nondescript while these theological eccentricities were slowly and emotionlessly emitted.

And what did you say, Chaplain?

What would you have said?

What a bright young chap I must tell you about now. What his religious background was I do not know or recall, at least now, but it seemed he had obtained a very vivid and vibrant experience. He wanted to be baptized. I explained to him the inadvisability of baptism in prison. I told him that water baptism was a testimony to the former life and companions, that he had buried that and was raised to a new life. The men in prison were not the ones he needed to give this testimony to but the ones he had lived his previous life with.

Another reason we do not baptize in prison, which I did not tell him of, was that we cannot discriminate or show favoritism, and if we would start baptizing inmates we would soon have a host of candidates on our hands that we knew not their lives nor whether they were indeed ready for such. Notwithstanding, he wanted to be baptized. I finally consented but told him that he was not to tell anyone or spread it around, but that if he would come to my office at a given time I would baptize him.

The time arrived and he appeared, ever so ready for this great step forward. I went to the restroom and filled a Styrofoam cup with tap water and set in on my desk. Then I asked him to give his testimony to me and he did so without hesitation or reluctance. I then proceeded to pray for him and when I came to the juncture where it was time for a going down into the water, I pronounced him baptized in the name of the Father, Son and Holy Spirit and dumped the cup of water on his head. Wide open came his eyes as he jumped and then looked at me very startled and said, "Wow! I'll get you sometime!" Paul said to the Corinthians, "besides, I know not whether I baptized any other." I know I did not.

A very large-boned and very black man was coming faithfully to the services. He had enough hair hanging down his back and bushing all over the place to have literally filled a half-bushel basket. He gave his heart to the Lord and was gloriously and happily saved. His face shone with the beauty of redemption. I had taken my good wife into the prison for a service, and I pointed him out to her as a wonderful specimen of God's redeeming grace. She could see the shine on his face, but after we left the prison she asked me, "When do you think God will talk to him about his hair?"

"I don't know, Sweetheart. I'm not God."

The very next Bible study he came to he was clean and shiny bald. Did God answer my wife's prayer? I don't really know. Did God even speak to him about it? I don't really know. One thing I know, whereas he was hairy, now he was bald.

Why this prison allows such extravagances in the growth of hair I don't know, but let me tell you about a couple of them. Out in the minimum camp there appeared for a short time a man from the Islands who had a very charming smile and handsome face, but he had terribly matted dreadlocks that hung halfway from his knees to the floor. After just a few Bible studies he came forward bearing that most amiable smile and said with a strong Caribbean accent, "Chaplain, I need to know more about this holiness, I need this holiness." Indeed, sir!

The other was in the prison proper and was also from the Islands somewhere. He also had similar dreadlocks, but divided into perhaps three or four sections, also hanging halfway from his knees to the floor. In addition to this he had a beard that was braided and hung down just as far as the dreadlocks. In order to take his chair in church or class he would have to reach behind and before— fortunately nature had equipped him with two hands— and gather dreads with one and beard with the other and pull them to the side, sit down, and then lay them across his lap.

After attending a few classes he desired to have a talk with me. We sat down and he explained that when he entered prison seventeen years previously, he had taken the Nazarite Vow and had cut no hair since. Then he proceeded to ask me to send a letter for him to President Bush. I explained to him that I was not allowed to take letters out for him and mail them.

"Oh," he remonstrated very reprovingly in his Caribbean accent, "but when the Holy Spirit speaks, we must obey."

I told him that the Holy Spirit would not tell him to do something contrary to the rules of the institution unless those rules violated the written Word of God. He was insistent. He had undergone a vision in which he had seen George Bush at the Wailing Wall in Jerusalem, and by that he knew he would become the President of the United States of America. The Holy Spirit most certainly must be obeyed! To date, George Bush, at least to my knowledge, has been deprived of this singular addition to his résumé.

Oh yes, and then I met one more— as if this chapter could ever have an end. He was perhaps in his late fifties and was adorned with all the white hair a man's head could develop, above and below. He claimed to be Jewish in origin and showed me a picture of his oriental wife who looked to be maybe half his age. Notwithstanding his Jewish derivation he claimed now to be a Christian, but obviously in the developmental stage. He shuffled about with a gait that would depict someone not fully landed on the surface of the earth. One Sunday evening he came shambling into the chapel, and as he passed the officer in charge he was ordered in no uncertain terms,

"Tie your shoes!"

He passed on by as though he heard nothing and as he passed me, muttered in his usual monotone, "Is someone having a problem with my shoes?"

I said, "Yes, the officer wants you to tie them."

Identical tone quality replied (of course head not turning for any of this conversation), "Tying shoes has never been my forte."

I asked another inmate to tie his shoes for him.

He joined my Christian Living classes and one morning stopped and asked in the same expressionless language, "Chaplain, may I have a few minutes to speak to the class about Passover?"

Since it was Passover week I didn't see it to be undesirable so said, "How long would you need?"

"Perhaps ten minutes."

I agreed.

After we had prayer I introduced him and let him come to the front of the class. He immediately snapped out of his accustomed style and an hour and a half later no one wanted him to sit down. He brilliantly related the Jewish Passover feast to the Christian faith with learning and with humor. One thing he observed was that at the Passover feast there comes a moment when the eldest son arises from the table and goes to the door and opens it to welcome in the coming Messiah. "So," said our guest speaker, "you see both Jews and Christians are waiting the return of the Messiah. Give the Jews some credit—at least they open the door!"

A short while after this class he was discovered with razor blades in his shoes and was sent to another prison.

Chaplain, did you ever figure him out? No. Have you?

Have I met one of everybody yet? Probably not.

Appendix
FROM AN INMATE MISSIONARY

AFTER FOUR VOLUMES of happenings in a State Prison by a chaplain, it cannot be wrong to hear from another perspective. Thus the pages that follow are being printed with permission of an inmate who came to this prison shortly after the chaplain started there. He is nearing the end of a thirty-year sentence and for all the time the chaplain has known him, he has walked in the beauty of holiness without one flicker of digression therefrom.

The stories that follow were written by him. They will undoubtedly give a whole new perspective of what lies inside of prison walls than is known or conceived by those outside. Whatever you may imagine is going on inside of prison may indeed be going on, but you will here see that something else very wonderful is going on, too.

These will also give a window into the now-redeemed heart of a former murderer. We are first giving you his own testimony in his own words, and then several stories written by him which will give adequate evidence that the Holy Spirit is preparing a Bride for the Lamb, even in the most unlikely places that human minds would expect them. All glory be to the Blood of the Lamb!

In all of the letters written in these volumes, we have carefully, by State instructions, avoided giving names to anyone written about. Names are given to the following stories, but they are changed so as to conceal identities. The writer's own name will not appear except to Him Who "knoweth them that are His."

The prison hospice program was initiated somewhere around fifteen years ago and has been an untold blessing to many men. Eternity alone will reveal how many men, dying alone in a prison hospital, we will meet in the Glory Land above. And much of the earthly credit goes to these men who have given of their time, their love, their prayers and themselves to reach way down into lives that no one else reached.

It would be safe to say that the love for a fallen brother which shines forth in these stories can only be surpassed by the God of Love Himself. These men who we have labeled "inmate missionaries" have accomplished a ministry impossible to anyone else. And not once have we heard one of them boast of themselves or their accomplishments. They are ever humbly conscious of the pit from which they themselves were dug.

We step aside now and ask our brother in Jesus to step forward.

My Personal Testimony

Nothing is Hidden: A Confession

"For there is nothing covered, that shall not be revealed; and hid, that shall not be known." (Matt. 10:26)

1989

ONE TERRIBLE AUGUST NIGHT, in five minutes of fiery rage, I killed my wife and my mother-in-law. After, as I returned to my senses, in an agony of sorrow and regret, I nearly killed myself as well. I wanted more than anything to undo what I had done. My dear wife and her good mother were gone and it was impossible to bring them back. Remorse, shame and fear crushed me. But I didn't have the courage to take my own life. Nor did I have the courage to turn myself in. Instead I made a decision to cover up my crimes.

This would mean lying to everyone I knew, everyone who cared about me all the time. It would mean living a lie. And before any of that it would mean disposing of the bodies. But this I did. I waited until the next night and I drove them out of state and hid them.

(I can't begin to explain how a formerly decent and law-abiding man could come to a decision to do this. Much less can I explain how he actually carried it out, but I did. In a kind of trance, not daring to think about what I did, ignoring my conscience, I did the ugly work of disposing of bodies and beginning a life of lies. I began to carry a horrible secret that ruled my life, while my soul grew harder and harder each day.)

It was after 4:00 a.m. as I returned to New Jersey after disposing of the bodies. A donut shop was the first place I found open. My nerves jangled painfully. Alcohol helped dull my mind but it didn't help my nerves. I needed to stop and rest for a minute, maybe try to eat something. I was a wreck.

The place was nearly empty; just a teenaged couple at the counter. I hid my condition as well as I could. I hoped my stagger looked like a walk. I leaned on the counter for support.

The teens giggled. I wanted to ignore them but they wouldn't give up. They wanted to be noticed. I turned and saw the boy grinning at me. Then, through his grin, he said it. It is unbelievable but it is true. That young man looked me in the eye and said, "Murderer!"

I nearly fainted. I was paralyzed with shock. Did I have blood on my hands? Had I left evidence on my clothes? Or did my face cry out that I had committed the most awful crime?

No, he was grinning. It was a joke. I slowly focused and saw the boy pointing. I followed his finger to the grill of my truck where a bird hung dead. All the boy knew was that I'd killed a dumb bird. Unbelievable. Slowly I drew another breath. Slowly strength came back to my legs. I returned the boy's grin with something like a snarl. His grin disappeared and I took my donuts and fled.

Pulling back onto the highway, the orange glow of dawn appeared before me. Another day was being born. It was beautiful, but it mocked me. That dawn sky mocked me because it explained the boy's statement, the word that had nearly floored me. And that explanation was, "Almighty God." Almighty God, whose glory spread before me, had sent that grinning teenager with a message as clear and damning as any Biblical prophet. Almighty God had spoken to me. He had called me a murderer. I knew that He knew and that nothing was hidden.

I knew it and despaired. There was only one sane thing for me then, but I could not do it. The only thing that made any sense at all was repentance, confessing my crimes, bringing all to light, and pleading for mercy. But I refused. God or no God, prophecy or no prophecy, my fate was decided. I'd done the deed and nothing could undo it. So there was no point in repentance, sane or not. Sanity held no advantage that I could see. My choice had been made— such as I wished it was not— and I would take the path of insanity from that point.

1990

I LISTENED AS A DETECTIVE began to expose my secret. It was unbearable. I'd carried my damning secret for more than a year, always fearing, yet unprepared for, the day it should be known. And now that day appeared to be before me. Dread was being fulfilled.

The wheels in my head spun sadly, seeking to analyze every word he spoke. I needed to know if he had evidence that removed all doubt. I didn't think I heard it. He described a weak case with little evidence— I hoped. Mostly, he had not found the bodies. My efforts that previous August night had been successful. The heart of the case against me, the heart of my secret, was missing. So my lie might remain standing. I believed that I might get up that day and walk out the door of the prosecutor's office. And if I could to that, if I could have just that much, I might stand a chance a continuing some kind of life. I might continue to breathe free.

I would have to run, of course. I would have to leave my life— my job, my friends, my family. But I had really left my life already, hadn't I? Hadn't I left everything on the day my secret was born? I'd done nothing but lie since then. I'd lied to everyone about everything all the time. And that was my decision, wasn't it? I could not change it now. No. If I got the chance I would run, and I would begin telling new lies to new people in new places. It was all I had.

But he didn't give me the chance. The detective finished going over my case, then he urged me to tell him what had happened. I couldn't. All I could do was squeak that I wouldn't answer questions. I said I wanted a lawyer. Then he dropped the bomb: he'd already been before a Grand Jury. He'd already gotten indictments against me. From somewhere he pulled a warrant ordering my arrest on two counts of murder. My last hope was crushed.

I was handcuffed and processed and taken to the county jail. Most of my memory of that day and of those that immediately followed is hazy. What I remember are worries and fears: what of my family and friends? Would I ever be with them again? Could I get out of this trouble? If no, could I survive prison?

I also remember that during that time I spent all my energy trying to look composed, to walk uprightly and without fear. I played the part (or so I thought) of a falsely accused man who was sure that the mistake would soon be cleared up. Of course it was a lie. It was the same lie, the same cover-up that

I'd been leading for a year. I couldn't give it up. It was all I had. I continued to play-act right up until the day of my bail hearing. I went to court hoping against hope that my bail would be reduced and I would be released. But before entering the courtroom my lawyer took me aside and told me they had found the bodies of my wife and mother-in-law.

My case suddenly looked very bad and I would not go home on bail. My act fell apart then. I was despondent. And back in my cell I began to seriously plan my suicide. I hadn't had the courage to do it on the night of my crimes, but now I lacked the courage *not* to do it. The thought of the shame of being known as a murderer and liar, and the thought of life in prison, was too much for me. I wanted to end it all.

On the evening I planned to take my life I heard a bang on my door. I was surprised to see a jail trustee, a big Hispanic man named Angel, quickly move away from my cell. I saw that he had pushed a Gideon's New Testament under the door.

I was moved. It was the first act of kindness I'd known from any inmate. I picked up the Bible and returned to my bunk. I didn't open it, however. I couldn't. I'd sought God right after my crimes, filled with grief and sorrow, but He was not to be found. I'd known that I was condemned. It was too late for me.

Later still that same night, waiting for darkness, a letter was pushed under my door. It was from my brother David, and it was from his heart. It told of his love for me no matter what. And it told of God's love and forgiveness. But all that I could see in my state of mind was that he did not believe my lies any longer. After all, why would an innocent man need unconditional love or forgiveness? And if my own brother believed I as a murderer, who wouldn't?

I was convinced of what I must do. And when the lights dimmed I knew it was time to go. I longed for the peace that would come with death. I wanted to escape the shame of what I'd done and the punishment I faced for it. I would be content to exist no more— to no longer be. I was ready.

I lay still for a long time to be sure the officers thought I was asleep, as I mentally prepared myself for the act. Then I paused to look into that black void before me.

But then… while I did that, while I looked into that void, I became aware of something there. I became aware that it was not a void at all. I sensed something terrible there in the darkness. I suddenly experienced the greatest fear I had ever known. The greatest fear by far. I sensed black burning coals just under my feet. I understood that the escape I planned was no escape at all. I was certain, rather, that I was on the verge of an endless torment. And I knew that torment was for me just because it was what I deserved for my sins. It was the perfect judgment of Almighty God. Nothing was hid and there was no escape from His righteous anger.

I trembled. I wept. And I absolutely changed my plan for suicide. That was NO option and must be avoided at any cost. Yet, I had nowhere else to go. I was on the edge of hell, desperately afraid of falling in but having no way to turn back. My life, my choices, had led me to that point and it still pushed me forward, threatening to push me in. It was like the whole world was rising up behind me, forcing me into the pit. Or, it was like a mountain covered in smoke and flame, from which I heard the voice of God booming, "Thou shalt not kill." The mountain pushed me unstoppably into the fires of hell.

Having nowhere to turn, being pressed between that terrible mountain and that place of torment, I did the only thing I could do: I cried out as a helpless child seeking rescue. I cried from my heart, "Help, Lord!"

And there in that cell, from that most low position, in answer to those desperate words, I experienced what I can only call a miracle. It was like a ray of light coming down, burning through the black smoke in my soul. It was a glimmer of light, a drop of love— God's love— breaking through. Even to me, even then, even there. For me it was like standing beside the Red Sea, watching it part before my eyes. I was shocked and amazed but I didn't wait to take advantage. I cried again to

God begging for forgiveness, confessing my sins, asking to be made right with Him. And to my great joy I felt Him respond in mercy. Smoke cleared and light increased and filled my soul. It was, I knew, the Light of God coming into my life to save me.

Joy! I could barely believe it. I had thought I would never know joy again. I thought I had lost all joy and everything good forever. I *deserved* to lose all! But no, as I lay there on my bunk in that cell I knew joy. I didn't understand it but I knew the love of God and the forgiveness of my sins, peace, contentment, happiness, hope. My troubles seemed to melt. The punishment I faced was nothing compared to God's love for me and eternal life with Him in heaven.

My mind and heart were changed then, and I wanted to know more about God and to get closer to Him. My first thought was the Gideon's Bible, that blessed gift from Angel. (How good was that name!) It had been closed to me when I received it, but that was changed. I hungered for it now.

I realized I had not held a Bible since my parent's deaths, half my life ago. I felt a pull of guilt for that, for having left God and His Word back then. How foolish. Still, thankfully, the past was past and I was being given a second chance, and a new life. Thank God.

So I opened the Bible. Not knowing where to begin I remembered my brother's letter. In it he had shared some Scripture— the Parable of the Lost Sheep. I found the reference: the Book of Luke, chapter fifteen. There I turned and I found these words of Jesus:

> What man of you, having an hundred sheep, if he lose one of them, doth not leave the ninety and nine in the wilderness, and go after that which is lost, until he find it? And when he hath found it, he layeth it on his shoulders, rejoicing. And when he cometh home, he calleth together his friends and neighbours, saying unto them, Rejoice with me; for I have found my sheep which was lost. I say unto you, that likewise joy shall be in

heaven over one sinner that repenteth, more than over ninety and nine just persons, which need no repentance.

There it was, hope for me. I believed that Jesus Christ, the Son of God, was my Shepherd. I believed that He had come into the world to save lost sinners, and He had found me. I was in His hands. And I believed He wanted me to repent and be joyfully restored to God. I most gladly repented then, promising to give my all to Him forever.

I felt God's smile upon me then, Praise His Name.

1991

As I BEGAN TO settle into the routine of the jail I also began facing some big questions that continued to nag my soul. Of many, these three questions stood out:

1. How could I be forgiven of murder when God's law demanded death for a murderer?

2. How could I change from a terrible sinner into a man of God?

3. What was the end of my wife and mother-in-law? I wrestled with this terribly. I would rejoice in God, then I would think on those poor women, and my joy would crash down.

Slowly and gently the Lord used His Word to give me understanding and comfort in these things. I was (and I am) happy and amazed to find answers to these great questions in the old teachings of Christianity. The Bible answers my questioning soul. The God of the Bible— the Father, the Son, and the Holy Spirit— was the God of my salvation. So—

1. I could be forgiven of my sins, even murder, because the *Son of God* died as a substitute for those who deserved death themselves. The Bible says of Jesus, "Who his own self bare our sins in his own body on the tree, that we, being dead to sins, should live unto righteousness: by whose stripes ye were healed" (1 Pet 2:24).

2. I could become a changed man, because the *Holy Spirit*

enters into the hearts of believers and acts powerfully in them, transforming them, giving them a "new birth." The Bible says of the Spirit, "But if the Spirit of him that raised up Jesus from the dead dwell in you, he that raised up Christ from the dead shall also quicken your mortal bodies by his Spirit that dwelleth in you" (Romans 8:11).

3. I could trust the fate of my wife and mother-in-law to God because the *Father* is the Creator, the true and only God of all the earth, ruling over everything, and He is their God as surely as He is mine. I could bow before Him and accept that in a way beyond my understanding. He always was and always is and always will be on the throne. The Bible says of Him, "For of him, and through him, and to him, are all things: to whom be glory for ever. Amen" (Romans 11:36).

Then there was another question I faced. It was the question of what to do about my charges. I'd confessed to God, but I had not yet confessed to men. The answer was simple, of course. It was the same sane thing I'd known that awful August night. It was to confess my crimes, plead guilty, and accept my sentence. But I kept hoping for God to step in and spare me. I hoped that God's mercy would deliver me from the consequence of my sins. So I waited and time passed.

But time and waiting had their effect. The truth in my soul slowly came out. I began to see that I would have to pay the price. And at last two things brought this front and center in my life.

First there was my testimony. By God I was given chances to speak to other prisoners about Jesus and the forgiveness of sins and the Kingdom of God. And some responded. They knew they were sinners in need of a Savior. I took this very seriously, but at the same time I felt hypocrisy for my failure to do the right thing and confess to my crimes. Where was the faith and obedience I talked about with others?

This came to a head when I was speaking to a young man crushed by guilt for what he'd done. We spoke about God and the saving work of Jesus Christ, but he would not be comforted. He would not believe that forgiveness could be shown to him. He believed his sin was too great. I told him as strongly as I could that I knew God's grace was sufficient for great sinners who had committed crimes as terrible as his. I promised him that I knew this from experience. But he was not convinced and he put it to me directly: did I know what it was to be guilty of murder?

Under the circumstances I could do nothing but tell the truth. To lie or to avoid the truth would have been a grave sin and a slap at the Lord who had shown me such mercy. So for the very first time I confessed to another person that I was indeed guilty of murder and more.

I do not know what this meant to the man to whom I spoke, but for me it opened floodgates. It became clear as day that the whole truth had to come out. I had to open the book on myself for all to read. That was the only way for me to go on, to know peace in my life, to serve any purpose. As I confessed to that needy man I'd have to confess to all.

At about this same time another thing also moved me to accept the consequences of my sins. One night as I read my Bible, seeking for wisdom and strength, God spoke to me. He spoke to me in His Word as I read these words of Jesus: "Render to Caesar the things that are Caesar's, and to God the things that are God's" (Mark 12:17).

These words came to me with a glorious force— a gentle and beautiful and comforting power. In them I heard the still, small voice of God, and I understood that the words were meant for me. I knew. I knew that I owed Caesar— the State of New Jersey— for the things I'd done. The law made it clear. I knew that I had to pay that debt by accepting their sentence for my crimes. And I knew that God's love and mercy did not change that fact. I loved Him and I knew that He loved me, but still it was my duty to give Caesar that which I owed.

I rose from that Bible reading ready to take the steps I'd known all along I must take. There was no more question. It was the most difficult thing I'd ever have to do, but by God, by His grace and power, I was finally prepared to do it.

I could barely move when the morning for my plea arrived. But while I waited to enter the courtroom, my thoughts went to the Lord Jesus Christ. I thought of His suffering, how He suffered for me because He loved me. That was what would help me and get me through the day.

In the courtroom at last, the Judge spoke about my plea. I understood it well enough. I would have to do every day of thirty years. Then I came to the hard part. We came to the point where I had to stand and tell the court exactly what I had done. I rose and told the truth about those wicked murders. I told my horrible secret to the world.

The Judge accepted my confession and found me guilty of two murders. But even as he did that and even as I left that courtroom and returned to prison, knowing that I would spend much of my life there, I felt great surprise. I felt a happy surprise at having passed through that fire. I knew that the hardest thing I would ever face was behind me. My nightmare, my greatest fear— the exposure of my secret— had come to pass and now it was behind me. I was amazed at the relief I felt, and the peace. I knew that while many trials and dangers were still before me, I had passed through a fire which prepared me for whatever else I might have to face.

I wept with joy at this truth, and I gave thanks to the Lord with every tear. He had done it; He had brought me through in His love and power.

2015

IN SEPTEMBER OF this year it will be twenty-five years since I was arrested for my crime; twenty-five years spent in prison.

In writing this story now, remembering these things from my past, I have been filled again with shame for so much that I have done, for awful crimes and terrible sins. I have so many regrets. Thinking about my wife and mother-in-law brings me painful sorrow. But I have no regrets about crying out to

God, repenting and seeking Him. I have no regrets about coming to Jesus Christ and casting my soul upon Him for salvation. And I have no regrets about confessing my crimes and accepting my prison sentence. Rather, I give thanks to God for enabling me to do these things. I give thanks that I have been allowed to come to Him freely, as His child, as His friend, accepted in the Beloved Son. And I give thanks that He has blessed and kept me, showed me grace, made me holy, given me peace. He has taught me and transformed me. The years in prison with Him have been blessed beyond anything I could have imagined. I truly love the Lord.

> I love the LORD, because he hath heard my voice and my supplications. Because he hath inclined his ear unto me, therefore will I call upon him as long as I live. The sorrows of death compassed me, and the pains of hell gat hold upon me: I found trouble and sorrow. Then called I upon the name of the LORD; O LORD, I beseech thee, deliver my soul. Gracious is the LORD, and righteous; yea, our God is merciful. The LORD preserveth the simple: I was brought low, and he helped me (Psalm 116:1-6).

Introduction

I OFTEN TELL PEOPLE that volunteering as a hospice caregiver is the best thing I have ever done. I do not mean that it is the most selfless thing or the thing that most benefits others (although considering how few selfless or beneficial things I ever did before, that would also be true). What I mean, is that it is the most personally rewarding, satisfying, fulfilling, meaningful thing I have ever done. It has most benefited me. The people I have met have blessed me enormously and the experiences I have had have been rich. And this is especially amazing when you consider that the people I speak of are prisoners, and the experiences concern death. Yet it is the truth. I have received much from this work and I am thankful for it.

In the summer of 2002 South Woods State Prison in New Jersey began providing hospice-type care to terminally ill inmates. They set aside a small portion of their hospital unit specifically to house these dying men and they brought in a team from a local hospice to train prisoner volunteers to act as caregivers for their fellow inmates. The caregivers have two primary objectives in their interaction with patients: companionship and life review. They spend time every day visiting with an assigned patient, seeking to befriend him and to be of help in any way they can. Most importantly they seek to be good listeners and to help the patient talk freely about himself, his life, his loves, his losses, and any other thing he may need to resolve in order to die peacefully. At the very end of a patient's life caregivers sit with him on a vigil. They stay with him around the clock so that he will not die alone. The hope is that although he cannot be with his family at the end, at least he may know that he is accompanied by a trusted friend.

Caregivers also meet together weekly in a class run by a prison social worker. This class allows for ongoing training, and it also allows men to share with one another their experiences. This is a needed "vent" for the individual and it serves to teach all. It is a time for sharing grief and for sharing joy, and it bonds the volunteers together intimately.

I have had the privilege of being a caregiver for the last nine years. In that time I have seen more than one hundred patients come through our program and we have seen more than eighty of them die. Some of them were with us for years, some for mere days. Our patients have been Black, White, Hispanic and Asian. They have been young and old, rich and poor, educated and uneducated, lifers and short-timers. And while each of these distinctions would have made a difference in the general population, in our program they have made no difference. Death is a great equalizer, it seems. Each and every one has red blood. Every one's waste smells badly. Each body wears away. None escape the fact that death is ugly and irreversible. This naturally makes the spiritual aspect of dying extremely important. This was covered at length in our training and I can state as a fact that none of the patients that I have known have faced death believing that he was to be no more. All have anticipated some kind of afterlife. Some have trembled at the thought, but none expected annihilation. I must note, however, that the hospice program is not a religious program. It is run by Social Services and our volunteers come from many different backgrounds and faiths. The primary emphasis of the spiritual training concerns respecting the spiritual position of the patient, not trying to change a man's mind or bring confusion or fear to their final days. And neither I nor anyone else that I know of has violated our training, or simple human decency, in this regard. However, speaking from my own experience again, most of the patients who have had the capacity to hold a conversation have wanted to speak about their souls and the hereafter, and most have been glad to hear what our personal convictions or faiths offer on the subject.

I am a Christian. I am forty-seven years old and I have been in prison for twenty-one years. I am serving a thirty-year sentence for two terrible murders committed in 1989. And I am guilty. I have done some ungodly things for which I know great sorrow and shame. But in 1990 God saved me. He brought me to repentance, and I put my faith in His Beloved Son who died for sinners and who rose again from the dead. From that time I have lived believing in Jesus Christ and trusting that He has taken away my sins and that He has given me a new and eternal life. I believe the Bible and its Gospel message, God's good news.

I say this so that it will be understood that the stories which I now share are those which have moved me as a Christian, and that I am writing now with the hope of affecting others for Christ as well. These are not all the stories from our program, nor are they meant to be. What interests me and what I want to share are stories that demonstrate God at work in the hearts of men. And I hope to do this simply by telling true stories from a prison hospice.

For all flesh is as grass, and all the glory of man as the flower of the grass. The grass withereth, and the flower thereof falleth away: But the word of the Lord endureth forever. And this is the word which by the gospel is preached unto you (1 Peter 1:24,25).

✝✝✝

Jessie

JESSIE WAS THE VERY first patient in our program. I was not assigned to care for him, but he would prove to impact our entire program in a large way and his story is important to the story of our prison hospice.

Jessie was only in his twenties but he was dying of AIDS. He was also a transsexual and looked very much like a woman.

I think that I can say there was a collective gasp among our group at meeting Jessie. Most of us had not had much experience with transsexuals and more, most of us were religious men and believed there was moral wrong in this lifestyle. There was no doubt that our group, and especially the three men assigned to care for Jessie, faced a daunting task— that of applying hospice care skills, which we had never yet used, in a situation of unique awkwardness, confusion, and even mild persecution.

As for the persecution, it must be said that prisons are less tolerant environments than others and that openly homosexual men are often harassed. So it was not surprising that there was a vocal percentage of men even in the hospital unit that spoke harshly and without sympathy toward Jessie. And this same group saw our men visiting him, spending private time in his room, showing him kindness and compassion, and word spread that our group was full of homosexuals. Some of our men received insults and when we met as a group we were labeled "the fag class."

This mild persecution was important for our newly-formed

group, because it made us see that there was a cost to the work. It made everyone consider why we were there and whether it was worth continuing, and a few men withdrew from the group. It was a valuable period of "sifting" for us. (Personally, although I felt an initial [discomfort] at being taunted it was quickly replaced by pity for the ignorance around me and I determined to serve despite such foolishness. I also felt a joy because it occurred to me that God was teaching me what I should and what I should not be ashamed of. I realized that I had much to be ashamed of in my life but that this, of all things, was not one of them. So what did I care if others tried to shame me? I knew that God knows. That was a big lesson for me.)

Still, that persecution was a far less important matter for our group than was our awkwardness and confusion toward Jessie. The men assigned to his care spoke at our group meetings about their struggles to get past the strangeness of visiting this man who looked and spoke and acted like a woman. Yet each week we saw these men growing closer and closer to him. Then we heard them begin to admonish themselves for their preconceived thoughts and initial revulsion toward him. And in time we heard them develop real affection for him. They told us about the terribly painful life he had lived since childhood; about the tremendous sense of shame that he carried; of his desperate unhappiness; of his great fear of death. And they sorrowed with him. And through this we all came to understand that he was a man like us, made in the image of God, and we came to feel that his disease was a tragedy. And in understanding this all awkwardness was overcome.

Then Jessie took a turn for the worse. He began to look and act like one who was dying. And with this there came an extraordinary moment for our group. We were together for a weekly meeting when one of his caregivers entered directly from his bedside. He obviously wanted to speak but could not. After a moment of struggling silence he burst into agonizing tears. His pain was plain to all and soon our whole group joined him weeping. A roomful of khaki-clad convicts sat crying for Jessie and for the sadness of those men who had grown so close to him. It was the moment when we grasped what it was that we were doing, I believe, when we understood what hospice care was really about. It was about suffering and death, and seeking to face those things in faith and love. This was the day that our hospice care group became a kind of family, and I doubt that any of us will ever forget that moment.

After Jessie passed away our group came together for a small memorial for him. And at that time his caregivers shared a piece of news with us. They told us that in his last days Jessie had made peace with God, and that he died unafraid. And for those of us who believed in the ever-living Savior, it was the best news we could have heard.

> For when we were yet without strength, in due time Christ died for the ungodly. For scarcely for a righteous man will one die: yet peradventure for a good man some would even dare to die. But God commendeth his love toward us, in that, while we were yet sinners, Christ died for us (Romans 5:6-8).

Kevin

KEVIN CAME TO South Woods' hospital from another prison. When he arrived he was in terrible, terrible shape. He was roughly forty years old but could have been eighty. He was emaciated, literally skin and bones. Only his neck and lower jaw differed. These were swollen large from throat cancer. A tracheotomy tube extended from a big, ugly red hole in his throat through which he breathed with difficulty.

The first time I entered Kevin's room I was taken back by his ruined appearance, but was quickly distracted from this by his great agitation. He was shifting and squirming and muttering angrily. He could not speak but he gave me an angry look. I entered the room slowly while he watched me warily. I tried to explain my purpose, my desire to be of help to him in any way I could. His eyes showed contempt and I trust that if he could have spoken he would have said something like, "How could *you* possibly help *me?*" To which I would have no answer.

I asked if he minded if I stayed with him. He hesitated before throwing up his hands to say, "What do I care?" He then turned his attention back to what had him muttering in the first place. He pulled a portion of the tracheotomy tube out of his throat. It was clogged with a sickening mix of blood and phlegm. (I say "sickening," because my stomach began to turn upon seeing it.) Kevin went about a process he had apparently performed many times before. With agonizing slowness he used a thin brush to clean out the tube before reinserting it. I felt relief when he had finished and the sickening tube was hidden again and his breathing became slightly less labored.

Kevin turned his head in my direction and seemed surprised to see me there. I realized then that he was very heavily medicated. I tried to reintroduce myself but he waved me off— he didn't care. The message I got was that I could stay if I wanted but that I wasn't to bother him. So I just sat quietly.

Less than five minutes later Kevin's breathing grew labored again. So he slowly withdrew the tube and began the same process of cleaning it again. This, I soon learned, was the extent of Kevin's activity. He spent fifteen minutes cleaning his tube so that he could breathe slightly easier for five minutes, and then repeated this again and again and again. All the while he muttered angrily.

My spirit grew heavier and heavier as that first morning passed. I struggled to physically endure the sight, to emotionally endure his anger, and to spiritually endure the helplessness of the situation. I did the only thing that I could do: I prayed.

I left Kevin that morning feeling quite useless, dreading the thought of returning again the next day. I received a lift from a nurse who said that I was the first person Kevin had allowed to stay in his room. He had chased everyone else out immediately. I was encouraged by this, yet I still wondered how I could possibly make a connection with that angry, dying man.

I returned the next day and Kevin again let me stay, but again ignored me. He resumed the process I had seen the day before. I wondered if he'd slept at all. I returned to prayer. The same scene was repeated for several days and my spirit grew heavier and heavier. I found myself overwhelmed. Walking to the hospital each day was drudgery, a chore I dreaded. I felt totally inadequate. I did not want to quit on Kevin but I just didn't think I could go on any longer. I just didn't have what it took to do such work.

One day as I left Kevin I found myself actually trembling. The helplessness was undoing me and I knew I was at the end of my rope. When I got back to my cell that day I fell down before God, praying more fervently than ever before that He would intervene, touch Kevin and deliver him from his suffering and his anger, and touch me and give me grace to persevere. I begged the Lord to somehow allow Kevin and me to connect so that I might share His love with him. And I rose from prayer relieved of a great burden. I had put the responsibility for these things entirely upon God.

The following day as I entered Kevin's room I thanked God to find him lying still for the very first time. He wasn't muttering or fidgeting with his tube. He looked at me with recognition and if not with gladness, at least without anger.

Then I saw a Christmas card on Kevin's desk. It was late January but it had just caught up to him because of his prison transfer. It was a card with a picture of Mary and the infant Jesus, with a scripture verse inside. Again, I thanked God. More, I began to sense His presence. He seemed to have settled in with us. I was strengthened with joy in Him.

I commented on the card to Kevin. He just shrugged. I pressed on, reading the scripture verse to him and asking,

"Are you a believer?"

He paused, then slowly raised a wavering hand. "Maybe. More or less."

I then told him that I was and that I had been since shortly after coming to prison some twelve years before. He didn't respond negatively so I said, "Can I tell you about it?" Again, he paused but again he slowly raised his wavering hand. So I shared my testimony, and I shared it in a way I had never done before, it seemed. I shared it knowing that God was with us, giving the opportunity, answering prayer. I knew that He made it a moment of grace and of power. I told Kevin of my life of sin, and of the crimes for which I came to prison. I told him of contemplating death in my jail cell and of the terror I felt in considering God's judgment, and hell. And I told him of crying out to God for forgiveness and of finding that God loved me, and that He forgave me because His Son died for my sins on the cross of Calvary. I told him of believing in the Resurrection of Jesus and of the new life that I had experienced with Him since that day.

Something about the testimony touched, I could tell. I saw it in his eyes. Because he hadn't stopped me and because he still looked at me intently I asked him if I could tell him more about Jesus. It thrilled me that he didn't merely offer a wavering hand but positively nodded his head. He had a desire to hear. I thanked God, amazed. I wanted to laugh, truly, but refrained, fearing that Kevin would misunderstand.

I pulled my Gideon's New Testament from my pocket and shared some of Jesus' own words from the Gospels, and several important points from Romans. My time was growing short and I wanted to be sure to share one last passage, Luke 23:39-43, the short story of Jesus and the thief on the cross. "And one of the malefactors which were hanged railed on him, saying, If thou be the Christ, save thyself and us. But the other answering rebuked him saying, Dost not thou fear God, seeing thou art in the same condemnation? And we indeed justly; for we receive the due reward of our deeds: but this man hath done nothing amiss. And he said unto Jesus, Lord, remember me when thou comest into thy kingdom. And Jesus said unto him, Verily I say unto thee, Today shalt you be with me in paradise."

I asked Kevin to think about that. Here was a man who had done wrong all his life until he was about to die as punishment for his crimes. But even then, by calling upon Jesus he was saved, he was promised paradise with the Lord. Then I told him that I hoped that he had an assurance like that, a sure hope of entering paradise. Kevin looked at me with tears in his eyes and he put his hands together on his chest in a position of prayer. I too was shedding tears then as I told him to do exactly as that thief had done, to say, "Lord, remember me when you come into your kingdom. Lord Jesus, forgive me of my sins. Accept me, please!" And Kevin closed his eyes to pray.

I believe Kevin found peace with God that day, and it is one of the greatest joys of my life. I cannot express how wonderful it was to have been a part of an event like that— to see God work miraculously in a man's priceless and everlasting soul. I left Kevin that day in utter awe of God. And I understood that I had been a useful vessel for Him only because that I knew that I was helpless and inadequate of myself. It was when I knew that I could do nothing and that I had to cast all upon Him, entrust all to Him, that He acted in answer to prayer. To Him belongs all glory, I know, the Savior of men.

When I returned to visit Kevin the next day he had lapsed into a coma. I stayed with him and held his hand and read the Bible to him, and for the first time since I had known him he looked peaceful. The following day I learned that he had died in the night. I was not sad but glad, for I had a real and living hope that Kevin was that day with Jesus in paradise.

> But God, who is rich in mercy, for his great love wherewith he loved us, even when we were dead in sins, hath quickened us together with Christ, (by grace ye are saved) and hath raised us up together, and made us sit together in heavenly places in

Christ Jesus: That in the ages to come he might show the exceeding riches of his grace in his kindness toward us through Christ Jesus.

Vinnie

As I entered Vinnie's room for the first time, before I had even introduced myself, he said, "My wife tells me it's time for me to become a Christian." I was taken back. This man knew nothing about me, yet he shared something like that. It was surprising, to say the least, but it surely seemed like a positive way to start.

Vinnie was a hardened convict who had been in prison much of his life for various crimes. In fact, Vinnie was infamous within the prison system for audacious things that he had done. But he had begun to settle down. He'd gotten out of prison several years before and he had married a Christian woman. They owned and operated a small farm together. I don't know what brought him back to prison but he said it was his past catching up with him and not any new crime. He was doing a short sentence, a "skid bid," and he wasn't really worried about it— until his liver failed and he learned that he had cirrhosis due to hepatitis. That's when his wife urged him to get right with God once and for all.

Still, he was not as prepared to become a Christian as his first words to me implied. He responded skeptically to nearly everything when we spoke about God. We went to the Bible but it did not satisfy him. He didn't accept its authority. It was not long before our conversation dried up.

However, a Catholic chaplain began visiting Vinnie often and he seemed buoyed by him. In time their interaction renewed Vinnie's spiritual interest, and he and I began speaking about the Lord once again. Most significantly, on one occasion he asked me about communion he had taken the night before. We had a long discussion about the broken body of Jesus and the new covenant in His blood, and he truly seemed persuaded to eat and to drink of Christ in faith.

Very soon after this Vinnie's condition worsened. His disease increased to the point that he was no longer lucid. He was not conscious of anything around him, it seemed, yet he was restless and uncomfortable. It was hard to see him like that, and hard to be with him. We had to watch him constantly or he would squirm right off the bed. Meanwhile, he seemed always distressed and we were continuously trying to speak words of encouragement and assurance. After being with him for hours, and for days, we were drained mentally, physically, emotionally and spiritually.

After several days like that I felt relief because he was calm when I arrived to sit with him. He lay very still and quiet. Yet that stillness soon brought a new discomfort. A strong sense of death began to pervade the room. While I sat with him it felt as if the Angel of Death was at hand. I was uneasy, and found myself watching the clock, hoping that my relief would arrive before the moment came.

The hours slipped away and I began to think Vinnie might survive another day, when he began to move again, as one awakened out of sleep. He began moving even more than he had the days before, and turning his head to look at me. He seemed to be with us in the land of the living, but it wasn't a good thing, it was chilling. His eyes had a kind of panic in them which I had never seen before, as if he knew that he was dying. Then a severe rattling sprang up in his breathing. This panicked him more and it panicked me, too— I'd learned that this rattling was often a precursor to death.

A nurse looked in at just that moment, saw him, and said that it would not be long now. Then she moved on.

The next fifteen minutes were horrible. They saw his breathing deteriorate more and more, and the rattle grow more pronounced. They saw the panic in his eyes increase, along with the thrashing of his limbs. Then the thrashing slowed, and his eyes closed. The rattle became hard to distinguish because his breathing was so shallow. Then, when I thought that he was all but finished, Vinnie sat bolt upright (scaring me witless), and with his eyes wide and fixed on the ceiling, he said plainly, "I don't give a f—!" Then he laid back down, let out a final rasping breath, and every muscle in his body seemed to relax. A thick black liquid poured out his nostrils and I knew beyond doubt that he was dead.

This was a powerful thing to experience. I was shaken by it and yet I felt enriched at the same time. I know I cannot describe it but it was surely a God-moment. God was there. I felt a reverence and awe. I felt a holy fear.

But was God there to save? I can't possibly say. It seemed to me at that moment that Vinnie's last words expressed defiance toward God even at the end. They seemed a challenge to the Lord. Yet others say there could be other explanations and that his words weren't necessarily meaningful at all. I accept that and I conclude that I simply don't know. But what I take away from my experience with Vinnie is that regardless of his condition, when he left this life he entered into the presence of God, where He faced a perfectly righteous judgment. This is a powerful thing, and it makes me stop and think. Surely there is nothing more important than being ready to meet God. Surely— *surely*— rebellion against Him on that day will be futile.

> Marvel not at this: For the hour is coming, in the which all that are in the graves shall hear his voice, and shall come forth; they that have done good, unto the resurrection of life, and they that have done evil, unto the resurrection of damnation (John 5:28,29).

Bob

WHEN I FIRST OPENED Bob's door to introduce myself I saw a sweet-looking elderly man smiling broadly. He reached out a weak hand and a weak voice told me his name. And this began a real friendship that lasted until his death. Of course, this made his death very emotional for me.

Bob was in his seventies and he had lung cancer. He had finished a difficult round of chemo and radiation therapy which left him very weak. But he was calm and content, peaceful and quiet, and he was genuinely kind and was loved by all the men around him.

The first thing that drew Bob and I close, I suppose, was our faith. Bob loved God and we got along wonderfully, worshipping and praising the Lord together.

Another thing that drew us close was that Bob was just the age that my own father would have been, and he reminded me of my dad in many respects, mostly in his fondness for story-telling. We quickly developed a simple routine of talking away the mornings over coffee.

Like my dad he did most of the speaking, and like him he seemed to have an inexhaustible source of topics. His life was a mine of interesting stories and information. One day he would tell me of traveling through the south in the days of segregation, another day he would explain the art of beekeeping, or cheese making. But his two favorite topics were my dad's topics as well— his experiences in World War II, and his family.

Bob had served in the Navy. He'd been in nearly every theatre of the war but his most action came in the Pacific. Dad had been a marine fighting in the Pacific and I imagined him appreciating Bob's stories, especially as Bob told of the day that his ship took a direct hit from a Kamikaze pilot. Bob still felt the horror as he told the story, and he still mourned deeply the many shipmates who died in that attack.

Above all else, however, Bob talked about his children and his grandchildren. He never tired of talking of them all. In listening to him I could not help but feel like part of his family, and I thought of him as part of mine. We truly and deeply bonded. We were able to be something to one another that we both missed terribly there in prison. (I should add that his family did visit him regularly and nothing made him happier. They were loyal and loving, just as he was, I'm glad to say.)

Bob was a very sick man, however. A great deal of our conversation came despite his great pain and difficulty breathing. Often I tried to make him lie down and rest. I sometimes felt like he was going to extra effort for my sake— and he probably was. But he always insisted that there was nothing he wanted to do more than have our conversations. They took his mind away from his pain, he said.

Still the pain showed through, sometimes. I could see that he was in misery. And as it did his cancer progressively got worse. I saw it slowly break him down. It was very hard to watch.

A day came when Bob could not sit up to greet me. We both knew then that his time was short. I was very sad as I sat with him then, but he truly wasn't. He was really ready. He told me he looked forward to dying. The only thing that pained him was the thought of leaving his family. And at one point Bob asked me to contact his children to tell them how much he loved them. "Later," he said, meaning after he had died.

That did it for me. As Bob drifted off to sleep, I began to think about the letter I would write to his family and in doing that my tears began to flow. I found myself sobbing at his bedside. It was an emotional release for me unlike any I could remember— and it was wonderful! Instead of trying to suppress it I went on sobbing for Bob and his family.

Moreover, I turned my thoughts also to my own deceased father and mother and wept for them as I'd never wept before, freely, unreservedly. A fountain seemed to burst open in my heart that cleansed me and purged me of a weight of black grief. It was a long overdue catharsis, an unburdening of a weight that had pressed me down for many years. I think I had never before been so sad, or so happy. I had never been so emotionally alive.

Bob died a few days later. I was not at his side, another man was. I honestly don't think he wanted to die in front of me. But we had said our goodbyes and when he passed he was ready, and so was I.

Thank you, beloved Lord.

> For this cause I bow my knee unto the Father of our Lord Jesus Christ, of whom the whole family in heaven and earth is named… that ye, being rooted and grounded in love, may be able to comprehend with all the saints what is the breadth, and length, and depth, and height; and to know the love of Christ which passeth knowledge, that ye might be filled with all the fullness of God (Ephesians 3:14-19).

Sam

SAM WAS A TYPE-A personality, a former college basketball star who talked a mile a minute to anyone and everyone who would listen. Soon after I'd met him he had told me all about his disease. He'd had AIDS for more than ten years but had it under control with medication. Then he developed lung cancer, which was killing him rapidly. He also told me much about his life. He considered himself a Baptist, but he had lived much of his life as a real gangster. And it seemed that his favorite pastime was telling stories about his life of crime, of violence and gunplay.

It was hard to imagine the laughing and friendly man that I visited, doing the evil things that he told me about, but I have learned that this is a fact of life in prison. Many men seem to be two people— the one who committed their crime and the one with whom I can have a long and very human conversation about hopes and fears and longings. The difference in men, I suppose, is that in some there is remorse for the things they have done, while in some there is not. Sadly, in Sam there was not.

As long as he was physically able, Sam remained very sociable, spending most of his time in the yard and the dayrooms, playing cards, joking, swapping stories with other men. On occasions he and I had opportunities for private conversation, but when that was the case he did most of the talking.

As months passed I grew more and more concerned for Sam's spiritual condition. Although he spoke plainly about his disease, he never spoke about death or his thoughts on eternity. On the contrary, he deliberately avoided those topics and swiftly steered conversation away from such things. Part of this, I believe, was that he was close to "maxing out" his sentence. In a few months he would go home. This allowed him to focus solely on that day of deliverance and to avoid dealing with any harsh truths beyond it.

Only when Sam went sharply downhill did this change. He found himself bedridden and weak and he became more interested in speaking about God. And for a time we spoke a great deal about God's law, sin and forgiveness, justice and mercy, the atoning sacrifice of Jesus Christ and His resurrection from the dead. I was glad that we spoke about these things, but I was terribly troubled by something he eventually revealed to me. Sam confessed that he believed in God, he believed that Jesus was the Savior of the world, he believed he was a sinner who needed Christ's salvation, but despite all that he still said plainly, "I know it's true but I'm just not going to bow to God." When I questioned him further he said that he would always be his own man, no matter what, even if he died, even if he went to hell. I pled with him to think about what he was saying, about the vanity of losing his soul for the sake of pride, but he would not be moved.

Then Sam's health declined so far that the doctors believed he would die within days. For several days he was very low, often unresponsive, and he seemed to be on the verge of death. During this time I sat with him for hours, speaking with him, reading to him, praying for him, but never finding any cause for further hope for his soul.

Then one day a zealous Christian brother announced that

Sam had accepted Jesus. He told me that he had led him in "the sinner's prayer" the night before. It was a deathbed conversion.

I don't doubt that what this man said was true, but something extraordinary happened next. Sam bounced back. He returned to strength and to his senses. He spent the next several weeks in complete lucidity, and in that time Christ meant nothing to him. In those weeks he wanted to hear nothing of God. He returned to anticipating his release from prison and boasted of his plans for sex and drugs. There was no evidence at all of a new heart but every evidence that Christ was *not* in him. There was no reason to think his deathbed conversion had meant anything.

Then, just a few days before Sam was due to go home, he again took a turn for the worse. This time, however, he did not bounce back. Instead, on the very day before he was to be released, he died in prison, and he died badly. With another friend at his side he sat up suddenly, thrashing about. He fought his way out from under his covers and attempted to get out of bed. The friend tried to stop him but he went over the rail and collapsed to the floor with an incomprehensible shout. Nurses were summoned but by the time they arrived, Sam had perished. And we who knew him and who know Jesus Christ had no cause for hope for him, but only anguish and pity.

> Wherefore God also hath highly exalted him, and given him a name which is above every name: That at the name of Jesus every knee should bow, of things in heaven, and things in earth, and things under the earth; And that every tongue should confess that Jesus Christ is Lord, to the glory of God the Father (Philippians 2:9-11).

Ricky

RICKY'S STORY CONCERNS another caregiver, Larry. Larry and I are close friends and we worked in the mornings together for some time, so I was able to closely observe his time with Ricky. I am glad I did.

It was obvious from the time he arrived that Ricky would be difficult. He had an unhappy disposition, a miserable kind of countenance that said "stay away." He had spent much of his life in prison, and had probably spent *all* his life in a world where self-preservation reigned all-important. He clearly did not want any help. Nor did he need it, at first.

Despite this, knowing that Ricky's hepatitis C would eventually drag him downhill, Larry attempted to insert himself into Ricky's life. At first he simply stopped at his room to say, "Hello." Ricky didn't want company and told him so, but he would return the next day and say, "Hello" again. After some time Ricky's guard came down just a little, and he allowed Larry to spend some time with him.

This didn't make Larry's job easier, however. It really just initiated the difficulties, for as Larry spent time with him, Ricky started talking and it was like the opening of floodgates. Larry soon found himself overwhelmed by Ricky's non-stop speech. And all his talk was ungodly, full of cursing and hatred and anger. He spoke of all kinds of evil he had known and participated in throughout his life.

Larry let him talk, of course, understanding that this outpouring of Ricky's was a venting, a necessary release for him. But he also knew that by dwelling always in the past Ricky was not facing his present condition nor considering his future. Larry tried to insert some good things in the conversation and to turn Ricky's thoughts to important matters, but he felt he had no influence at all.

During this time, which lasted for months, I could see frustration and sadness building up in Larry as we left the hospital each day. I sympathized indeed. I had experienced something of this with other patients, but none comparable to Ricky.

Larry continued with Ricky, however, and somehow he continued to make progress. Slowly, very slowly, Ricky's guard came further down. Larry began to find more opportunity to speak to Ricky about his real needs, and the short time left for him to seek peace in his soul. And while Ricky didn't respond to much of this outwardly, he did allow Larry to talk that way more and more. And one day when Larry had left early I looked in on Ricky and I "caught" him reading his Bible. He did not know that I saw him but when I told Larry about it his strength seemed to be renewed. After that we both made it a point to look in on him and we both found him in his Bible often.

Then Ricky took a turn for the worse. His body was bloated with the impurities that his liver was not filtering. He found himself bedridden, with faithful Larry at his side. And from that point on Ricky's Bible reading was no longer secret. Larry read to him from God's Word every day.

Still, it was hard to know how he really felt. Was he simply a captive audience? Larry surely didn't want that. We discussed the fact that Ricky never initiated any kind of God-centered conversation, and we recognized this as a sad sign. We knew that our desire for his relationship with God was insufficient. We knew that his heart had to be turned.

Then one morning to our surprise and delight, Ricky asked us to pray with him. We immediately went to his bedside, took his hands and prayed. And when we had finished Ricky looked happy. And I don't say that lightly. Ricky was never demonstrative, but from that time on he *looked*_like a man at peace. He no longer looked as if he were at war with the world. And our prayers were a regular part of his life from then on, because he wanted them to be.

Ricky hung on for more than a month. And we struggled to hang on with him. It was a grueling experience, seeking to comfort such a sick man through such a prolonged death. But at the end it was a wonderful thing.

I sat with Ricky from 2:00 a.m. until 8:00 a.m. on his final day. Despite the length of his struggle and some previous false alarms, I knew that he was at the very end. He had not been conscious in days. He was barely breathing, and what breath escaped was accompanied by the now-familiar rattle. I continued speaking to Ricky, assuring him that I was there, and assuring him that it was okay to stop fighting. But I also kept telling him that Larry would soon be there. And amazingly Ricky kept on breathing, kept holding on, until at 8:00 a.m. I saw Larry come through the door.

Larry could see that it was all over and he hurried to Ricky's side. He said goodbye to Ricky and he told him that he loved him. Then he told him to go home to heaven to be with Jesus. And with that, at that very moment, Ricky took his last breath and died.

What a blessed thing to see. The more I thought about it the more I admired the power and the glory of Christian love. I saw it with my own eyes, how Larry had faithfully demonstrated love to a man who appeared to be unlovable. I'd seen that love chip away at Ricky's formidable walls. I'd seen it endure setbacks and hardships, but persevere. And I saw that love finally overcome.

I know that Christ was in Larry and that He used him to show His love to another needy sinner, and that man was overcome. Love won him over and he responded in love— love for Christ his Savior, and love for the dear humble man that God put into his life. He loved him and he waited for him to say "goodbye" before he went home. And I don't think I have ever seen anything more beautiful.

> Charity suffereth long, and is kind; charity envieth not; charity vaunteth not itself, is not puffed up, Doth not behave itself unseemly, seeketh not her own, is not easily provoked, thinketh no evil; Rejoiceth not in iniquity, but rejoiceth in the truth; Beareth all things, believeth all things, hopeth all things, endureth all things (1 Cor. 13:4-7).

Alberto

I WAS A CAREGIVER TO Alberto for more than six years, far longer than any other patient, and when he died I felt it more than I felt any other.

Alberto was seventy-seven years old when I met him— ancient by prison standards. Actually, I had seen him around before that, tottering around the prison with a cane. But at seventy-seven he suffered a major stroke which rendered him paralyzed on the left side, and the doctors assigned him to the palliative care program.

Al was unique in many ways. He was unique in the length of time he remained on palliative care. He was unique in how good-natured he was, smiling and uncomplaining. (Except for rare occasions, bouts of verbal rage which were unique for their ferocity!) He was unique for how well-respected and cared-for he was by the other men on the hospital unit. And he was unique in that he was born and raised in Sicily, and despite living thirty-nine years in New Jersey he never learned more than a handful of English.

Needless to say, when he and I met, communication was difficult because of the language barrier. Hand signals were predominant in establishing a routine, a routine that was very important. Every day when I arrived I helped Al get out of his bed and into his wheelchair. I helped him use the bathroom, get cleaned up, and get dressed for the day. Every day I took him outside where he could smoke a cigarette while I pushed him around the perimeter of the recreation yard, then I sat him in the vicinity of some other older men. And for all our years together that routine never substantially changed. Al needed more help doing basic things as the years passed, and after a bout with pneumonia he quit smoking completely, but basically our routine never altered.

What did change profoundly was our relationship. Through

the weeks and months and years our communication steadily increased. I learned to understand some Sicilian— mostly from Al directly, but also from an Italian/English dictionary and from *Italian for Dummies.* I also learned to understand his heavy accent so that I could make out his attempts at English. Some mutual Spanish also helped, and the result was a kind of pidgin language unique only to Al and I. But it worked. Through the years officers and doctors and social workers relied upon me to translate for Al. And Al was satisfied, too. *"Capice* mee too much," he would say, or "You understand me well."

But translating was only a small part of the importance of our communication. For as we learned to understand one another, Al had someone to talk to, and that was a big deal. The poor man had been in prison for more than ten years without that. Occasionally a man came through that spoke Italian, but these men didn't have the time or the will to sit with and get to know the old man. But in me he had someone he could tell about his family, his life, his crime. And how emotional he would get as he told his stories! He wept freely, and I suspect that he needed that very much. I confess that I often understood only the gist of his stories. I didn't have nearly enough Italian to follow him in detail, when he got on a roll. But still I was an ear for him, and I know he valued that.

I would add that Al was a very religious man, raised by a Catholic mother. I would often say something to him about a figure in the Bible— say Jonah or John the Baptist— and he would recall the whole story, passionately sharing the history in detail. Christmas and Holy Week were also very important to him and he would always tell me of the significance of the holidays when they came. He never had a dry eye when telling me of the sufferings of Christ on Good Friday.

I grew to love Al, truly. On the days when I couldn't be with him because of appointments or lock-downs, I missed him as much as he missed me. And the way that he would light up upon seeing me the next day always touched my heart. He simply became a part of my life, and a best part, too

Over the years he had a few medical scares. Three times he had pneumonia and grew very weak, but he pulled through. Finally, however, he developed an infection that he just couldn't beat. They sent him to an outside hospital to try to get him right, but when they sent him back to South Woods, they sent him back to die. He had had another major stroke and he came back completely paralyzed and unable to speak.

Al was put on a twenty-four-hour-a-day watch as I and three other men rotated at his bedside. He was still lucid, acknowledging us with his eyes and with his familiar smile, but nothing more.

Sitting on vigil with him I spoke with him, and read the Bible and prayed with him. I even anticipated another bounce back like we had seen from him often. But it soon became apparent that it was not to be. A fever returned and he became less and less responsive. Finally I began to say goodbye to him— but what tears followed! These were some of the most emotional days I have ever spent, sitting there with my dying friend. Even as I looked to God and trusted in His Sovereignty, and as I trusted Al to His living hands, yet I would look at Al, weak and dying, and I would weep in sorrow.

When I left Al the final time he was barely breathing. I knew he could not hang on much longer. So as I walked to the hospital the following day I tried to prepare to hear that he was dead. I entered the hospital and approached the officer's desk, but as I looked down the hallway I could see that Al's room was sealed shut. I knew too well what that meant. I did an about-face and hustled out of the hospital. I was afraid that if anyone said anything to me I would burst out in tears. As quickly as I could, with eyes set only on the ground before me, I returned to my tier and to the privacy of my cell.

There I fell down before God in prayer. And from my heart (rather than my head) came these words: "Death is wrong!" I startled myself with those words, a bit. I had to stop and examine them. It felt almost as though I had accused God. But no, that wasn't it. I was not accusing God of being wrong, nor suggesting that death was unjust. I was saying that death was wrong because it wasn't part of God's good creation. Death only entered in because sin had entered in. But, praise God, I knew that Jesus Christ came into the world to undo the wrong done by sin and death! He died for our sin, and He rose from death! This is the Gospel, the good news! Our Lord has won the victory and one day soon He shall make all things right again! We wait for a kingdom where sin and death have no place, where God Himself shall be with us, in perfect righteousness and life.

I rose from prayer that day with a tremendous joy. I had joy for the great lesson I had received, the blessed reminder of the Gospel truth. But I also had joy because it had been good to pour my heart out to God, that this was not only permitted but was pleasing to Him. And He was pleased to answer me and to comfort my mourning heart.

I still miss Al, of course. But I am thankful that I had a chance to know him. And I am thankful that I had a chance to help him, and to do some genuine good for another person. I said in the Introduction that volunteering as a hospice caregiver is the best thing I have ever done, and I meant that wholeheartedly. Working with prisoners, facing death— it is the best thing I have ever done.

> Yea, though I walk through the valley of the shadow of death, I will fear no evil: for thou art with me; thy rod and thy staff they comfort me. Thou preparest a table before me in the presence of mine enemies: thou anointest my head with oil; my cup runneth over. Surely goodness and mercy shall follow me all the days of my life: and I will dwell in the house of the LORD for ever (Psalm 23:4-6).

Conclusion

IN THE INTRODUCTION, I MENTIONED that we have had more than

100 patients since this hospice program began. Well, we have also had even more volunteers at one time or another. And many of these men have awed me and have proven that great goodness exists even within the confines of prison. Not all, of course. We have had our share of men who proved to be only self-centered, self-interested, selfish. But I have seen many men act in a tenderness and self-sacrifice and compassion that would surely amaze an outsider.

I have seen men sit vigil for many long nights in hard plastic chairs in brightly lit rooms with men they barely knew, and do so without complaint. I have seen others roused from their beds to their complete surprise, but arrive at a bedside with a sincere smile on their face. I have seen others persevere despite angry patients who spent their anger on the caregivers, yet maintain their sense of humor.

I have seen others— many others— ignore the most foul sights, sounds and smells in order to care for their patients, and to preserve the dignity of men who could no longer do so for themselves. I've seen many hold the hands of dying men, softly comforting them as they passed away. I've seen so many prayers and tears, so much gentleness and love. I have seen so many bring smiles to the faces of sick and hurting men, and do anything for them that they could do.

And these men were criminals, every one. Many had spent long, hard years in prison. And they all were volunteers, and one could have quit at any time, walked away, and said, "Not me." I think on these things and I am amazed, and I am grateful to have known these men and to have seen the things that they have done.

The final man I must now remember was another patient, Joseph. I did not know Joseph long, but it was he who, unknowingly, inspired me to begin writing these stories.

The moment I met Joseph, I knew that I was speaking with a Christian brother. We immediately bonded in a way that defies explanation: A back-and-forth love and trust existed even from the beginning.

Joseph was a big, handsome and apparently healthy young man. But he was full of cancer. On his second day with us he told me of his sickness. He told me that just four months earlier he did not even know that he was sick. He went to the doctor because he did not feel well and shortly thereafter they determined he had prostate cancer. He went to the hospital for surgery but when they went inside his body, they found the cancer had spread throughout his internal organs. He was beyond hope. They gave him only months to live.

After sharing this, Joseph shook his head and said, "It hit me like a train."

What could I say? How do you respond to that? I hesitated, at a loss, but then I thought of something that a wise brother in Christ often shares with me. I said, "Brother, you know that you are in the hand of God, and He doesn't make any mistakes, and He hasn't forgotten about you."

Joseph nodded his head slowly. Then he smiled, nodded again, and said spiritedly, "You know, I have the same joy today that I had nine years ago when Jesus saved me."

It thrilled my soul. It dawned on me that before my eyes was a living and breathing example of what I always hoped to see in the hospice care program. I had seen many Christian patients, and some that I hope sought Christ as they approached their death. But I had never before seen one that faced death boldly, with faith that overcame the world, who rejoiced in the prospect of leaving this world and entering heaven. Joseph was such a man, blessed of God.

Joseph was not finished thrilling my soul, either. They scheduled him for another trip to the hospital, to attempt a risky operation. The day before he left, the last time I would see him, he and I were talking about God when I was moved to ask him what exactly he prayed for. He thought about it for several moments, then said, "My prayer is that I will bear a faithful testimony for Jesus Christ, no matter what."

What better answer could any man, at any time, under any circumstance, give?

Joseph died the following day at the hospital. I don't know if he even made it to the operating table. But when I learned of his death I realized that he had borne the faithful testimony to Jesus that He sought. And it also occurred to me that I could continue bearing Joseph's faithful testimony for him by sharing his story with others.

I began telling everyone about Joseph and about how He rejoiced in glorifying Christ to the end. And soon I found people telling me that I should put his story on paper. Eventually I sat down to do so, but as I did, I found the story grow. I found that talking about Christ's work in one man in our hospice program led inevitably to telling about His work in others. The story was bigger than Joseph alone.

Still, Joseph and his story hold a special place in my heart. His faith encouraged me, and it encourages me still, especially in my work in the prison hospice. Thinking about him and his "good" death makes me all the more eager to see other men get ahold of the truth that our Lord and Savior is alive. He has risen from the dead victoriously and those who love Him are certain of sharing in the victory with Him. Death is a defeated enemy that holds no power over those who are washed by the blood of Jesus Christ, the Lamb of God. He takes away the sin of the world. Praise the One and Only God!

> O death, where is thy sting? O grave, where is thy victory? The sting of death is sin; and the strength of sin is the law. But thanks be to God, which giveth us the victory through our Lord Jesus Christ (1 Corinthians 1:55-57).

Members of Schmul's Wesleyan Book Club buy these outstanding books at 40% off the retail price.

Join Schmul's Wesleyan Book Club by calling toll-free:

800-S₇P₇B₂O₆O₆K₅S₇

Put a discount Christian bookstore in your own mailbox.

**Visit us on the Internet at
www.wesleyanbooks.com**

You may also order direct from the publisher by writing:
**Schmul Publishing Company
PO Box 776
Nicholasville, KY 40340**

Made in the USA
Las Vegas, NV
02 April 2022

46716336R00195